Teacher's M[illegible] 3

On Your Way

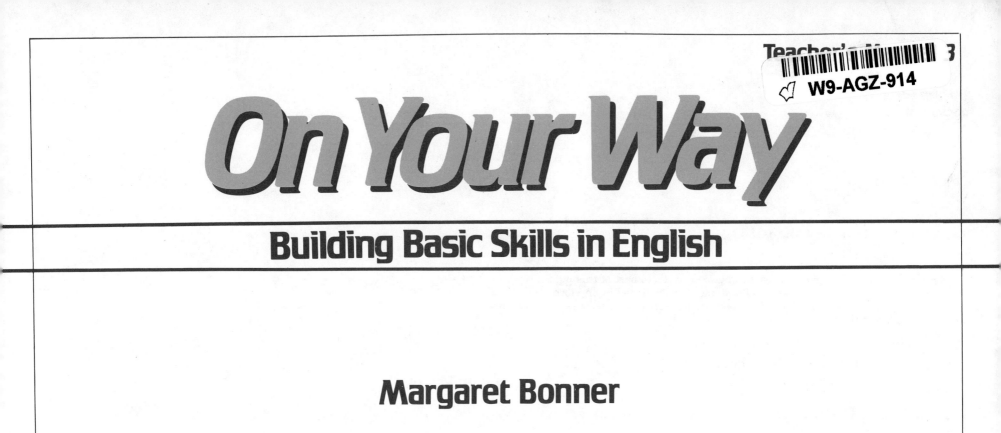

Building Basic Skills in English

Margaret Bonner

Longman

On Your Way Teacher's Manual 3

Longman Inc., 95 Church Street, White Plains, N.Y. 10601

Associated companies:
Longman Group Ltd., London
Longman Cheshire Pty., Melbourne
Longman Paul Pty., Auckland
Copp Clark Pitman, Toronto
Pitman Publishing Inc., New York

Distributed in the United Kingdom by Longman Group Ltd., Longman House, Burnt Mill, Harlow, Essex CM20 2JE, England, and by associated companies, branches, and representatives throughout the world.

Executive editor: Joanne Dresner
Development editor: Nancy Perry
Production editor: Helen B. Ambrosio
Text and cover designs: Lynn Luchetti
Cover illustration: Bill Schmidt
Production supervisor: Joanne Jay

ISBN: 0-582-99877-8

89 90 91 92 93 94 9 8 7 6 5 4 3 2 1

Printed in the U.S.A.

Contents

Introduction

Innovative and flexible, ON YOUR WAY is a new series in English as a second or foreign language that integrates grammar, functions and life skills. Created especially to help students develop the language facility they need to function in an English-speaking environment, it is designed for adult and young adult learners from the beginning to the intermediate levels. This unique three-level program presents natural language in context and gives students the practical skills they need to get along in English.

Each level of ON YOUR WAY includes a **Student's Book,** a **Teacher's Manual,** a **Workbook** and a set of **Cassettes.** Each level can be taught in approximately forty-eight to seventy-two hours of classroom instruction, depending on how the workbook and supplementary suggestions in the Teacher's Manual are used.

KEY FEATURES

Integrating Basic Skills

The field of English-language teaching has undergone many changes. Methods come in and go out of fashion. Often what is good gets thrown out with what has proven less successful. ON YOUR WAY has taken the strengths of grammatical and functional approaches and integrated them to give students the best of both worlds.

The material in ON YOUR WAY is organized by grammar points. ON YOUR WAY, however, is not a rigidly grammatical course. Students learn grammatical forms not as isolated items but as building blocks that help them learn English comfortably and that they can transfer to real-life situations. In ON YOUR WAY, students learn grammar as they talk about their various personal interests, express their opinions and feelings, exchange information about their daily lives, solve problems and accomplish tasks.

ON YOUR WAY never loses sight of its primary goal—to provide students with a rich environment that will help them learn to communicate in English.

Structural Control and Natural Language

The grammatical items presented in ON YOUR WAY have been selected and graded according to structural clarity and functional usefulness. Students learn the most frequently used forms of each structure in contexts that illustrate how English is used by native speakers.

Life Skills and Cultural Information

Each unit of Student's Book 1 and alternate units in Books 2 and 3 have a section that focuses on the practical skills students need to function competently in an English-speaking environment. Students learn to use language appropriate to such situations as banking, housing, medical care, transportation and employment. In addition to asking for and giving information in conversational roleplays, students learn to understand and fill out forms.

While ON YOUR WAY provides a great deal of information about U.S. culture, it also recognizes the importance of giving students opportunities to refer to their own cultural experiences. Through discussion questions, systematically introduced in Books 2 and 3, students are able to explore cross-cultural differences and similarities.

A Clear Methodology

ON YOUR WAY is clear and easy to use. Teachers can immediately see the communicative purpose of each exercise. Little preparation is necessary since the activities are easy to set up and explain. They are arranged so that they provide a pedagogically sound progression—from controlled exercises to open-ended personalizations in which individuals talk about their own situations. Students also do written exercises that reinforce the language they have been practicing orally. A great deal of variety in exercise type and topic holds students' interest.

ON YOUR WAY has a flexible design to meet the needs of various class sizes. All the oral exercises can be practiced with the whole class. For more variety, these exercises can be done as small-group or pair work. In addition to giving individuals more time to talk, small-group or pair work lets students interact with each other and practice the language on their own.

Recycling

Students are given repeated opportunities to practice previously learned language in new contexts. Great care has been taken to re-enter vocabulary, expressions and grammatical items to help students gain proficiency and confidence in English.

Listening Comprehension

From the beginning of the course, ON YOUR WAY provides students with many opportunities to develop their listening comprehension skills. Previously practiced material is presented in a variety of listening exercises. These range from simple clozes and dictations to more complex tasks such as completing charts or writing messages based on information students hear.

Writing

In Student's Book 1, writing is used to reinforce the language students have learned in conversational exchanges. A variety of exercises teaches students about punctuation, capitalization and sentence formation. Students follow simple models and write notes, messages and postcards.

In Student's Books 2 and 3, separate **Writing** sections are found in alternate units. Here students learn about sentence and paragraph formation, paragraph unity and the organization of ideas. They study the style and format of different kinds of written material—messages, notes, formal and friendly letters, postcards, newspaper articles and academic writing. Then, following models, students practice expressing themselves in all of these written styles.

Reading

In Student's Book 1, students read short paragraphs that recycle language they have learned in conversational exchanges. They also are exposed to such types of real reading as ads, menus, forms and brochures.

In Student's Books 2 and 3, there is a separate **Reading** section in alternate units. The specially written reading passages relate to the theme of the unit and as often as possible recycle the vocabulary and structures of the unit. They also present new language for students to recognize only. The exercises in the **Reading** sections develop such skills as previewing, understanding vocabulary from context, inferring, finding the main idea and skimming.

STUDENT'S BOOK 3

There are twelve units in the Student's Book. After every second unit, there is a two-page section that reviews grammar, functions, vocabulary and expressions. The **Review** sections can be used in class or at home for self-study.

The Story

Each Student's Book has a separate story that presents interesting characters in true-to-life situations and provides students with a real context for the language they learn.

Student's Book 3 is an exciting mystery story. A reporter for a Houston newspaper gets involved in trying to solve a mystery while she is covering a news story. In addition to the main plot, the storyline focuses on such everyday events as looking for a job, bringing up children, visiting someone in the hospital and being concerned about family and friends.

Organization of the Units

Each Student's Book unit is divided into three parts: **Introduction, Practice** and **Life Skills** or **Reading** and **Writing.**

I. Introduction

Conversation. Each unit begins with an *Introductory Conversation* which sets the scene for the story and presents new structures, vocabulary and functions in context.

Comprehension check, synonym search, Warm Up and *Develop Your Vocabulary.* The conversation is followed by three activities. The first is a basic *comprehension exercise* which quickly checks students' understanding of the conversation. Students do not have to produce new structures here and can often answer in one or two words.

The second exercise is a *synonym search* where students are given several words or phrases and must find words or phrases with the same meaning in the *Introductory Conversation.*

The third exercise is a conversational *Warm Up* which practices such functions presented in the *Introductory Conversation* as inviting, asking for and giving information, complaining or making an excuse. The *Warm Up* allows students to get involved immediately in the purpose of the unit as well as to identify more closely with the characters.

Students have the opportunity and should be encouraged to practice the conversations using their own information. To this end, *Warm Ups* are accompanied by a *Develop Your Vocabulary* box. This box, which also accompanies exercises throughout the unit, presents vocabulary and expressions which students may wish to substitute into the conversations. The teacher or other students can provide additional vocabulary and expressions based on what students want or need to say.

II. Practice

Grammar. This section is divided into two to four parts which focus on different grammatical structures. Each structure is first presented in a paradigm which makes its meaning, form and use clear. The paradigm is followed by contextual exercises which allow students to practice the structures for communicative purposes.

Functions. Throughout the book, language is presented functionally to convey and practice the grammar in natural exchanges. Language is always presented in segments that make its use clear. To keep the language natural, it is sometimes presented independently of a grammatical paradigm; the grammar in such exchanges is not meant to be explained or analyzed. For example, in Unit 8 students practice complaining and sympathizing using the embedded clause *I know what you mean.*

A: It's hard being unemployed.

B: I know what you mean. Being unemployed is terrible.

III. Life Skills

The last part of each even-numbered unit is called **Life Skills.** This section focuses on the development of skills and strategies for getting along in an English-speaking environment. **Life Skills** takes the students from asking for and giving medical information in Unit 2 to finding out about employment benefits in Unit 12.

Exercises and Special Features

Exercises

All of the exercises in the Student's Book are intended for small-group, pair or individual work. Exercises intended for group work can incorporate the entire class for purposes of presentation and review. In this way, you can preview an activity before small groups of two or three students come together for communicative practice.

Apart from the listening activities described below, every unit consists of a variety of oral-exchange exercises, fill-in exercises, completion exercises and written exercises based on authentic tasks. These are followed by exercises that personalize the practice.

Special Exercises

There are several special exercises that are repeated regularly throughout the book:

1. *Just for Fun* provides a variety of exercises which include games, puzzles and creative tasks. These student-centered activities give the class an opportunity to practice what they have learned in a relaxed and enjoyable way.

2. *Review and Build* exercises combine previously learned grammar and/or functions with new material that is currently being practiced. For example, in Unit 9 the students review adjectives while they practice adverbs of manner.

3. *Put It All Together* ends the **Practice** section of each odd-numbered unit. This listening activity incorporates all the grammar points presented in the unit. The task, which is always related to the storyline, gives the students the opportunity to hear all the new language components come together in natural discourse while it checks comprehension of these structures.

4. *On Your Own* is a student-centered activity. In this section, students have the chance to discuss issues raised in the unit and to express their own feelings and opinions about them. When relevant, students can examine cross-cultural differences and similarities.

Listening

There are two or three types of listening activities in each unit. They each have a different purpose:

1. *Cloze listenings* focus on isolated grammatical items and vocabulary words or on sentence completion.

2. *Dictations* require that students write in correct form what they have heard spoken in natural speed, rhythm and intonation.

3. *Real-life listening tasks* allow students to listen to a recorded message or to "eavesdrop" on a conversation. Students complete a comprehension task or get information in situations similar to those they might encounter on their own.

For Your Information

For Your Information sections provide students with information that is both functional and cultural. For example, Unit 4 gives information on store refund policies and also on clothing sizes in the United States. In Unit 12 students are given information on paycheck deductions and help with reading their pay stubs.

Additional Material

Review

Two-page **Review** sections follow every second unit. They provide students with more practice in the grammar, functions, vocabulary and expressions of the preceding two units. The **Review** sections can be used in the classroom or at home for self-study.

Pronunciation

Pronunciation exercises are found at the back of the book and are recorded on cassette. As often as possible, the exercises are based on the vocabulary and expressions of the unit. They practice sound-symbol correspondence, stress, reduction, blending, rhythm and intonation.

COURSE COMPONENTS

The following components accompany each Student's Book:

- a **Teacher's Manual,** made up of the Student's Book, with notes on each page on how to present and practice the material. Each unit begins with a summary of the structures, functions and vocabulary presented. This *Language Summary* is followed by the *Pronunciation exercises* from the Student's Book and additional *warm-up exercises* in a section called *Getting Started.* Optional exercises, games and pronunciation practice and the answers to exercises are included in the *Teaching Notes.* At the back of the **Teacher's Manual** are found the *Tapescript,* which contains all of the material on cassette, *Answers to the Workbook Exercises* and *Midterm* and *Final Tests.*
- a **Workbook,** which reinforces writing skills taught in the Student's Book and provides written practice of the key structures, functions and vocabulary of each unit. A variety of exercises, including games and puzzles, is designed for individual work. The **Workbook** exercises can be done in class with students working alone or in pairs, or they can be assigned as homework.
- **Cassettes,** consisting of recordings of the *Introductory Conversations, Listening exercises, Pronunciation exercises* and *Listening Comprehension Tests.*

ORGANIZATION OF THE TEACHER'S MANUAL

Each unit of the Teacher's Manual is organized into three main parts: **Language Summary, Pronunciation** and **Teaching Notes. Midterm** and **Final Tests** are found at the back of the Teacher's Manual.

An audio cue [cassette icon] indicates sections of the Student's Book that have been recorded on cassette.

Language Summary

The **Language Summary** includes the new *structures, functions, vocabulary items and expressions* and *Life Skills topics* for the unit. Expressions are ungraded items which have been introduced to give students language used naturally in a given situation. Unless they are also the grammar focus of the exercise, these expressions should not be grammatically analyzed. Some of the vocabulary and expressions marked *for recognition only* will appear later for active use.

Pronunciation

There is a set of **Pronunciation** exercises for each unit of the Student's Book. They give practice in recognizing and distinguishing sounds and in reproducing stress patterns of Standard American English. These exercises are found after the **Language Summary** in each unit of this Teacher's Manual, and their **Tapescripts** are at the back of this book. The **Teaching Notes** in each unit point out appropriate places in each lesson for practicing pronunciation points. However, you may prefer to do all the exercises after the unit is completed. General procedures for using the exercises begin below.

Teaching Notes

The **Teaching Notes** appear alongside the reduced Student's Book pages to which they refer. They present suggestions for preparing students for each exercise (including teaching new vocabulary, expressions and structures) and suggestions for using each of the exercises. In addition, there are extra warm-up exercises (in a section called *Getting Started),* optional exercises and activities, answers to each of the exercises and suggestions for more pronunciation practice.

Tests

A **Midterm** and a **Final Test** are located at the end of the Teacher's Manual. They are reproducible and should be given after Units 6 and 12 respectively. Clear and simple, these achievements tests are designed to measure the students' acquisition of the functions, competencies and grammar presented in the Student's Book.

Each test consists of 50 items, some of which are multiple choice, some fill-ins. All items are contextualized. There is also an optional **Listening Comprehension** section for each test, consisting of 10 multiple-choice items. These listening comprehension tests are recorded on the cassettes following the pronunciation exercises for Units 6 and 12. You may play the cassette or read the Tapescript of p. 000 and p. 000 of this Teacher's Manual.

GENERAL PROCEDURES FOR USING THE EXERCISES

In all units except Unit 1, the **Teaching Notes** include several warm-up exercises to be done before beginning that unit. They are found in the *Getting Started* section. There will usually be short dialogs from a previous unit, but there will sometimes be games or other activities. The purpose of the warm-up exercises is to review an important skill or structure, to give the students opportunity for relaxed and natural communication and to give students a sense of having mastered a skill before going on to new material.

Introduction

Introductory Conversation

Preteaching. Suggestions are given in each unit for teaching structural and vocabulary items that are necessary for a complete understanding of the material. You may wish to teach them before you present the conversation, or you may prefer to let students listen to the new material in context first. Look at each conversation carefully and vary your approach to suit the material.

Preparation. Talk about the conversation and the illustrations by asking *who-* and *what-*questions, e.g.: *Who's in the picture? Who's doing (a particular activity)? What's happening in the picture? What's that?*

Give a listening goal. Write one or more focus questions on the board and ask the students to find the answers while listening to the conversation. These questions direct the students' attention to essential information in the conversation and let them know they can get the gist of a conversation without knowing every word. The focus questions will also direct their reading in Step 5 of the procedures.

Procedures

1. Ask the students to cover up the conversation. It is important that the students develop skills in using nonverbal cues, so they should get used to looking at the illustrations and listening without reading the written conversation. Explain they will have a chance to look at the conversation later.

2. Play the cassette or read the conversation to the students. The students listen and look at the illustrations.

3. Ask for answers to the focus questions.

4. Repeat Step 2, but this time ask the students to look at the conversation as they listen.

5. Ask the students to read the conversation silently. This helps reinforce aural learning. It also gives the students the opportunity to see the conversation as a whole and identify language difficulties.

6. Discuss language difficulties and new vocabulary. Possible language difficulties are pointed out in the *Preteaching* section of individual units, and suggestions are given on how to explain them.

7. Now read the conversation aloud or play the cassette sentence by sentence. Ask the class to repeat each sentence after you or the cassette. Then ask individuals to repeat the sentences. Encourage the students to ask you to repeat words or lines for better understanding or to practice correct pronunciation.

8. Have the students practice the conversation in small groups. Check around the class, listening in as the groups practice.

9. *Optional:* If the students are willing, one or more groups can act out or improvise the conversation for the class.

Say *That's right, That's wrong . . .*

This is one of three types of comprehension checks following the *Introductory Conversation.*

1. Read each sentence aloud.

2. Ask for volunteers.

3. Call on a student to answer or have the class answer in chorus.

4. *Optional:* Have the students work in pairs or small groups. One student reads the question aloud, and the other student or students answer.

Correct the information

This and the following comprehension check are new to the series and are more challenging than earlier ones. Procedures are the same as in the exercise above, but you must allow a little more time for students to locate the answers in the *Introductory Conversation.* Have students respond in short answers as they would naturally in conversation. For example, in Unit 1 the answer to *Pete is the reporters' boss* would be *No. Angela is.*

Give a reason

For this comprehension check, students should again respond in short answers. For example, in Unit 5, *Pete wants Linda to take a break* should be answered with *Because she's been working too hard.* Procedures are the same as in the above exercise.

Find a word or phrase . . .

In this vocabulary exercise, students search for synonyms in the *Introductory Conversation.* They are prompted to infer the meaning of new words and expressions from context. Vocabulary treated in this exercise is not defined in the preteaching section.

1. Call on volunteers for each item and write the answers on the board as they are given.

2. If time permits, write additional examples of how to use these new words.

Warm Up

This is a short conversational exchange that provides simple practice with one or more of the functions of the *Introductory Conversation.* Additional vocabulary is introduced to vary and personalize the *Warm Up* in the box labeled *Develop Your Vocabulary.*

1. Explain the situation of the *Warm Up* dialog, usually by referring to the illustrations or situation of the *Introductory Conversation.*

2. Read the dialog aloud. Italics indicate substitutions are to be made for that word or phrase, so be careful not to stress italicized words.

3. Divide the class into two groups. Ask one group to take the part of A and the other the part of B. Ask the two groups to repeat after you in chorus. Then have them switch roles.

4. *Develop Your Vocabulary.* Write the substitutions on the board and explain new vocabulary as necessary. Suggestions are given in each unit for introducing new vocabulary. Then ask the class what other words or expressions they have heard or used in this situation. Write their contributions on the board.

5. Pronounce the new vocabulary and have the students repeat in chorus.

6. Ask pairs of students to practice the dialog, guiding them in the substitutions by pointing to the vocabulary on the board.

7. If time allows, divide the class into pairs for further practice. Selectively check students while they are practicing.

Practice

Study Box

1. Read each item aloud. Write it on the board and underline any part you want to call to the students' attention.

2. Give a simple explanation of the grammar, using the suggestions in the **Teaching Notes** for each unit. Whenever possible, use blackboard diagrams to reinforce and clarify your explanations. For example, to show how the verbs differ in direct and reported speech:

"My sister's sick," she said. She	said	her sister	was	sick.
"I can't meet her," she said. She	said	she	couldn't	meet her.

3. Read the sentences in the *Study Box* sentence by sentence and have the students repeat them in chorus.

4. *Optional:* Do a short drill. For example, cue students to produce sentences with *not enough* or *too:*

T: Janie can't watch that TV show. She's only three years old.
S: Janie's too young to watch that TV show.

Exercises

Look at the pictures

1. Explain new vocabulary by referring to the pictures and to the suggestions in the **Teaching Notes.**

2. Pronounce each new word and have the students repeat it.

3. Say one sentence or read the dialog sentence by sentence and have the students repeat after you in chorus.

4. Call on one student at a time to make a sentence or call on pairs to do the dialog until the exercise is completed.

5. The instruction to look at the pictures and talk about the activities illustrated in them encourages students to engage in freer and more open-ended conversations. Using the suggestions in the **Teaching Notes,** help students find alternate ways to ask or answer the questions and ways to prolong the conversation.

6. Divide the class into pairs for further practice.

7. Some exercises ask students to write the exercise after they have practiced orally. See the procedures for **Writing sentences,** on p. 00. This is also an optional way to extend an oral exercise.

Ask and answer questions

This is a short dialog in which substitutions are made. Sometimes the additional vocabulary is in a *Develop Your Vocabulary* box; at other times the students are asked to personalize the dialog and supply their own information. Adapt the following procedures depending on the exercise.

1. Read the dialog aloud and have the class repeat after you in chorus. Remember that the italics indicate substitutions are to be made, and do not stress those words or phrases.

2. Divide the class into two sections. One section takes the part of A; the other takes the part of B. Have them repeat the dialog after you and then switch roles.

3. If new vocabulary is being introduced, write it on the board and explain it using the suggestions in the ***Teaching Notes*** or by referring to the illustrations. Add any additional vocabulary suggested by the students or that you feel is appropriate.

4. Pronounce the new vocabulary and have the students repeat after you in chorus.

5. Call on pairs of students to practice the dialog. Guide them in using substitutions by cuing them from the work on the board, or ask them to use their own information if the dialog asks for personalization of the material.

6. The students continue to practice in pairs.

Match the sentence with the picture

1. The students work in pairs or small groups so that they can discuss the picture. They write their answers on a piece of paper.

2. Write the answers on the board as the students call them out. Ask the students why they chose a particular answer—what feature in the picture was their cue?

3. The students correct their own work or exchange papers with a classmate.

Complete the sentences/paragraph

1. Ask the students to look over the exercise to see what kind of information or structure is being asked for.

2. Students work individually or in pairs to write the answers in their notebooks or on a separate piece of paper.

3. Call on volunteers to read the completed sentences. As they read, write the correct fill-ins on the board.

4. Students check their own work, or exchange papers and check a classmate's work.

Make sentences

This exercise is done orally.

1. Model the sentence or read the model in the Student's Book and point out the structure the students are working on.

2. Call on volunteers to do the remaining sentences.

3. Divide the class into small groups or pairs for further practice.

4. *Optional:* After oral practice, have students write the sentences, and then put them on the board for correction.

Writing sentences

Writing exercises that call for connected sentences are included in the **Practice** sections as well as the **Writing** lessons in alternate units.

1. Model the sentences on the board or read the model in the Student's Book with the class and point out the features that students are being called upon to imitate in their own writing. Specific suggestions are given in the **Teaching Notes** for each unit.

2. The students work individually on the exercise.

3. Several students put their work on the board.

4. Correct the board work and answer the students' questions.

5. The students exchange papers and read each other's work. Leave time to answer the questions this activity will elicit.

6. In addition to putting work on the board, teachers may choose to collect and correct the writing exercises as well. If so, remember it is better not to correct every error, but to concentrate on the structures practiced in the exercise.

Listening

There are three types of listening exercises: *cloze, task* and *dictation. Dictations* will be read through twice on the cassette—once at natural speed, and then at natural speed but with beeps that signal you to stop the tape and give the students time to write. The general procedure for *dictations* is the same as for *cloze* and *task* exercises, but the students may require an additional listening.

If you do not wish to use the cassette, you can simply read the **Tapescript** for the listening exercises to the students. The **Tapescript** is found at the back of this book, and the procedures for the exercises are the same whether you choose to read the exercises or play the cassette.

Note: Play the cassette or read the **Tapescript** as many times as necessary.

1. Draw the students' attention to the illustrations or describe the situation in order to set the context of the conversation. Suggestions are given in the **Teaching Notes** for introducing unfamiliar vocabulary. New words and expressions can be explained here, or you may decide to wait until the cassette has been played through once (or you have read the material once) and the students have heard the new material in context.

2. Ask the students to read the instructions and the follow-up questions. Make sure they understand what information they need to listen for.

3. Tell the students that there may be words in the listening that they do not understand but that they should be able to complete the exercise anyway.

4. Now play the cassette or read the passage aloud. Encourage students to pick up as much information as possible on the first listening.

5. If necessary, go over any language problems that impede understanding.

6. Play or read the passage again for the students to check their answers. Repeat a third time if necessary.

7. Send the students to the board to write the answers or have the students call out the answers to cloze or task exercises as you write them on the board. When the board work is correct, students can check their own work or exchange papers and check a classmate's.

Life Skills

Procedures for the most frequent exercises in this section of the unit are given below. **Life Skills** contains many of the exercise types used in the **Introduction** and **Practice** sections. The **Teaching Notes** for each exercise will refer to the appropriate procedure.

Look at the document

In this exercise, students are asked to extract information from a list or a document such as a map and then to use this information in a dialog, a completion exercise or a writing task.

1. Have students read the instructions and look at the document to get an overview of the kind of information it contains.

2. Ask focus questions that will elicit the type of information in the material.

3. Pronounce any new vocabulary, such as place names, and ask students to repeat in chorus.

4. Introduce any new vocabulary, using the suggestions in the **Teaching Notes.**

5. Have students work in groups or pairs to find the information. For some exercises, suggest that they jot the information down to use in exercises that follow.

6. Practice the exchange or the sentences by reading the model sentence or dialog and having the class repeat in chorus.

7. Call on volunteers to ask and answer questions or make sentences.

8. Students continue to work in pairs for further practice.

9. *Optional:* After the exercise has been done orally, have students work individually and write the sentences. Then send several students to put the work on the board. After the board work has been corrected, they can exchange papers and check each other's work.

Complete the chart

This exercise may be done either in groups or individually.

1. Ask the students to complete the chart on a separate piece of paper. If they are working in groups, each group may want to appoint a "secretary" to record answers for the group.

2. As the groups work, go around the room to help.

3. Send several students or a group to put the work on the board.

4. If the exercise includes a personalization, ask for volunteers and put their answers on the board.

5. Correct the board work and ask for questions.

6. *Optional:* Have students or groups exchange papers to check each other's work. This will give them an opportunity to share any personal information elicited by the exercise.

Roleplay

This exercise follows one involving a dialog, so students will already have practiced a conversation that provides the basis for their roleplay.

1. Review the functions being practiced, e.g., asking for information.

2. Explain to the students that they are to act out a similar situation. They should use the conversation freely, for ideas.

3. Use the suggestions in the **Teaching Notes** for adapting the material in the exercise for roleplays. Also, tell students they can give themselves particular characteristics or circumstances to make the roleplay more interesting.

For Your Information

This section includes important information that will help students in day-to-day survival and communication. Suggestions for presenting and practicing this material are given in the **Teaching Notes** for individual units.

Teachers in an English-speaking country other than the U.S. may adapt this information to their own situation, using the material as a guide for choosing important skills and for structuring exercises. In non-English-speaking environments, the material is, of course, helpful for those planning to use their new skills in the future. However, even students who are not planning to immigrate to or visit an English-speaking country will find that this section provides interesting cultural information for discussion and comparison.

1. Read the information to the class and discuss cultural features of the information, perhaps by asking for comparison with the students' own culture.

2. Pronounce any new words and phrases for the students and have them repeat in chorus.

3. Follow procedures in the **Teaching Notes** for particular exercises.

On Your Own

This section presents discussion topics suggested by the material in the unit. The **Teaching Notes** focus on a number of points of discussion for each topic, and teachers will want to add their own suggestions. At this point, mistakes in grammar should be ignored, or at most, major errors related to the grammar just covered may be pointed out after a student has completed a comment. The point here, however, is to encourage free conversation.

1. Begin the discussion by relating the topic to the unit with some general comments. For example, in Unit 4, you can say: *Ken has been unemployed for three months. What should he do?* Then go on to ask individuals some of the questions in the Student's Book. Write a few major points on the board as students answer.

2. Once the discussion is underway with the whole class, divide the class into small groups to continue the discussion.

3. Go from group to group participating as appropriate. In groups that have trouble getting started, use some of the suggested points in the **Teaching Notes** to spark discussion. Encourage students to talk about their own experience with a topic, not just offer generalized opinions.

4. Groups may wish to appoint a secretary to jot down major points discussed and a spokesperson to present the group's views to the whole class at the end of the discussion.

Reading

Suggestions are given in the **Teaching Notes** of each unit for an introductory discussion of the **Reading** and for teaching new structural or vocabulary items that are necessary for a complete understanding of the material. The introductory discussion develops skills in predicting content. It motivates the class by awakening students' interest in the subject and by making them aware of their own opinions. You may wish to teach the new structural or vocabulary items before the class reads the selection, or you may prefer to let students see the new material in context first.

Preparation. All the selections in Book Three represent typical newspaper readings—news stories, an advice column, a recipe, reviews, classified ads. First, discuss the type of reading and elicit what kind of information or point of view the students expect from this kind of article. Discuss the selection, its format, headline and its illustration by asking *wh-* questions: *Who's/What's in the picture? What will you find out by reading this article? When do you look for this kind of information?*

Give a reading goal. Write one or more focus questions on the board and ask the students to find the answers while reading.

Procedures

1. Ask students to read the selection silently.

2. Do the *Comprehension* exercise. This exercise focuses on main ideas in the reading and helps students recognize important points. Do the exercise as a whole class or in groups, depending on whether the class finishes the reading at about the same time.

3. After discussing any problems in comprehension, ask the class to reread the selection, starting at the beginning and skimming rapidly. This rereading will help students integrate points covered in the comprehension exercise.

4. In groups or as a whole class, do the *Skill* exercises. The **Teaching Notes** of each unit refer you to the relevant general procedures in other sections of the Teacher's Manual.

5. Discuss the selection, eliciting students' opinions on the ideas presented. The discussion can be in small groups or as a whole class. See the general procedures for *On Your Own*.

Comprehension

Answer the questions

1. Read a question. Give students a chance to locate the relevant section of the text, if necessary.

2. Call on a volunteer to answer.

3. Alternatively, students work in groups or pairs. One student asks the question and another answers.

4. If the questions lend themselves to more extended discussion, call on volunteers to discuss why they made a particular choice.

Complete the sentences

Follow Steps 2–4 of *Answer the questions* above.

Special skills

In addition to *Comprehension* exercises, each unit focuses on a particular reading skill or strategy. The **Teaching Notes** for each exercise will provide procedures or refer you to the relevant general procedures in other sections of the Teacher's Manual.

Matching

1. Have students look over the exercise to see what kind of information is being asked for.

2. The class works individually or in pairs to complete the exercise. Ask students to write the answers on a separate piece of paper.

3. Ask volunteers to read the matched sentences. Write the answers on the board as students call them out.

Put the sentences in the right order

The procedure is the same as *Matching* (above). For Step 3, ask a volunteer to read the complete exercise in order. Then put the letters of the ordered sentences on the board. Discuss what clues in the text led students to order the sentences as they did.

Optional: Do this exercise as a game, in small groups:

1. Write each sentence on a slip of paper or card, making as many copies as there are groups. Assign each sentence a letter or number.

2. Distribute a set of cards to each group.

3. Appoint a secretary, or have each group choose a secretary who will write down the order of the sentences.

4. Explain that each group is to put the sentences in the correct order. Group members must read their sentences aloud, *not* pass the cards around. The secretary writes down the order of the sentences by referring to the number or letter.

5. Write the answers on the board as the class calls them out.

Writing

Each **Writing** section focuses on one skill and assigns a writing task that will give practice in this skill in a natural and useful way. Each skill is introduced briefly, with an example. A prewriting activity, either controlled writing or discussion, follows. The students then do the writing task, which is based on a model. The **Teaching Notes** for each unit give specific suggestions for teaching each of these steps and often will suggest ways of creating a communicative context for the writing task.

Procedures

1. Introduce the skill, using the suggestions in the **Teaching Notes** for the unit. Give additional examples if necessary.

2. Introduce any new vocabulary, using the suggestions in the **Teaching Notes.**

3. Discuss how and when the type of writing in the task is used. Ask students for their own experience in this type of writing.

4. Have students work in pairs or small groups for the prewriting activities or discussions. Have several students put any written exercises on the board for comparison. For discussion activities, call on several groups for their contributions.

5. Point out features in the model you wish students to imitate.

6. Students work individually to do the writing task. Suggestions are given in the **Teaching Notes** of individual units for follow-up activities.

7. The teacher may collect and mark these papers, or have students read each other's work in groups. If the papers are collected, some may be copied and distributed for the class to read. Remember—when marking student work, do not correct every error, but concentrate instead on the grammatical structures discussed in the unit and focused on in the writing lesson.

Pronunciation

Pronunciation exercises are found at the back of the Student's Book and at the beginning of each unit of this Teacher's Manual.

The **Pronunciation** exercises give practice in the pronunciation of Standard American English. They practice distinguishing and pronouncing similar sounds, especially where distinctions in meaning are involved such as between the past and present tenses or between *can* and *can't.* They also practice stress and intonation, from the blending of unstressed syllables to the intonation of particular sentence patterns such as *if*-clauses. As much as possible, the pronunciation points are integrated with the functions and structures of each unit. The **Teaching Notes** for each unit will suggest appropriate places within the unit to introduce and practice these points, or you may decide to practice pronunciation all at once before or after each unit. In each case, you should introduce the pronunciation point to be practiced and give some examples.

The **Pronunciation** exercises are recorded on cassette, but if you do not wish to use the cassette, you can simply read the **Pronunciation** exercises to the students. The **Tapescript** is found at the back of this book, and the procedures for the exercises are the same whether you choose to read the exercises or play the cassette.

Note: Play the cassette or read the **Tapescript** as many times as necessary.

Recognizing and distinguishing sounds

These exercises teach students to recognize or distinguish particular sounds and to understand them in the context of natural spoken English. After practicing them in completion exercises, the students use them in conversations or sentences.

1 Listen and write

The students differentiate between sounds and perform related tasks.

Procedures

a. Model the sound or sounds and give more examples.

b. Go over the instructions to make sure that students understand what information is being elicited.

c. Play the cassette (or read the tapescript) and have the students write the answers on a piece of paper.

d. Elicit the answers and write them on the board. Students check their own work or exchange papers and check each other's.

e. *Optional:* Read the sentences yourself and ask students to repeat.

2 Listen and complete
Students listen to a conversation or sentences that contain the sounds they are learning to recognize and then fill in the blanks to complete the conversation or sentences.

Procedures
a. Model the sound or sounds and give more examples.

b. Discuss any differences in meaning involved if two sounds are being distinguished.

c. Ask the students to read the exercise to understand the information they are going to be asked for.

d. Play the cassette (or read the tapescript) through once for the class to listen to only.

e. Play the cassette (or read the tapescript) through a second time and have the students write the answers on a piece of paper.

f. Elicit the answers and write them on the board. Students check their own work or exchange papers and check each other's.

3 Listen and repeat
Students listen to and repeat a conversation or sentences that contain the sound they learned to distinguish and pronounce in the previous exercise.

Procedures
a. The students listen to the cassette (or to you) and repeat the sentences in chorus.

b. After the class practices in chorus, call on individuals to say the sentences.

Stress and intonation
Exercises in this section give students practice in recognizing and reproducing the appropriate stress in words, phrases and sentences. This includes blending of unstressed words or syllables and the intonation of particular sentence patterns.

1 Listen and notice
Students listen to a conversation or sentences that demonstrate the stress or intonation pattern in natural spoken English.

Procedures
a. Write an example of the pronunciation point on the board. Mark the stressed or unstressed syllable to be practiced or show the intonation pattern. Then model the pronunciation and give more examples.

b. Refer to the **Teaching Notes** for that unit and point out any differences in meaning involved.

c. Play the cassette (or read the tapescript).

d. *Optional:* Read the sentences yourself and call on individuals to repeat after you.

2 Listen to the sentences and mark the stressed word/cross out the unstressed word or syllable
After listening to a conversation, sentences or words that demonstrate the stress pattern, students mark stressed or unstressed words or syllables in an exercise.

Procedures
a. If appropriate, explain that the pronunciation of a word in a sentence may change depending on whether it is stressed or unstressed. Students will listen to the words and, depending on the exercise, mark either the word where they hear the stress fall or the syllable that is not stressed.

b. Write a sentence or word on the board as an example. Pronounce it and mark the stress.

c. Ask the students to copy the sentences or words onto a separate piece of paper.

d. Play the cassette (or read the tapescript) and have students mark the words or syllables.

e. Elicit the answers and write them on the board for students to check their own work.

f. If necessary, play the cassette again (or read the tapescript again) for students to resolve any difficulties.

g. Play the cassette once more (or read the tapescript) and ask students to repeat each sentence in chorus.

h. *Optional:* Read the sentences or words yourself and ask individuals to repeat them after you.

3 Listen and complete these phrases/sentences
Students complete conversations or sentences, or provide appropriate punctuation for the stress or intonation pattern they are practicing. Procedures are the same as for *2 Listen to the sentences . . .*

4 Listen and repeat
Students repeat a conversation or sentences that demonstrate the stress or intonation pattern they are practicing. Often this is done as the final step of a completion exercise.

Procedures
a. Play the cassette (or read the tapescript) and ask students to repeat in chorus.

b. After the class practices in chorus, call on individuals to say the sentences.

STRESS AND INTONATION

If Pete finds an apartment,

he'll move.

Have you seen Linda?

Intonation:

These lines show how the level of the voice rises and falls.

They ought to give Linda a medal.

Why didn't you call the police?

Stress:

The dots show where the voice is loudest; this is usually the most important part of the sentence. A small dot indicates normal sentence stress; a large dot means that the word or syllable should be given extra stress to show emphasis.

Transcriptions have been made by using a modified version of the International Phonetic Alphabet taken from Clifford H. Prator, Jr.'s *Manual of American English Pronunciation*, 1957. (Note that the symbol /ṭ/ has been added.)

PRONUNCIATION GUIDE

SYMBOL	ENGLISH EXAMPLES	
Consonants		
b	boat	/bot/
d	dark	/dark/
f	far	/far/
g	gold	/gold/
h	home	/hom/
k	cold	/kold/
	kodak	/kȯdæk/
l	let	/lɛt/
m	man	/mæn/
n	next	/nɛkst/
ŋ	ring	/riŋ/
	sink	/siŋk/
p	part	/part/
r	rest	/rɛst/
s	send	/sɛnd/
	city	/sɪṭɪ/*
ʃ	ship	/ʃɪp/
t	ten	/tɛn/
ṭ	better	/bɛ̇ṭər/**
θ	think	/θɪŋk/
ð	that	/ðæt/
v	very	/vɛ̇rɪ/
w	went	/wɛnt/

SYMBOL	ENGLISH EXAMPLES	
Consonants		
y	you	/yu/
z	zoo	/zu/
	rose	/roz/
	knows	/noz/
ʒ	pleasure	/plɛ̇ʒər/
	vision	/vɪ̇ʒən/
tʃ	children	/tʃɪ̇ldrən/
dʒ	jury	/dʒʊ̇rɪ/
	edge	/ɛdʒ/
	age	/edʒ/
Vowels		
a	far	/far/
	hot	/hat/
æ	am	/æm/
e	late	/let/
	raise	/rez/
ɛ	get	/gɛt/
	bread	/brɛd/
	said	/sɛd/
i	see	/si/
	receive	/rɪsi̇v/
	reach	/ritʃ/
ɪ	in	/ɪn/
	become	/bɪkə̇m/

SYMBOL	ENGLISH EXAMPLES	
Vowels		
ɔ	for	/fɔr/
	all	/ɔl/
	ought	/ɔt/
o	go	/go/
	coat	/kot/
u	rule	/rul/
	too	/tu/
ʊ	put	/pʊt/
	could	/kʊd/
	good	/gʊd/
ə	but	/bət/
	bird	/bərd/
	other	/ə̇ðər/
	ago	/əgȯ/
	reason	/ri̇zən/
Diphthongs		
aɪ	I	/aɪ/
	cry	/kraɪ/
aʊ	now	/naʊ/
	house	/haʊs/
ɔɪ	boy	/bɔɪ/
	noise	/nɔɪz/

*When /ɪ/ occurs at the end of a word, the pronunciation is usually between /ɪ/ and /i/.
**/ṭ/ is pronounced like a quick English /d/.

UNIT 1

Language Summary

Functions

Giving advice
Why doesn't she look for a job as a computer operator?
Introducing
Sam, have you met Carlos? It's a pleasure to meet you, Carlos.
Talking about ability
Angela can use a computer.
Talking about habits
Does Linda usually write about politics? Yes, she does. But now she's writing about arson.

Introduction

Vocabulary

arson
arsonist
burn down *trans*
cover *v*
(= report on)
do over
erase
except *prep*
firefighter
go out (= be extinguished)
if
introduce
newsroom
politics
power *n*
prefer
put out
(= extinguish)
quickly
reporter
spread *v*
story (= report)
sure *adv*
typewriter
warehouse
who *rel pron*
whole *adj*

Expressions

How do you do?
It's a pleasure to meet you.
the only one
Welcome to . . .

Practice A

Structures

Simple present tense contrasted with present progressive tense*
Linda usually writes about politics. But now she's writing about arson.

*Structure introduced in Student's Book 2 and reviewed here.

Vocabulary

full
meal

For recognition only
election
get back *intrans*
(= return)
space (= room)
staff *n*

Expressions

For recognition only
Any news from . . . ?
I can't wait to see you.

Practice B

Structures

Modals: *Can, should, might**
Pete can use a computer.
Tom should learn to use one.
He might not like it.

Vocabulary

afraid
bilingual
caterer
chauffeur
chef
language
tailor
translator

For recognition only
film *n* (= movie)

Practice C

Structures

Separable two-word verbs
The firefighters couldn't put out the fire.
They couldn't put the fire out.
They couldn't put it out.

Vocabulary

assignment
bring back
call up *trans*
drop off *trans*
get back *trans*
hand in
look over *trans*
(= examine)
look up *trans*
mistake *n*
point out
revised
think over

Expression

by *6:00*

Put It All Together

Vocabulary

For recognition only
destroy
injure
kill
save *v*

For recognition only—on cassette
jump *v*

On Your Own

Vocabulary

For recognition only
compare
consider
cost *n*
editorial
type *n* (= kind)
where *conj*

Reading

Skills

Predicting
Understanding pronouns

Vocabulary

For recognition only
advise
available
found *past part*
however
immigrate
realize
true
uncommon
valuable

Expressions

For recognition only
back home
in a way
in all this time

Writing

Skill

Expressing contrast or contradiction

Task

Writing a letter describing a problem

Vocabulary

available
difference
difficulty
however
immigrate
obey

For recognition only
visa

Pronunciation

Pronunciation points

1. Practicing final /s/ and /z/
2. Understanding object pronouns
3. Special emphasis in sentences

Pronunciation exercises. *The pronunciation exercises for Unit 1 also appear in the Student's Book on p. 112.*

Part 1. *Practicing final /s/ and /z/*

Listen and complete these sentences.
See Intro. p. xiii, Recognizing and distinguishing sounds 2 and 3

1. Tom ______ ______ ______.
2. He doesn't like ______.
3. He ______ to use a typewriter.
4. Linda usually ______ ______ about ______.
5. Now ______ doing a story about all ______ ______ ______.

Answers: 1. writes, sports, news 2. computers 3. prefers 4. writes, stories, politics 5. she's, those, warehouse, fires

Now listen again and repeat the sentences.

Part 2. *Understanding object pronouns*

Listen to these sentences and complete each one with the correct object pronoun.
See Intro. p. xiii, Stress and intonation 3 and 4

1. Look ______ up in the dictionary.
2. Why don't you call ______ up?
3. Drop ______ off at the library.
4. Pete's handing ______ in.
5. Yes, do ______ over.
6. Please point ______ out to me.

Answers: 1. it 2. her 3. him 4. them 5. it 6. her

Now listen again and repeat the sentences.

Part 3. *Special emphasis in sentences*

Listen to these sentences and mark the word that has the *most* stress in each sentence.
Example: I think it's right.
See Intro. p. xiii, Stress and intonation 2 and 4

1. Well, I think so.
2. But you speak Spanish.
3. It's very difficult.
4. I won't understand anything.

Answers: The words with the most stress are marked in the sentences above.

Now listen again and repeat the sentences.

See p. 136 for the Pronunciation Tapescript.

Teaching Notes

Introduction

1. **Introductory Conversation.** See Intro. p. vii.

Preteaching

Group vocabulary items by content:
newsroom Where the reporters and editors of a newspaper work.
reporter Reports news for newspaper, radio or TV.
politics Issues relating to government.
story Here, a report in the newspaper.
the only one Here, means none of the other reporters use the typewriter now.
erase Demonstrate by writing on and erasing from the blackboard.
warehouse Large building used to store things.
arson The crime of starting fires on purpose.
arsonist Someone who starts fires on purpose.
spread (v) Demonstrate with a diagram on the blackboard.
firefighter Ask students to infer the meaning.
put the fire out The firefighters do this.

Preparation

Set the context by asking if any students have been in or have worked in a newsroom. Ask: *What was it like? Did the editors and reporters use computers?* Ask focus questions: *Which reporter dislikes the computer?* (Tom does.) *Is Linda covering politics now?* (No. She's covering an arson story.)

Exercise 2. See Intro. p. viii, Correct the information.
Answers: 1. Angela is the reporters' boss. Pete's a new reporter. 2. Tom dislikes computers. He prefers typewriters. 3. Linda thinks the fires are arson. 4. The fires are hard to put out. 5. Arsonists set fires. Firefighters put out fires.

Exercise 3. See Intro. p. viii, Find a word or phrase . . .
Answers: 1. power 2. do over 3. covers 4. prefers

Exercise 4. See Intro. p. viii, Warm Up.
Have students introduce themselves to students around them. Then they can work in small groups introducing each other. Elicit questions students can ask to extend the introductions, e.g.: *Where do you work? What do you do for a living? How long have you studied English? Where are you from?*

Develop Your Vocabulary: *Do you know . . . ? I'd like you to meet . . .*
Review various relationships: This is my husband/sister/brother/aunt/uncle/sister/sister-in-law/colleague/classmate.

Pronunciation point: Practice the stress and intonation pattern:

Sam, meet Bill. Bill works in my office.

Laura, meet Fumiko. Fumiko is in my math class.

UNIT 1

Welcome to the Houston Herald

1 This is the newsroom of the Houston *Herald* daily newspaper. Angela Lentini, the editor, is welcoming Pete Gómez, a new reporter. Listen to their conversation.

1

ANGELA: Well, this is our newsroom, Pete.
PETE: I'm glad to see you're using computers.
ANGELA: We just started using them last year, and our reporters are happy with the change.

2

TOM: Except for me, Angela.
ANGELA: Pete, meet Tom Kirby, our sports reporter, and the only one who still prefers to use a typewriter.
TOM: How do you do, Pete?
PETE: Nice to meet you, Tom. You know, it's easier to do your stories over on the computer. You should try it some day.
TOM: I just don't like machines that can erase your work if the power goes out.

3

ANGELA: And this is Linda Smith. She usually covers politics, but right now she's working on something special.
LINDA: That's right. I'm doing a story about all those warehouse fires.
PETE: Do the police think it might be arson?
LINDA: Well, *I* think so. The fires always happen at night, and they spread very quickly. The whole building burns down before the firefighters can put the fire out. It sure sounds like the work of an arsonist to me.

2 Correct the information.

1. Pete is the reporters' boss.
2. Tom likes computers.
3. Linda thinks the fires are an accident.
4. The fires are easy to put out.
5. Arsonists put out fires.

3 Find a word or phrase in the conversation that means:

1. electricity
2. do again
3. reports on
4. likes better

4 Warm Up

Introduce two people.

A: *Sam*, meet *Bill. Bill works in my office.*
B: *It's a pleasure* to meet you, *Bill.*
A: Good to meet you too.

DEVELOP YOUR VOCABULARY

Have you met *Carlos?*
I'd like to introduce you to *Reiko.*
This is my *wife, Ingrid.*
. . .

Practice

A.

> Linda usually **writes** about politics.
> Right now she**'s writing** about something special.

Usually

Now

1 The pictures show what Linda Smith usually does and what she is doing now. Ask and answer questions about Linda's habits.

1. arson / politics

A: Does Linda usually *write about arson?*
B: No, she doesn't. She usually *writes about politics.*
OR
A: Does Linda usually *write about politics?*
B: Yes, she does. But now she's *writing about arson.*

2. office / home
3. full meal / sandwich

Find three more differences between the pictures and talk about them.

2 Angela Lentini is introducing Pete Gómez to some other members of the news staff. Listen and write what she says about each person.

1. Cathy Wilson

She 

2. Brad Kimball

He ______________________________.

3. Minh Tran

He ______________________________.

Practice A

Study Box. See Intro. p. viii.

Simple present tense contrasted with present progressive tense. Explain that the simple present tense is used for repeated, habitual actions. Ask for examples of students' daily schedules, and write some examples with various subject pronouns.

I usually get up at 7:00. We usually drive to work.
He often works until 6:00 P.M.

Point out the final *-s* for the third person singular.

Explain that the present progressive tense is used for action happening at the moment. Write an example on the board:

Today we're beginning a new book.

Remind students that a form of *be* is needed to complete the verb.

Pronunciation point: Use the Study Box questions to contrast the intonation patterns:

Linda usually writes about politics.

Right now she's writing about something special.

Exercise 1. See Intro. p. ix, Look at the pictures.
Review the patterns for statements and questions on the board and point out that the base form of the verb is used in the question.

subject	verb	aux.	subject	verb
He usually	writes about crime.	Does	he usually	write about crime?

full meal Refer to the picture.

Answers: 2. A: Does Linda usually write/work in the office? B: Yes, she does. But now she's working at home OR A: Does Linda usually write/work at home? B: No, she doesn't. She usually writes/works in the office. 3. A: Does she usually eat/have a full meal? B: No, she doesn't. She usually just eats/has a sandwich. OR A: Does she usually just eat/have a sandwich? B: Yes, she does. But today she's eating/having a full meal.

Some other differences are: Linda usually uses a computer, but now she's using a typewriter. She usually drinks tea, but now she's drinking coffee. She usually works at her desk, but now she's working at her kitchen table.

Pronunciation point: Use this exercise to practice the intonation patterns that were pointed out in the Study Box sentences.

Exercise 2. See Intro. p. ix, Listening.
Elicit types of newspaper workers—columnists, editors, photographers. Then tell students they will find out what these people do.

Answers: 1. . . . articles on health and food. Now she's writing a story on new restaurants. 2. . . . does a lot of different things. He's helping Linda with the arson story right now. 3. . . . takes great pictures. He's also working on the arson story.

Exercise 3. See Intro. p. ix, Complete the sentences/paragraph.
Go over the information in the Note Box and give examples:

I have an old car.
We know these words already.
She thinks today's lesson is interesting.
I need a pen right now.
You seem tired.

**election* When people vote for (choose) an official such as a mayor or president.
**get back* Means *return.* Refer to the context.
**space* Refer to the context—where Pete writes that he and Michael need a bigger apartment.
**staff* Employees. Point out that *staff* is usually singular in American English.

Answers: 2. 'm working 3. 'm writing 4. like 5. seem 6. is helping 7. need 8. works 9. stays 10. comes 11. know 12. think 13. want.

Exercise 4. See Intro. p. ix, Writing sentences.
Review adverbs of frequency, *always, sometimes, never, usually, rarely,* that are associated with the simple present tense.

Optional warm up: Write some cues on the board and have students work in pairs to ask and answer questions about their daily schedule and habits, e.g.: *What time do you eat breakfast? When do you go to work/school in the morning? Do you always eat lunch in the same place? Do you ever go to the movies or theater in the evening? What do you usually watch on TV?* Students can write the results of their conversation or report in groups of four.

Optional: For Step 5 of the general procedures, when students exchange papers and read each others' work, encourage them to converse about the information in their sentences. They can ask why and elicit examples from each other, e.g.:

A: My friend Taki usually likes to study alone.
B: Why does he like to study alone? Do you ever study together?

*Words marked with asterisks are for recognition only.

3 Pete Gómez is writing a letter to his girlfriend, Suzanne. Complete his letter with the simple present or the present progressive form of the verb.

Note: These verbs are not usually used in the progressive form.

be	like, love, want
have (=possession), own	need
have to	seem
know, think	

The Houston Herald

Dear Suzanne,

I'm typing (1. type) this letter because I _____ (2. work) late at the office. I _____ (3. write) a story for the Sunday paper about the next election. I really _____ (4. like) it here. The other reporters _____ (5. seem) very nice. One of them, the sports reporter, Tom Kirby, _____ (6. help) me find a bigger apartment. Michael and I really _____ (7. need) more space.

The staff here _____ (8. work) harder than we did at the Dallas Star. Tom says that he often _____ (9. stay) late, and another reporter, Linda Smith, _____ (10. come) in every Saturday. I _____ (11. know) it's going to be hard, but I _____ (12. think) I can learn a lot here.

Well, I should get back to work. I _____ (13. want) to finish this article before I go home. I really miss you and can't wait to see you next week.

Love,
Pete

P.S. Any news from Montreal? How's your family doing?

4 Write about a friend's or relative's habits. Then tell a classmate.

1. My friend _____ (name) usually _____.
2. He (She) never _____.
3. He (She) _____ at 6:30.
4. It's 5:00 now. I think _____ (friend's name).

B.

Pete **can** use a computer. Tom **can't.**
Tom **should** learn to use one. He **shouldn't** be afraid to.
He **might** like it. He **might not.**

Note: We do not contract *might not.*

1 Talk about the pictures. Use the words below them.

1. Angela can use a computer.

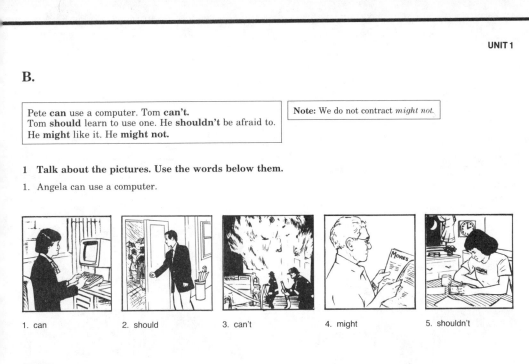

1. can

2. should

3. can't

4. might

5. shouldn't

2 Linda Smith and Tom Kirby are having lunch. Read the sentences below. Then listen to their conversation and choose the correct answers.

1. Linda thinks she _might_ (might / should) see a movie.
2. Tom thinks she ________ (should / shouldn't) see a Spanish movie.
3. Tom ________ (can / might) understand Spanish.
4. Linda says she ________ (might not / can't) understand a film in Spanish.
5. Tom thinks she ________ (might / might not) understand a lot.
6. Linda thinks she ________ (should / might) work more tonight.
7. Tom thinks Linda ________ (shouldn't / can't) work so much.
8. He thinks she ________ (should / can't) have a good time.

3 Talk about someone who doesn't like his or her job.

A: *My sister* really hates *her* job.
B: Then *she* should find a new one. Can *she type?*
A: Yes, *she* can.
B: Why doesn't *she* look for a job as *a computer operator? She* might like that better.

OR

A: No, *she* can't.
B: Hmm. Then *she* can't be *a computer operator.* Well, can *she* . . . ?

Student B can use these ideas:

drive . . . taxi driver, chauffeur
sew . . . tailor
speak two languages . . . bilingual secretary, translator
work with numbers . . . cashier, bookkeeper
cook . . . chef, caterer

Practice B

Study Box. See Intro. p. viii.

Modals: *Can, should, might.* Review the meanings of the modals: *can* indicates ability; *might* suggests something is possible. Explain *should* by giving a situation and asking for advice, e.g.:

T: This room is cold. What should we do?
A: We should close the window.
B: We should ask for more heat.

Point out that the base form of the verb follows the modal. Review formation of questions: *Pete can use a computer. Can Tom use one? Where should we go for lunch today?* Write questions on the board and have students discuss their answers in pairs or small groups, e.g.: *Can you play a musical instrument/drive a car? What languages can you speak? What errands should you do this week? Should you write some letters soon? What might happen after you finish this class? What movie might you see this weekend?*

be afraid Means have the feeling that something bad might happen.

Pronunciation points: Contrast pronunciation of *can* /kən/ and *can't* /kænt/. Point out the stress pattern in:

Pete can use a computer. /pitkənyuzəkəmpyuṭər/

Exercise 1. See Intro. p. ix, Look at the pictures.
Elicit the storyline and who these characters are. Encourage students to prolong their discussion of the pictures, especially with modals, e.g.: *Why should Angela use the computer and not a typewriter?* (She can work fast that way. She can correct her work on the computer.) *What will happen if Pete forgets his umbrella?* (He might catch cold/get sick.)

Answers may vary: 2. Pete should take his umbrella. 3. The firefighters can't put out the (warehouse) fires. 4. Tom might see a movie. 5. Linda shouldn't work so hard/stay up so late.

Exercise 2. See Intro. p. ix, Listening.
Answers: 2. should 3. can 4. can't 5. might 6. should 7. shouldn't 8. should

Optional: Ask students' opinions of this situation: *Should Linda work that hard? Can she be successful at her job if she takes Tom's advice?*

Exercise 3. See Intro. p. ix, Ask and answer questions.
tailor Someone who makes or repairs clothing. Also give *dressmaker* and *seamstress,* words usually used for women.
language Give examples: *English, French, Chinese.*
bilingual Means able to speak two languages. Refer to the context.
translator Someone who changes conversations or documents from one language into another. Again, refer to the context.
chef Someone who cooks professionally.
caterer Someone hired to prepare and serve food.

Practice C

Study Box. See Intro. p. viii.

Separable two-word verbs. Explain that in two-word verbs the entire phrase is the verb. Point out that if a noun is used for the object, the object can go either in between the verb and the preposition or after the phrase. But if the object is a pronoun, it must appear between the verb and the preposition.

Students should infer the meanings of verbs from Ex. 1.
bring back Hand a book to a student. Then say, *Please bring back the book tomorrow.*
do over Means *do again.* Tell students, *If you make mistakes on your homework, you can do it over.*
find out Means find information. Linda wants to find out who started those fires.
hand in Means give completed work to someone. Students hand in their homework. Reporters hand in their stories.
pick up Means buy or get something, often on the way to another place, e.g., *He picked up theater tickets on his way home.*
think over Means think about before making a decision, e.g., *I'm thinking over your job offer.*

Pronunciation points: Point out the stress patterns for the two positions of the noun as object:

put out the fire   put the fire out

Point out stress and reduction when the object is a pronoun:

Put it out. /pʊt̬ɪt̬aʊt/ Call her up. /kɔlərəp/

Call him up. /kɔlɪməp/ Call them up. /kɔlðəməp/

Practice the position of the object and the pronunciation points with Part 2 of the **Pronunciation** exercises.

Exercise 1. See Intro. p. ix, Match the sentence with the picture.
mistake (n) Demonstrate by misspelling a word on the board and correcting it.

Answers: 1. c 2. a 3. e 4. d 5. b

Exercise 2. See Intro. p. ix, Look at the pictures.
Answers: 1. Angela's pointing it out. 2. Linda's looking it up. 3. Minh's calling her up. 4. Angela's looking it over. 5. Pete's dropping him off.

Exercise 3. See Intro. p. ix, Complete the sentences/paragraph.
Answers: 1. OR hand their stories in 2. look them over 3. point out problems OR point problems out 4. do over their stories OR do their stories over 5. bring them back

C.

The firefighters couldn't	**put out** the fire. **put** the fire **out.** **put** it **out.**

Note: You have to separate these verbs when you use pronouns.
You cannot say:
The firefighters couldn't ~~put out it.~~

Other separable two-word verbs:		
bring back	find out	look up
call up	get back	pick up
do over	hand in	point out
drop off	look over	think over

1 Choose the sentences that describe the pictures.

1. ____ Angela's pointing out a mistake.
2. __a__ Linda's looking up a word.
3. ____ Minh's calling up his wife.
4. ____ Angela's looking over an article.
5. ____ Pete's dropping off his son.

2 Now use a pronoun in each sentence like this:

Linda's looking it up.

3 Angela Lentini is telling Pete Gómez about procedures for writing an article at the *Herald.* Complete the sentences. Be sure to put the pronouns in the correct place.

1. The reporters have to __hand in their stories__ (hand in (their stories)) by 3:00.
2. Then the editors ____________ (look over (them)).
   They ____________ (point out (problems)).
4. Sometimes the reporters have to ____________ (do over (their stories)).
5. Then they have to ____________ (bring back (them)) by 6:00.

4 Now ask and answer questions about procedures at the *Herald.*

1. When / have to hand in stories

A: When do the reporters have to hand in their stories?

B: They have to hand them in by 3:00.

2. Who / look over the stories
3. What / point out
4. What / reporters sometimes have to do
5. When / have to bring back revised stories

5 Ask a friend about his or her schoolwork.

A: Do you ever *look up words in the dictionary?*

B: Yes, I *look them up when I don't understand them.*
OR No, I never *look them up.*

You can use these ideas:

hand in assignments late
look over your homework
call up classmates for help
point out other students' mistakes

Note: Not all two-word verbs can be separated:
Look at the book.→ **Look at** it.
They'**re talking about** Angela. → They'**re talking about** her.
He always **waits for** the bus. → He always **waits for** it.

PUT IT ALL TOGETHER

Linda called Pete to tell him about another fire. Listen to their conversation and decide which story will be in tomorrow's newspaper.

1 The Houst— **Fire Kills 5, Injures 50**

2 The Houst— **Fire Destroys School**

3 The Houston Herald **Arsonist Burns Factory Down**

4 The Houston Herald **Firefighters Save Building**

ON YOUR OWN

Discuss these questions with your classmates.

1 Do you usually read the newspaper? If so, which one(s)? What's your favorite section?

2 How do the newspapers from your country compare to the newspapers where you are now living? Consider the cost, size, ads, editorials, special sections, and number and type of photographs.

Exercise 4. See Intro. p. ix, Ask and answer questions.
revised stories Stories the reporters have done over.

Answers: 2. A: Who looks over the stories/looks the stories over? B: The editors look them over. 3. A: What do they/the editors point out? B: They point out problems. 4. A: What do reporters sometimes have to do? B: They sometimes have to do over their stories/do their stories over. 5. A: When do they have to bring back revised stories? B: They have to bring them back by 6:00.

Exercise 5. See Intro. p. ix, Ask and answer questions.
Additional ideas are: *find out the right answers in class, drop off your work when you can't come to class, pick up good ideas in discussions with other students, do over work when it has mistakes.*

Optional: Students work in groups and use separable two-word verbs to create *how-to lists* for passing (or failing) a course, e.g.:

1. You should always hand in assignments on time (late).
2. You should always (never) look over your homework.

Put It All Together. See Intro. p. ix, Listening.

Point out telegraphic headline style, which leaves out articles and other words and gives a sense of immediacy by using the simple present tense instead of the past or present perfect tense. Explain the first headline: *A fire has killed five people and injured fifty people.* Point out that five people are dead, and fifty people are hurt.

**destroy* and **save* Elicit the contrast between them, *Which building is still standing?*

Call on volunteers for the answer (3), and then discuss why the other choices are wrong:
1. No one was in the factory. 2. It was a factory, not a school. 4. Linda doesn't think the firefighters can save the building.

On Your Own. See Intro. p. xi.

To introduce the context of the story, bring in major English language newspapers and discuss the different sections, especially those discussed in Unit 1 (crime, politics, food, self-help). Students can also bring in papers in their own languages.

1. Ask the students to bring in their favorite section of a newspaper, either English language or their native language.

2. Compare foreign language newspapers with English language newspapers. Ask groups to report on their discussions.

Reading

See Intro. p. xi.
*immigrate Means move to another country.
*available Means easy to get.
*in a way Refer to the context (line 10). The statement is true, but only in one way—because he hasn't learned English.
*in all this time Means during this long period of time.
*found Here, the past participle of *find*.
*back home Here, means in their native country.
*however Means *but*. Used in more formal writing.
*uncommon Means *unusual*, something you rarely see.
*realize Means understand or accept the idea that . . .
*valuable Refer to the context (line 44). The writer can use her English there to find a good job, gain status, etc.

Exercise 1.
If students have already discussed this type of column in their **On Your Own** activity, remind them of their discussion. In addition, bring in a similar column from a local newspaper and use it to discuss the prediction questions and give more examples of the features of an advice column.

Answers. It's an article about personal problems. We recognize it by the title of the article, the picture of the columnist, the letter format and the name used by the person who wrote in. We expect to find advice about personal problems in it.

Exercise 2. See Intro. p. xi, Answer the questions.
Answers: 1. The writer's husband. 2. The writer's husband. 3. The writer. 4. The writer. 5. Dr. Cousins. 6. The writer.

Exercise 3.
Have the students write the pronouns and their antecedents on a separate piece of paper. Then call for volunteers and write the answers on the board.

Answers: Letter 1. *he*/my husband, *our*/my husband's and my, *him*/my husband, *his*/my husband's, *this*/the question of whether life is better here or back home Letter 2. *one*/problem, *here*/in the United States, *there*/your country, *you all*/you and your children

Exercise 4. See Intro. p. xi, On Your Own.
Begin the discussion by calling on individuals and writing some of their ideas on the board. You can talk about why people don't want to learn a new language when they immigrate, specific reasons for going or staying (unemployment, social and medical services, education opportunities and cost, closeness of relatives), whether immigration is easier for men or women. Then go on to Step 2 of the general procedures.

Reading

1 Predicting. What kind of article is this? What helped you to recognize it? What kind of information do you expect to find in an article of this kind?

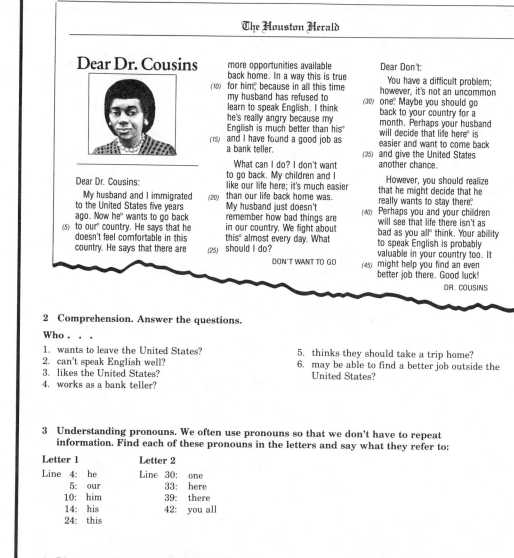

The Houston Herald

Dear Dr. Cousins

Dear Dr. Cousins:

My husband and I immigrated to the United States five years ago. Now he° wants to go back to our° country. He says that he doesn't feel comfortable in this country. He says that there are more opportunities available back home. In a way this is true for him° because in all this time my husband has refused to learn to speak English. I think he's really angry because my English is much better than his° and I have found a good job as a bank teller.

What can I do? I don't want to go back. My children and I like our life here; it's much easier than our life back home was. My husband just doesn't remember how bad things are in our country. We fight about this° almost every day. What should I do?

DON'T WANT TO GO

Dear Don't:

You have a difficult problem; however, it's not an uncommon one° Maybe you should go back to your country for a month. Perhaps your husband will decide that life here° is easier and want to come back and give the United States another chance.

However, you should realize that he might decide that he really wants to stay there°. Perhaps you and your children will see that life there isn't as bad as you all° think. Your ability to speak English is probably valuable in your country too. It might help you find an even better job there. Good luck!

DR. COUSINS

2 Comprehension. Answer the questions.

Who . . .

1. wants to leave the United States?
2. can't speak English well?
3. likes the United States?
4. works as a bank teller?
5. thinks they should take a trip home?
6. may be able to find a better job outside the United States?

3 Understanding pronouns. We often use pronouns so that we don't have to repeat information. Find each of these pronouns in the letters and say what they refer to:

Letter 1

Line 4: he
5: our
10: him
14: his
24: this

Letter 2

Line 30: one
33: here
39: there
42: you all

4 Discussion. What do you think? Discuss these questions with your classmates.

1. Do you think Dr. Cousins gave the woman good advice?
2. What would you advise her to do?

Writing

Skill: Expressing contrast or contradiction
Task: Writing a letter describing a problem

1 **We often use *however* instead of *but*, especially in formal speech and in writing.**

She wanted to immigrate, but she couldn't get a visa.
She wanted to immigrate; however, she couldn't get a visa.
OR She wanted to immigrate. However, she couldn't get a visa.

Rewrite these sentences using *however*. Write each sentence two ways.

1. We found an apartment, but it won't be available until June 1.
2. The students didn't understand all the words, but they were able to read the article.
3. Miguel wants to go home, but his wife and children are happy here.
4. Nguyen wants to work, but he can't find a good job.
5. There are many opportunities in this country, but there are also many difficulties.

2 **Complete these statements.**

1. All students need to do homework; however, . . .
2. Wives and husbands should talk over their differences; however, . . .
3. It's good to be ambitious. However, . . .
4. Immigrating to a new country can be exciting; however, . . .
5. Children should obey their parents. However, . . .

3 **Write a letter to Dr. Cousins similar to the one on page 8. Do not sign your real name. Give the letter to your teacher. Your teacher will give you another student's letter so that you can answer it. Try to use *however* in your letter and in your response.**

For pronunciation exercises for Unit 1, see page

Writing

See Intro. p. xii.

Exercise 1. See Intro. p. ix, Writing sentences.
Point out that both *but* and *however* express contrasts, and give an additional example: *I want to learn to speak English fluently, but my family only speaks Chinese at home.* Elicit some examples from the class. Point out the difference in punctuation. With *but*, the two clauses are joined by a comma. With *however*, they become two separate sentences or are joined by a semicolon. *However* is always followed by a comma.

difficulty A problem in the sense of something that is not easy to do, e.g., learning a new language and culture.

Answers: 1. We found an apartment; however, it won't be available until June 1. OR We found an apartment. However, it . . . 2. The students didn't understand all the words; however, they were able to read the article. OR The students didn't understand all the words. However, they . . . 3. Miguel wants to go home; however, his wife and children are happy here. OR Miguel wants to go home. However, his . . . 4. Nguyen wants to work; however, he can't find a good job. OR Nguyen wants to work. However, he . . . 5. There are many opportunities in this country; however, there are also many difficulties. OR There are many opportunities in this country. However, . . .

Exercise 2. See Intro. p. ix, Writing sentences.
difference A problem in the sense of different opinions or attitudes about a subject. The husband and wife in the letter to Dr. Cousins had differences.
obey Means do what someone tells you to do.

First elicit and put on the board examples for sentences 1 and 2, e.g.: *All students need to do homework; however, they also need time for fun. Wives and husbands should talk over their differences; however, sometimes they also need advice from someone else.* For less advanced classes, discuss the ideas in each sentence before students write.

Optional: Have students work with partners to discuss ideas and then write sentences together.

Exercise 3.
Have students reread the letter to Dr. Cousins. Elicit the structure of the letter and put a brief outline on the board:
Para. 1: Statement of problem. Husband's reasons for returning.
Para. 2: Request for help. Wife's reasons for staying.
Point out Dr. Cousins' reply uses *however* in the first paragraph to contrast ideas in the sentence. In the second paragraph, she uses *however* to contrast the main ideas of the two paragraphs.

For their letters, students might want to use topics they discussed in **Reading** Ex. 4.

For **Pronunciation** exercises for Unit 1, see p. 3.

UNIT 2

Language Summary

Functions

Asking for and giving explanations
Why did you sell your car? Because I wanted to buy a new one.
Asking for and giving information about a hospital patient
Can you please tell me the condition of Bill Thomas? Yes, his condition is listed as critical.
Talking about how long someone has done something
How long have you been a student here? Oh, for about two months.

Introduction

Vocabulary

cigarette	hit *past part*	optician
division (= department)	informant	scene (= place)
excellent	information	show up *intrans*
give up *trans*	officer	

Expressions

by the way	down there	get out of

Practice A

Structures

Present perfect tense with *for* and *since**
Minh has lived in the U.S. since he left Vietnam.
He's lived here for a long time.

Vocabulary

prison	quarter (period of time)	widow

For recognition only

institute	unconscious	witness *n*
spoken *past part*		

Expressions

a long while	for ages	the past *two years*
a short time	quite some time	

For recognition only

be in trouble	poor kid	

*Structure introduced in Student's Book 2 and reviewed here.

Practice B

Structures

Present perfect tense contrasted with simple past tense*
When did Pete move to Texas?
How long has he lived in Houston?

Vocabulary

college	journalism	suburbs
editor	member	

For recognition only

lunch hour	present *n* (time)	university
marital status		

For recognition only—on cassette
taught *past part*

Expression

in town

Practice C

Structure

Infinitive of purpose
Linda went to the factory to meet an informant.

Vocabulary

brick	pin *n* (for fastening)	rectangle
helmet	pot holder	rubber band
hold down	prepare for	straw (for drinking)
improve	protect	wall
needle *n*		
paper clip		

Life Skills

Health care
Filling out a medical ID card
Requesting patient information from the hospital
Giving a medical history

Vocabulary

anemia	guarded *adj* (condition)	none
asthma	hemorrhaging	nurses' station
concussion	intensive care (unit)	recovery (room)
condition	list *v*	related *adj*
connect	maternity	stable *adj* (= unchanging)
convulsion		wing (part of building)
critical		
fair *adj* (not good, not bad)		

For recognition only

- allergy
- drug *n*
- emergency room
- known *adj*
- medical
- medication
- penicillin
- visiting hours

Expressions

- heart disease
- high fever
- shortness of breath

On Your Own

Vocabulary

For recognition only

- hospitalization
- surgery

Expression

For recognition only

- second opinion

Pronunciation

Pronunciation points

1. Distinguishing /b/ and /v/
2. Distinguishing *has/hasn't* and *have/haven't*
3. Special emphasis in sentences

Pronunciation exercises. *The pronunciation exercises for Unit 2 also appear in the Student's Book on p. 112.*

Part 1. *Practicing* /b/ *and* /v/

Linda is talking to her new neighbor Vicky. Listen to their conversation and complete it.

See Intro. p. xiii, Recognizing and distinguishing sounds 2 and 3

VICKY: How long ________ (1) you ________ (2) in Houston, Linda?

LINDA: Oh, ________ (3) ________ (4) here all my life. I was ________ (5) in Houston. What about you?

VICKY: We ________ (6) to Texas in ________ (7) ________ (8) I got a ________ (9) job here.

LINDA: ________ (10) the way, ________ (11) you met ________ (12) and Alice? They ________ (13) in apartment 2 ________ (14).

VICKY: Yes. They seem ________ (15) nice.

Answers: 1. have 2. lived 3. I've 4. been 5. born 6. moved 7. November 8. because 9. better 10. By 11. have 12. Bill 13. live 14. B 15. very

Now listen again and repeat the conversation.

Part 2. *Distinguishing* hasn't *and* haven't

Listen to these sentences and complete them with *has, hasn't, have* or *haven't.*

See Intro. p. xiii, Recognizing and distinguishing sounds 2 and 3

1. Alice ________ seen Bill.
2. The doctors ________ examined him.
3. ________ he woken up?
4. The police ________ found the driver.
5. Alice ________ called her sister.

Answers: 1. hasn't 2. have 3. Hasn't 4. haven't 5. has

Now listen again and repeat the sentences.

Part 3. *Special emphasis in sentences*

Listen to these questions and mark the word that has the most stress in each question.

See Intro. p. xiii, Stress and intonation 2

1. Why didn't **you** call the police?
2. Why didn't you call the **police**?

Answers: The words with the most stress are marked in the sentences above.

Now listen again and match the questions with these answers.

a. Because Minh already called them.
b. Because I thought it was a job for the fire department.

Answers: 1. a 2. b

See p. 137 for the Pronunciation Tapescript.

Teaching Notes

Getting Started

Working with a new partner, students introduce themselves and tell what they do. Then, ask students to talk about something they are doing now that is out of the ordinary for them. Give some examples:

> Hi. I'm Maribel. I'm a computer programmer. I usually work in an office, but this week I'm working at home.
> OR I usually go to night school, but this semester I'm studying during the day.
> OR I usually drive to work, but today I took the bus.

Introduction

1. Introductory Conversation. See Intro. p. vii.

Preteaching

Officer A term of respect for a police officer, like *Ms.* or *Mr.*
division Here, means *department.*
by the way An expression used to change the subject slightly.
down there Means *there.*
excellent Means *very good.*
was hit by A car hit Bill.

Preparation

Elicit the storyline: *What does Linda do for a living? What story is she covering now?* Ask the focus questions: *Does Linda take photographs for her stories?* (No. Minh Tran does.) *Why didn't Bill Thomas meet Linda?* (He was hit by a car. OR He's in the hospital.)

Exercise 2. See Intro. p. viii, Say *That's Right . . .*
Answers: 1. That's wrong. 2. That's right. 3. That's right. 4. That's wrong. 5. That's wrong.

Exercise 3. See Intro. p. viii, Find a word or phrase . . .
Answers: 1. scene 2. show up 3. informant

Exercise 4. See Intro. p. viii, Warm Up.
optician Someone who makes glasses.
give up Means stop doing or using something.

Have students work with the same partner they had for **Getting Started.** They can use both the information in the idea box and the information they elicited from each other for this exercise.

UNIT 2 It Looks Like Arson

1 Linda Smith is at the police station talking to an investigator about the fire. Listen to their conversation.

1

LINDA: Do you think it was arson, Officer Brady?
BRADY: Well, I've been in the arson division since 1965, and it looks like arson to me. By the way, what were *you* doing down there on a Sunday afternoon?
LINDA: Actually, I went to meet an informant.
BRADY: How long have you been a reporter?
LINDA: For about five years. Why?
BRADY: I read your article in today's *Herald.* You're very good. Great photographs too.
LINDA: Thanks. Our photographer Minh Tran is excellent.
BRADY: Well, be careful. Things might get dangerous.

1

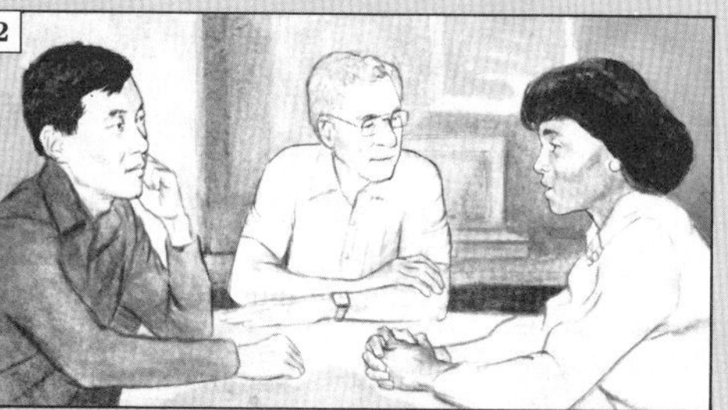

2

TOM: What did the police say?
LINDA: They think it *was* arson. They also wanted to know why I was at the scene of the fire.
MINH: Why *were* you there?
LINDA: To meet Bill Thomas, a neighbor of mine. He had some information for me, but he didn't show up.
TOM: How long did you wait?
LINDA: About a half an hour. Then I saw the smoke.

3

LINDA: Linda Smith.
ALICE: Linda, this is Alice Thomas. Billy's in the hospital. He was hit by a car.
LINDA: What? I'll be right there.

2 Say *That's right* or *That's wrong.*

1. Officer Brady works for the fire department.
2. Officer Brady thinks the fire was arson.
3. Linda didn't meet the informant.
4. Linda has been a reporter longer than Officer Brady has been a police officer.
5. Alice Thomas was in a car accident.

3 Find a word or phrase in the conversation that means:

1. location
2. arrive
3. a person who gives information

4 Warm Up

Think of something you know about a classmate and ask him or her about it.

A: Why did you *sell your car?*
B: Because I wanted to *buy a new one.*

Student A can use these ideas:

register for this class	give up *cigarettes*
go to *the optician*	become *a taxi driver*
immigrate to this country	

Practice

A.

Minh **has** Minh**'s**	**lived** in the U.S.A.	**since**	1975. he left Vietnam.
		for a long time.	

1 Talk about Minh's life. Use *for* and *since*.

1. Minh has lived in the United States since 1975.

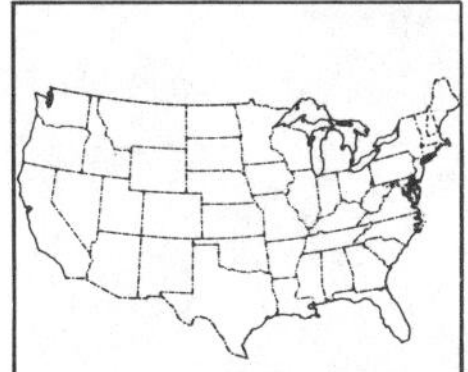
1. live / 1975

2. be / a long time

3. have / he came to this country

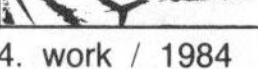
4. work / 1984

5. know / 3 years

2 Linda is at the hospital talking to Alice Thomas. Complete their conversation with *for* or *since*.

LINDA: Have you seen Bill yet?

ALICE: No, he's been unconscious since (1) they brought him in. The doctors have been with him ____ (2) more than two hours now.

LINDA: Don't worry. People are often unconscious after they've had an accident. Did the police tell you what happened?

ALICE: No, they don't know. They've only spoken to one witness ____ (3) Bill's been here. Oh, Linda, he's been so happy ____ (4) he started school. He's studied every night. And he hasn't been in trouble ____ (5) a long time.

LINDA: I'm sure he'll be all right, Alice.

Practice A

Study Box. See Intro. p. viii.

Present perfect tense with *for* and *since*.

1. Present perfect tense. Point out that the present perfect tense is formed with *have* or *has* + the past participle of the verb. Explain that this tense is used to talk about actions that began in the past and continue into the present. Put a time line and sentences on the board to demonstrate:

Past (Present perfect)	**Present**
X ________	X ________
1980	1990 (present year)

We have studied English for ten years.
We have studied English since 1980.

2. Contractions. Point out that the contractions *'ve* and *'s* are usually used in conversation.

3. *For* and *since*. *Since* is used with a particular point in time, which can also be expressed in a clause, e.g.: *since 9:00 P.M., since 1980, since I got to this country. For* is used with a period of time, e.g.: *for an hour, for ten years.*

Write some cues on the board:

be married   be an accountant   lived here   worn glasses

Have students make up sentences with *for* and *since.* Encourage them to use contractions.

T: she
S: She's been married for a year.

Pronunciation point: Put some of the students' sentences on the board and use them to point out and practice the final /z/ and /v/ for the contracted forms. Exercises from Parts 1 and 2 of the **Pronunciation** exercises can also be used here.

Exercise 1. See Intro. p. ix, Look at the pictures.
Answers: 2. He's been married for a long time. 3. He's had a motorcycle since he came to this country. 4. He's been working at the *Herald* since 1984. 5. He's known Linda for three years.

Exercise 2. See Intro. p. ix, Complete the sentences/paragraph.
**unconscious* Means *not awake.* Remind the class that Bill was hit by a car.
**witness (n)* Someone who sees an accident or crime and can give information about it.
**be in trouble* Here, means break the law, i.e., have problems with the police or other authorities.

First, elicit from the class who Linda, Alice and Bill are.

Answers: 2. for 3. since 4. since 5. for

Exercise 3. See Intro. p. ix, Listening.
prison Means *jail.*
**Institute* A school, often one for technical skills.
**poor kid* Pete feels sorry for Bill.

Answers: 2. 6 3. 12 4. 16 5. 17 6. 19 7. 19 8. 20 9. 21 10. 21

Now use the information. . . See Intro. p. ix, Ask and answer questions.
widow A woman whose husband has died.

To get the number of years, subtract Bill's age at each event from 21, his age now.

Pronunciation point: Part 1 of the **Pronunciation** exercises can be used here.

Answers: 2. A: How long has Bill's mother been a widow? B: For fifteen years. OR Since he was six. 3. A: How long has Bill been out of prison? B: For two years. OR Since he was nineteen. 4. A: How long has he been a mechanic? B: For two years. OR Since he was nineteen. OR Since he got out of prison. 5. A: How long has Bill had his high school diploma? B: For one year. OR Since he was twenty. 6. A: How long has he studied at Houston Business Institute? B: For two months.

Exercise 4. See Intro., p. ix, Ask and answer questions.
for a long while/quite some time/ages These expressions mean *a long time,* but are not specific.
quarter Here, means a school term of about twelve weeks.
for the past two years Means from two years ago until now.

Develop Your Vocabulary: Add *a little while* and *not long,* meaning a short, but indefinite, period of time.

Remind students that *since* can be used with a clause, e.g.: *I've worn glasses since I was in the third grade. I've had this jacket since I came to this country.*

Optional: Have students write some milestones in their own lives over the last five or ten years, e.g.:

1980	I came to this country.
1982	I got my Associate's Degree.
1984	I got married.

They can then exchange papers and write sentences with *for* or *since* about each other, e.g.:

Luis has been in this country since 1980.
OR He has been in this country for ten years.

3 Linda is telling Pete about Bill Thomas's life. Listen to their conversation and write Bill's age for each event and his age now.

Event	Bill's Age
1. family moved next to Linda	4
2. father died	___
3. police arrested him for the first time	___
4. quit school	___
5. went to prison for arson	___
6. got out of prison	___
7. became a mechanic	___
8. got his high school diploma	___
9. started studying computer programming at Houston Business Institute	___
Bill's age now	___

Now use the information to ask and answer questions about Bill's life. Begin with *How long.*

1. Linda / know Bill's family

A: How long has Linda known Bill's family?
B: For 17 years. OR Since Bill was four.

2. Bill's mother / be a widow
3. Bill / be out of prison
4. he / be a mechanic
5. Bill / have his high school diploma
6. he / study at Houston Business Institute

4 Ask a classmate about his or her life.

A: How long have you *been a student here?*
B: Oh, for *about two months.* OR Since *February.*

DEVELOP YOUR VOCABULARY

for:	
a long while	two quarters
quite some time	the past two years
only a short time	ages
one semester(s)	. . .

Student A can use these ideas:

wear *glasses*	work for *the phone company*
have *that jacket*	speak *Spanish*
live in *Chicago*	

B.

When **did** Pete **move** to Texas?	**In 1977.** Thirteen years **ago.**
How long **did** he **live** in Dallas before he moved to Houston?	**For** thirteen years.

How long **has** he **lived** in Houston?	**For** two months. **Since** March.

1 **Pete is asking Linda about Angela Lentini. Listen to their conversation and decide if Angela completed the action or is still doing it.**

	Completed past	Present
1. teach journalism		✓
2. be married		
3. live in the suburbs		

	Completed past	Present
4. live in town		
5. ski		
6. play the piano		

2 **Before he got his job at the Houston *Herald,* Pete Gómez had an interview with Angela Lentini. Look at Pete's résumé and the notes that Angela took during the interview.**

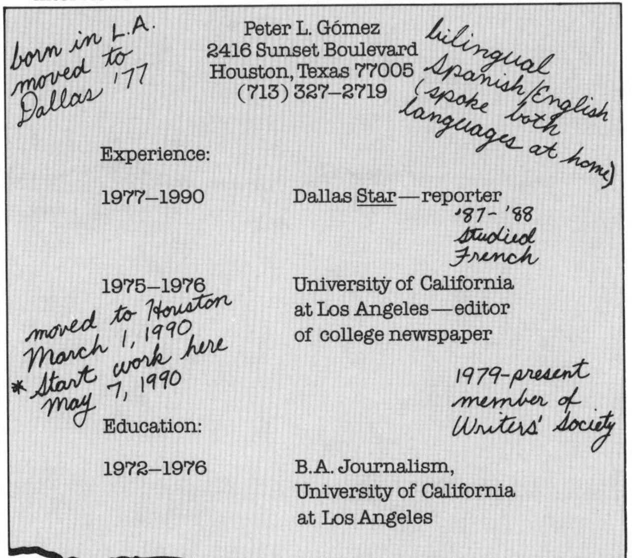

Peter L. Gómez
2416 Sunset Boulevard
Houston, Texas 77005
(713) 327–2719

born in L.A.
moved to Dallas '77

bilingual Spanish/English (spoke both languages at home)

Experience:

1977–1990 Dallas Star—reporter
'87–'88 studied French

1975–1976 University of California at Los Angeles—editor of college newspaper

moved to Houston March 1, 1990
* Start work here May 7, 1990

1979–present member of Writers' Society

Education:

1972–1976 B.A. Journalism, University of California at Los Angeles

Now find out about Pete's life. Pretend the date is May 9, 1990, and ask and answer questions like these:

A: How long *did he live in Dallas?*
B: He *lived there for thirteen years.*

A: How long *has he lived in Houston?*
B: He*'s lived there for two months (since March).*

Ask about these facts:

go to UCLA
speak Spanish
work for Dallas *Star*
write for Houston *Herald*
study French
be member of Writers' Society
be editor of college newspaper
live in Texas

Practice B

Study Box. See Intro. p. viii.

Present perfect tense contrasted with simple past tense.

1. Simple past tense. Review the word order for statements and questions and point out that the base form of the verb is used in questions and negative statements:

Pete went to school in California.
Did he stay after he graduated?
No. He didn't stay.

2. Uses of simple past and present perfect tenses. Explain that the simple past tense is used to talk about actions completed in the past. Contrast it with the present perfect tense, used for actions begun in the past but extending to the present. Point out how these distinctions work for the Study Box sentences: Pete lived in Dallas, but he doesn't live there anymore (simple past). He moved to Houston in the past, and he still lives there (present perfect).

3. Time markers. Point out that *ago* is used for a situation that ended in the past, and *for* and *since* are used for situations that continue into the present.

Exercise 1. See Intro. p. ix, Listening.
journalism The profession of gathering, writing and editing the news.
suburbs Areas close to the city. People usually live there and commute to work in the city. Use an example from your own area. Contrast with *in town* (in the city).
**taught* Here, the past participle of *teach.*

Explain or elicit the situation: *Pete is a new reporter, and he wants to find out about his boss.*

Answers: 2. present 3. past 4. present 5. past 6. present

Exercise 2. See Intro. p. x, Look at the document.
university, college Universities and colleges are both institutions for higher learning. A college is often part of a university and gives the Bachelor's Degree, while a university can also give Master's Degrees and Doctorates.
member Means part of a group, e.g., *Students are all members of the class.* Introduce *join,* or become a member of, a club.

Discuss a *résumé*—a summary of one's education and experience. People send these out to possible employers. Introduce *from . . . to* to describe a period of time ending in the past, e.g., *He went to UCLA from 1972 to 1976.*

Optional: Students roleplay the interview, figuring out the questions Angela asked from her notes.

Exercise 3. See Intro. p. ix, Complete the sentences/paragraph. **lunch hour* Compare with *rush hour*, a time when many people are doing the same thing.

If the question arises as students do this exercise, point out that certain verbs will not be used in the present perfect tense with *for* or *since* because the action happens at a point in time—*We opened our restaurant* OR *I decided to come here*—rather than over a period of time.

Answers: 2. did decide 3. came 4. 've lived 5. did open 6. 've been 7. Was 8. was 9. started 10. 's eaten 11. Did have 12. started 13. has been OR was

Optional: Teachers can write their own versions of this fill-in exercise, using small news items about their own areas. These rewritten interviews or prose passages can present information for discussion about the history of the place or interesting social or political events. For example, about a new Japanese high school opened in a northern suburb of New York: *How long has the school been there? Why did you decide to build it? How many students graduated last year?*

Exercise 4. See Intro. p. x, Complete the chart and p. ix, Ask and answer questions.

Optional: Have students fill out a résumé like Pete's in Ex. 2. They can then exchange résumés and interview each other.

3 Cathy Wilson interviewed the owner of a Japanese restaurant in Houston. Read the first part of the interview and complete it with the simple past or present perfect form of the verbs.

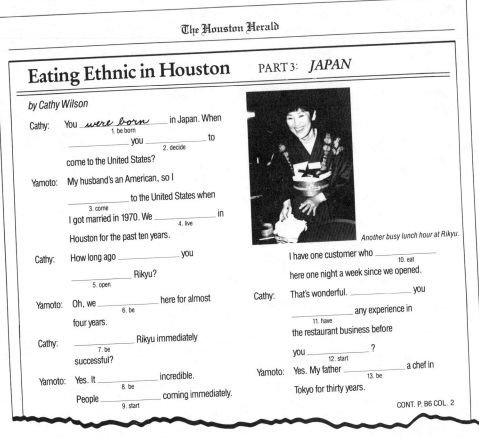

The Houston Herald

Eating Ethnic in Houston PART 3: *JAPAN*

by Cathy Wilson

Cathy: You were born (1. be born) in Japan. When ______ you ______ (2. decide) to come to the United States?

Yamoto: My husband's an American, so I ______ (3. come) to the United States when I got married in 1970. We ______ (4. live) in Houston for the past ten years.

Cathy: How long ago ______ you ______ (5. open) Rikyu?

Yamoto: Oh, we ______ (6. be) here for almost four years.

Cathy: ______ (7. be) Rikyu immediately successful?

Yamoto: Yes. It ______ (8. be) incredible. People ______ (9. start) coming immediately.

Another busy lunch hour at Rikyu.

I have one customer who ______ (10. eat) here one night a week since we opened.

Cathy: That's wonderful. ______ you ______ (11. have) any experience in the restaurant business before you ______ (12. start)?

Yamoto: Yes. My father ______ (13. be) a chef in Tokyo for thirty years.

CONT. P. B6 COL. 2

4 Complete this chart about yourself or someone you know.

NAME: ______________

Past	Present
address	....
....	....
occupation	....
marital status	....
interests	....

Now exchange charts with a classmate and interview him or her. Ask and answer questions like these with *how long:*

(past) How long did you live at ______________?
(present) How long have you lived at ______________?

C.

Why did Linda go to the factory?	She went **to meet** an informant.
Why does Minh wear a helmet?	**To protect** his head.

1 Match the questions in column A with the responses in column B to give reasons for these characters' actions.

A	B
1. __b__ Why did Linda go to the factory?	a. To look for mistakes.
2. ____ Why did Pete move to Houston?	b. To meet an informant.
3. ____ Why did Tom look at the newspaper?	c. To finish an article.
4. ____ Why is Pete going to Dallas next weekend?	d. To get a better job.
5. ____ Why did Bill's mother call up the *Herald?*	e. To see his girlfriend, Suzanne.
6. ____ Why does Angela look over the articles?	f. To protect his head.
7. ____ Why did Pete stay at work late?	g. To tell Linda about the accident.
8. ____ Why does Minh wear a helmet?	h. To find a good movie.

2 Ask a classmate why he or she signed up for this class.

A: Why did you sign up for this class?
B: To *improve my English.* How about you?
A: . . .

Student B can use these ideas:

meet new people	get out of the house
prepare for an exam	make new friends
get a promotion at work	

Just for Fun

3 What can you use these objects for? Think of as many uses as possible for each of these items. Use your imagination!

1. You can use bricks { to make a wall. / to draw a rectangle. / to hold papers down. / . . .

1. bricks

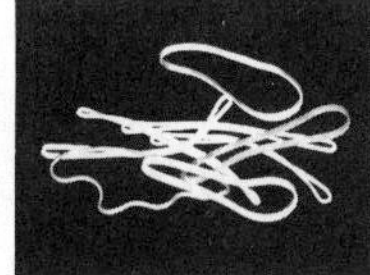

2. rubber bands

3. straw

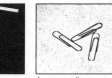

4. paper clips

5. pot holders

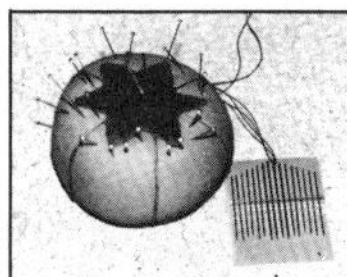

6. pins and needles

Practice C

Study Box. See Intro. p. viii.

Infinitive of purpose. Point out that the infinitive *to* + base form of the verb is used in these sentences to answer the question *Why:*

Linda went to the factory because she wanted to meet an informant there. Minh wears a helmet because he needs to protect his head when he's riding his motorcycle.

Create a number of contexts, using student's names. Then ask questions, e.g.:

Lara had a math test last week. She wanted to do well, but it was noisy at home, so she studied in the library. Why did she go to the library? (To study for her math test.)

Sam was buying a lot of books at the bookstore. When he got to the cashier, he took out his wallet. Why did Sam take out his wallet? (To pay for his books.)

Rolf had a large electricity bill last month, and now he turns all the lights out when he leaves the house. Why does Rolf turn out all the lights when he leaves the house? (To save money.)

Pronunciation points: Practice the stress pattern in:

She went to meet an informant. /ʃiwɛ̇ntəmi̇ṭənɪnfɔ̇rmənt/ and the stress and reduction in:

To protect his head. /təprətɛ̇ktɪzhɛ̇d/

Part 3 of the **Pronunciation** exercises can be used here.

Exercise 1. See Intro. p. xii, Matching.
Answers: 2. d 3. h 4. e 5. g 6. a 7. c 8. f

Exercise 2. See Intro. p. ix, Ask and answer questions.
Optional: Extend the exercise by having students work with the information in the résumés they completed for Ex. B4 on Student's Book p. 14. Suggest questions in various tenses, e.g.: *Why are you studying accounting? Why might you study French next year? Why should people join clubs at school?*

Optional: Bring in pictures from magazines and have students ask and answer questions about people's purposes in doing things. These can be real situations, e.g.: *Why is the mayor making that speech? To ask people to vote for him.* Or they can be imagined ones suggested by advertisements.

Exercise 3.
Do this exercise as a game. Divide the class into teams. Time them for each item. Whichever group finds the most uses for an item wins that round. In the case of a tie, have the class vote for the most imaginative uses.

Life Skills

In this unit students will learn terms and information important when seeking medical care. They will practice obtaining information over the telephone about a hospital patient and giving information about their own medical history.

Exercise 1.
**medical problems/medication* If someone has a heart problem, for example, and must take medicine for it every day, this should be on the card.
none Means Bill has no medical problems and is taking no medication.
**known drug allergies* This asks if you are sensitive to any medicines. Bill can't take penicillin, for example.
**penicillin* Have students use their dictionaries for this and *antibiotic.*

Remind students that Bill was unconscious when he was taken to the hospital, yet the doctors were able to find out important information such as his drug allergy.

Optional: Have students interview each other for this information.

Exercise 2. See Intro. p. ix, Listening.
connect Point out that the operator rings the nurses' station.
nurses' station The desk in the middle of the floor, where nurses work and keep their records.
condition Linda is asking how Bill is. Introduce the conditions listed in the next exercise: *good, fair* (not good, not bad), *guarded* (being watched carefully), *stable* (unchanging) and *critical* (very bad).
related (adj) That is, *Are you a relative?*
listed Point out the list of patients in Ex. 3.
visiting hours The hours when you can visit a patient.
wing Here, part of a building.

Answers: 1. Bill 2. Thomas 3. hospital 4. floor 5. Fifth 6. Linda 7. Smith 8. condition 9. patient 10. friend 11. his 12. hours 13. 1:30 14. 3:30 15. afternoon 16. 6:00 17. 8:30 18. room 19. 501 20. East 21. family

UNIT 2

Life Skills

Health care

1 **When Bill Thomas arrived at the hospital emergency room, the doctors knew who to call because Bill had an identification card in his wallet. Look at Bill's card and then fill out one of your own.**

MEDICAL I.D.

Patient's Name: Bill Thomas Date of Birth: 5/14/69
Address: 6411 Rolling Brook Lane, Houston Tx, 77038
Tel.: (Home) 225-7390 (Business) 255-0621
In Emergency Notify: (Name) Alice Thomas
(Relationship) Mother (Tel.) 858-7390
Medical Problems: none
Present Medication: none
Known Drug Allergies: Penicillin

2 **Linda Smith is calling the hospital to get some information about Bill. Listen and complete the conversation.**

OPERATOR: City Hospital.
LINDA: Hello, I'd like some information about ____(1) ____(2). He's a new patient at your ____(3).
OPERATOR: One minute. I'll connect you to the nurses' station on his ____(4).
(The operator rings the nurses' station.)
NURSE: ____(5) floor, Nurse Spencer.
LINDA: Hello. This is ____(6) ____(7). Can you please tell me the ____(8) of Bill Thomas?
NURSE: Are you related to the ____(9)?
LINDA: I'm a close ____(10) of the family.
NURSE: I see. Well, ____(11) condition is listed as critical.
LINDA: Oh. Can you tell me what the visiting ____(12) are?
NURSE: They're from ____(13) to ____(14) in the ____(15) and ____(16) to ____(17) at night.
LINDA: And what ____(18) is he in?
NURSE: ____(19). It's on the fifth floor, ____(20) Wing. But only ____(21) can see him now.
LINDA: Thank you.

3 **Here is a list of some other patients at City Hospital.**

NAME	ROOM	FLOOR	WING	CONDITION	VISITING HOURS
Johnson, Tommy	3021	3	Children's	guarded	8:30 A.M.-8:30 P.M. parents and grandparents only
McKormick, Karen	recovery	8	East	critical	none
Rifkin, Lynn	1121	11	Maternity	good	11:30 A.M.-1:00 P.M. 7:00-8:15 P.M. 24 hours fathers
Rivera, Juanita	intensive care	8	East	stable	1:30-3:30 P.M. 6:00-8:30 P.M.
Shakter, David	906	9	West	fair	1:00-4:00 P.M. 6:00-8:30 P.M.

Now roleplay phone conversations like the one in Exercise 2. Use the information in the list above.

4 **Dr. Valdez is asking Mrs. Thomas some questions about Bill's medical history.**

DR. VALDEZ: Has Bill ever had a concussion?
MRS. THOMAS: No, he hasn't.
DR. VALDEZ: Has he ever had pneumonia?
MRS. THOMAS: Yes. He had pneumonia five years ago.

DEVELOP YOUR VOCABULARY

anemia
hemorrhaging
convulsions
a high fever
shortness of breath
asthma
heart disease
allergic reaction to a drug
. . .

Now roleplay a similar situation with a classmate. Give information about yourself or someone you know.

ON YOUR OWN
Discuss these questions with your classmates.

1 Have you ever been to a hospital emergency room? When should you go to one?

2 Do you have health insurance? If so, what does your insurance cover (routine doctors' visits, second opinions, hospitalization, surgery)?

3 How does health insurance here compare to health insurance in your country?

For pronunciation exercises for Unit 2, see page 112.

Exercise 3. See Intro. p. x, Roleplay.
recovery Room where patients go after surgery.
intensive care A special unit of a hospital where patients in critical condition can be watched very carefully.

Point out the special conditions for visiting a patient: a child in guarded condition can be seen only by parents and grandparents; fathers have unlimited visiting hours for maternity patients; there are no visiting hours for patients in recovery. Bring these conditions into play by assigning roles such as "friend of the family" for Tommy Johnson or "aunt" for Lynn Rifkin.

Exercise 4. See Intro. p. ix, Ask and answer questions.
Go over these medical terms, but have students use their dictionaries to make sure they understand them. Point out that many of these are medical emergencies.
anemia A condition in which the blood does not have enough red blood cells.
hemorrhaging Uncontrolled bleeding.
convulsions Abnormal, violent muscle contractions.
a high fever A body temperature much higher than normal. Normal body temperature is 98.6° F or 37° C.
shortness of breath Short, fast breaths with a feeling of not getting enough air, similar to what happens when you exercise hard.
asthma A serious condition that makes breathing very difficult.
allergic reaction to a drug A problem that arises when you are sensitive to a drug.

Develop your Vocabulary: *Chest pains, high blood pressure, severe headache, stiff neck, rash* (skin problem), *croup* (a severe breathing problem in small children).

Make sure students know how to reach emergency medical service in your area, e.g., by dialing 911, and how to report their names and addresses clearly and accurately.

On Your Own. See Intro. p. xi.

1. Explain that the hospital emergency room is the part of a hospital that deals with problems that must be treated right away, like accidental injuries. People often go to the emergency room late at night or on holidays when their regular doctors do not have office hours and their illness or injury seems serious. Point out that many of the conditions listed in Ex. 4 would warrant a trip to the emergency room if a doctor were not available, e.g.: asthma, chest pains, a high fever with a stiff neck.

2. Other issues regarding health insurance include co-payment (What part do you pay?), prescription drugs and laboratory tests.

3. Students can also discuss public health insurance such as Medicare and Medicaid here and in their own countries, as well as the issue of insurance if you are injured on the job, e.g., Worker's Compensation.

For **Pronunciation** exercises for Unit 2, see p. 13

REVIEW 1

Exercise 1.
2. is 3. doesn't know 4. are shaking 5. isn't wearing 6. writes 7. doesn't like 8. thinks 9. covers, is/'s writing 10. need

Exercise 2.
2. a 3. e 4. f 5. d 6. b

Exercise 3.
2. might 3. can't 4. Can 5. might not 6. might 7. can 8. should 9. might 10. can

Exercise 4.
2. Please bring it back by 7:00. 3. The firefighters put it out quickly. 4. He forgot to turn them off. 5. I'll call you up when I arrive. OR When I arrive, I'll call you up. 6. He picked me up outside the theater.

REVIEW 1

1 Read the conversation on page 2 again and complete these sentences with the present progressive or the simple present form of the verbs.

1. Angela *is introducing* (introduce) Pete to the staff of the Houston *Herald.*
2. Angela ______ (be) the editor of the *Herald.*
3. Pete ______ (know–*neg.*) the *Herald* staff.
4. In picture 2, Tom and Peter ______ (shake) hands.
5. Tom ______ (wear–*neg.*) a jacket today.
6. Tom always ______ (write) his stories on a typewriter.
7. Tom ______ (like–*neg.*) computers.
8. Pete ______ (think) computers are easy to use.
9. Linda usually ______ (cover) politics, but right now she ______ (write) a story about a fire.
10. The police ______ (need) more information about some warehouse fires.

2 Match the questions in column A with the responses in column B.

A		B
1. *c*	What do you do?	a. Nice to meet you.
2. ___	How do you do?	b. Yes, I am.
3. ___	What are you doing?	c. I'm a writer.
4. ___	Do you do a lot of work?	d. Fine, thanks.
5. ___	How are you doing?	e. I'm writing a book.
6. ___	Are you doing a lot of work?	f. Yes, I do.

Now answer the questions in column A with your own information.

3 Complete the conversation with *can/can't, should/shouldn't* or *might/might not.*

PETE: You *shouldn't* (1) climb on the table. You ______ (2) fall. Why don't you go and do your homework?

MICHAEL: I started it, but I ______ (3) finish it. It's too hard. ______ (4) you help me with it?

PETE: Sure. I'll help you with it later, after I finish my work. But it ______ (5) be before 10:00. I'm very busy.

MICHAEL: OK. I have a test next week, and I'm afraid I ______ (6) fail.

PETE: Don't worry. I'm sure you ______ (7) pass. Just study more. You really ______ (8) study a few hours every day.

MICHAEL: You're right, Dad. It ______ (9) be difficult, but I'm sure I ______ (10) do it.

4 Make sentences with these words.

1. over have to do you'll it
You'll have to do it over.
2. bring please back it 7:00 by
______
3. out it the firefighters put quickly
______
4. forgot he off them turn to
______
5. when I'll you call up arrive I
______
6. outside me he theater picked the up
______

5 Answer each question with a sentence from Exercise 4.

1. A: Where did you meet Bill last night?
   B: ____________
2. A: Why are all the lights on?
   B: ____________
3. A: Was the fire very bad?
   B: No. ____________
4. A: When will you be back?
   B: I'm not sure. ____________
5. A: Did you like my story?
   B: I'm sorry. ____________
6. A: When will you need your car?
   B: ____________

6 Can you remember the story? Make true statements by combining the two parts of the sentences with *for* or *since*.

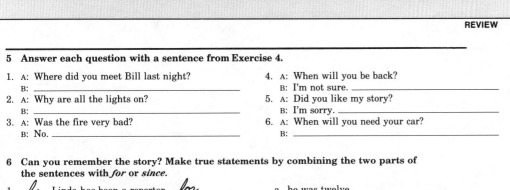

1. f. Linda has been a reporter for
2. ____ Pete has worked at the *Herald* ____
3. ____ Linda has been friends with Bill's family ____
4. ____ Bill has been in trouble ____
5. ____ Angela has lived in Houston ____
6. ____ Angela hasn't skied ____

a. he was twelve.
b. her accident.
c. they moved into her apartment building.
d. she left Canada.
e. a few days.
f. five years.

1. Linda has been a reporter for five years.

7 Look at the time line of Linda's life. Write questions in the simple past or the present perfect and answer them.

attended University of Chicago (1981–1985) — worked at Chicago *Sun* (1985–1986) — left Chicago (1986) — worked at Houston *Chronicle* (1986–1987) — started at *Herald*/met Minh (1987) — 1990

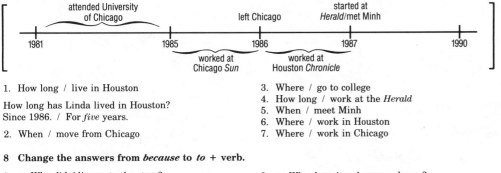

1. How long / live in Houston

How long has Linda lived in Houston?
Since 1986. / For *five* years.

2. When / move from Chicago
3. Where / go to college
4. How long / work at the *Herald*
5. When / meet Minh
6. Where / work in Houston
7. Where / work in Chicago

8 Change the answers from *because* to *to* + verb.

1. A: Why did Alice go to the store?
   B: Because she needed some milk. (buy)

To buy some milk.

2. A: Why is Bill studying computer programming?
   B: Because he would like a better job. (get)
3. A: Why does Angela wear glasses?
   B: Because she can't see well.
4. A: Why does Michael have to go to the language lab?
   B: Because he needs to practice pronunciation.
5. A: Why did Suzanne join the French Club?
   B: Because she wanted to meet new people.

Just for Fun

9 Which word doesn't belong?

1. photographers editors reporters (informants)
2. politics buildings sports health and food
3. robbery arson murder accident
4. eraser computer typewriter pencil
5. journalism arson history mathematics
6. article headline editorial conversation

19

Exercise 5.
1. He picked me up outside the theater. 2. He forgot to turn them off. 3. The firefighters put it out quickly. 4. I'll call you up when I arrive. OR When I arrive, I'll call you up. 5. You'll have to do it over. 6. Please bring it back by 7:00.

Exercise 6.
2. e, Pete has worked at the *Herald* for a few days. 3. c, Linda has been friends with Bill's family since they moved into her apartment building. 4. a, Bill has been in trouble since he was twelve. 5. d, Angela has lived in Houston since she left Canada. 6. b, Angela hasn't skied since her accident.

Exercise 7.
2. When did she move from Chicago? In 1986. OR *Four* years ago. 3. Where did she go to college? (She went to) The University of Chicago. 4. How long has she worked at the *Herald?* Since 1987. OR For *three* years. 5. When did she meet Minh? In 1987. OR *Three* years ago. 6. Where has she worked in Houston? At the Houston *Chronicle* and the Houston *Herald.* 7. Where did she work in Chicago? At the Chicago *Sun.*

Exercise 8.
2. To get a better job. 3. To see well/better. 4. To practice pronunciation. 5. To meet new people.

Exercise 9.
2. buildings *(not a section in a newspaper)* 3. accident *(not a crime)* 4. eraser *(not a writing instrument)* 5. arson *(not a field of study)* 6. conversation *(not found in a newspaper)*

UNIT 3

Language Summary

Functions

Changing the topic of conversation
I had dinner with friends last night. That reminds me . . . have you talked to Maria lately?

Reminiscing
What were you doing the first time you met your girlfriend? I was standing at a bus stop.

Reporting what someone said
I wanted my sister to wake me up at 9:00.

Talking about the past
Has your life changed a lot since you moved here? Oh, yes. I didn't use to like American food, but I do now.

Introduction

Vocabulary

advantage
cross *v*
disappear
find out
found *past part*
get back (= return) *intrans*
hit *s past*
license plate
light *n*
reach *v* (= contact)
sidewalk
take off *intrans* (= leave quickly)
turn out *trans* (= extinguish)
used to
witness *n*

Expressions

be in trouble
hit-and-run accident
Speaking of . . .
That reminds me . . .

Practice A

Structures

Past progressive tense contrasted with simple past tense*
What was Tom doing when the lights went out?

Vocabulary

come back (= return)
examine
go out (= be extinguished)

For recognition only
blackout
both
cassette recorder
coma
flashlight
generator

Expressions

best friend

For recognition only
on the news

Practice B

Structure

Used to
Angela used to ski, but now she doesn't.

Vocabulary

childhood
weekly

Expression

get into trouble

Practice C

Structure

Verb + object + infinitive
Angela wanted Brad to help Pete.

Vocabulary

commissioner
encourage
mayor
renovation
rewrite
wake up *trans*
warn

Put It All Together

Vocabulary

For recognition only
artist
definitely

For recognition only—on cassette
gasoline
guilty
location
right *adj* (= directly)

Reading

Skill

Understanding vocabulary through context

Vocabulary

air conditioner
heavy (greater than usual)
massive
occur
rescuer
spectator
traffic light
unusually
use *n*

*Structure introduced in Student's Book 2 and reviewed here.

For recognition only

admit
affect
blacked out *adj*
blow up *intrans* (= explode)
event
experience *v*
full blast *adv*
genius
glass (material)
handful
modem
power plant
repairperson
restore
rush *v*
smash *v*
spokesperson
take (= bear)
turbine
unusual

Expressions

give birth
just as

For recognition only

stand still

Writing

Skill

Putting events in order

Task

Writing a story

Vocabulary

alarm *n*
fight *v*
go off (as a gun)
note *n* (short letter)
pull
security guard
window (in a bank)

Expressions

as soon as
in line

Pronunciation

Pronunciation points

1. Practicing the regular simple present and past tenses
2. Understanding *used to*

Pronunciation exercises. *The pronunciation exercises for Unit 3 also appear in the Student's Book on p. 113.*

Part 1. *Practicing the regular simple present and past tenses*

A. Listen to these verbs in the present and past tenses. How many syllables do you hear—1, 2 or 3?

See Intro. p. xii, Recognizing and distinguishing sounds 1 and 3

	Present	Syllables:	Past	Syllables:
Ex:	**connect**	**1 2**	**connected**	**1 2 3**
1.	try	1 2	tried	1 2 3
2.	use	1 2	used	1 2 3
3.	protect	1 2	protected	1 2 3
4.	finish	1 2	finished	1 2 3
5.	visit	1 2	visited	1 2 3
6.	need	1 2	needed	1 2 3
7.	talk	1 2	talked	1 2 3
8.	work	1 2	worked	1 2 3
9.	hate	1 2	hated	1 2 3
10.	happen	1 2	happened	1 2 3
11.	start	1 2	started	1 2 3
12.	want	1 2	wanted	1 2 3

Answers: 1. 1, 1 2. 1, 1 3. 2, 3 4. 2, 2 5. 2, 3 6. 1, 2 7. 1, 1 8. 1, 1 9. 1, 2 10. 2, 2 11. 1, 2 12. 1, 2

Now listen again and repeat each word.

B. 1. Which words in Exercise A have the same number of syllables in the present and in the past?

See Intro. p. xii, Recognizing and distinguishing sounds 1

__________ __________ __________
__________ __________ __________

Answers: try, use, finish, talk, work, happen

2. Which words in Exercise A have *more* syllables in the past than in the present?

See Intro. p. xii, Recognizing and distinguishing sounds 1

__________ __________ __________
__________ __________ __________

Note that these words end in a *t* or *d* sound in the present tense.

Answers: protect, visit, need, hate, start, want

C. Listen and repeat this conversation.

See Intro. p. xiii, Recognizing and distinguishing sounds 3

A: What did you do yesterday?
B: I visited my aunt. She wanted me to help her paint her bedroom.
A: What did you do after you painted the room?
B: Oh, we just talked about people we used to know.

Part 2. *Understanding* used to

Listen and repeat these sentences. Notice that *used to* and *use to* are pronounced the same way.

See Intro. p. xiii, Stress and intonation 4

1. Angela used to live in Toronto.
2. Pete used to be married.
3. Tom didn't use to speak Spanish.
4. Did Linda use to paint?
5. Minh didn't use to ride a motorcycle.

See p. 138 for the Pronunciation Tapescript.

(continued on next page)

Teaching Notes

Getting Started

The whole class plays a game to practice the infinitive of purpose. Make up a set of cards with questions and a set with answers. Students get one or more of both question and answer cards. They go around the room to try to find someone with a good answer to their questions. Tell students that some answers fit a number of questions, so they may find several good answers as they move around the room.

Questions: Why did you sign up for this class? Why are you studying English? Why did you move to *(name of city)?* Why did you buy the newspaper today? Why do you watch *(name of popular TV show)* every week? Why did you call the telephone company yesterday? Why did you stop smoking? Why should I listen to the radio or TV in the morning? Why are you taking driving lessons? Why do you play tennis every weekend?

Answers: To meet new people. To get a promotion. To join my family. To look for a job. To look for an apartment. To find out what happened to *(name of character).* To complain about my bill. To feel healthier. To find out the weather. To get my driver's license. To get some exercise.

Introduction

1. Introductory Conversation. See Intro. p. vii.

Preteaching

reach you Tom tried to telephone Linda.
found Past participle of *find.*
hit-and-run accident Students should infer the meaning from the pictures.
sidewalk Refer to the picture.
used to Talks about some situations that ended in the past.
be in trouble In Bill's case, this means to be doing things against the law and having problems with the police.
turn out the lights Demonstrate.
disappear Demonstrate by writing on and erasing from the board.
advantages Means good points. Ask the students, *What is the advantage of the typewriter in this situation?*
cross Here, means walk from one side of the street to the other.

Preparation

Elicit or review the storyline and vocabulary: *Linda is covering an arson story. She was talking to an officer in the arson division when she learned that her informant is in the hospital.* Ask focus questions: *Where was Linda last night?* (At the hospital.) *Who will get Linda information about the warehouses?* (Brad will.)

Exercise 2. See Intro. p. viii, Correct the information.
Answers: 1. Tom wanted to talk to Linda last night. 2. She was at the hospital with Bill's mother. 3. He was walking on the sidewalk. 4. The witnesses didn't see the license plate. 5. She's going to Dallas now. She'll be back on Friday.

 (continued on next page)

UNIT 3 Who Turned Out the Lights?

1 The Houston *Herald* reporters are working hard to finish their stories for tomorrow's edition of the paper. Listen to their conversation.

1

TOM: I tried to reach you last night, Linda.
LINDA: I was at the hospital with Bill's mother.
TOM: Have the police found out what happened?
LINDA: Yes. It was a hit-and-run accident. Bill was walking on Bank Street when a car came up on the sidewalk, hit him and took off.
TOM: Were there any witnesses?
LINDA: Yes, but they didn't see the license plate.
TOM: It doesn't sound like an accident to me. Bill used to have some pretty bad friends. Do you think he's in trouble again?
LINDA: I'm not sure.

2

ANGELA: I'm leaving for Dallas now. Linda, I asked Brad to get you that information you need about the warehouses. Have you finished the Cooper article, Tom?
TOM: Not yet. I'll show it to you when you get back on Friday.

3

LINDA: Speaking of getting back—I should get back to work.
TOM: Hey! Who turned out the lights? Look outside, the whole city's dark!
LINDA: And all my work just disappeared from the computer.
TOM: See, a typewriter still has some advantages.

2 Correct the information.

1. Linda wanted to talk to Tom last night.
2. Linda was at the hospital alone last night.
3. Bill was crossing the street when a car hit him.
4. The witnesses saw the license plate.
5. Angela is going to Dallas on Friday.

3 Find a word or phrase in the conversation that means:

1. return
2. have gotten information
3. people who see a crime or an accident
4. left quickly

4 Warm Up

Tell a classmate what you did last night, and he or she will change the subject, like this:

A: I had dinner with friends last night.
B: That reminds me . . . have you talked to Maria lately?

DEVELOP YOUR VOCABULARY

Speaking of { restaurants / Linda / movies
shopping / going to the store }

By the way, . . .
. . .

Practice

A.

What **was** Tom **doing**	when the lights went out?	He **was typing** an article.
What **did** Tom **do**		He **looked out** the window.

1 Talk about what people were doing at the time of the blackout and what they did right after the lights went out.

1. A: What was Tom doing when the lights went out?
   B: He was typing an article.
   A: What did Tom do when the lights went out?
   B: He looked out the window.

1

2

3

4

5

2 Pete is talking on the phone to his girlfriend, Suzanne. He's telling her about the blackout. Listen and complete their conversation.

SUZANNE: I heard about the blackout on the news. Are you and Michael OK?

PETE: Oh, we're both fine.

SUZANNE: What _____(1) _____(2) _____(3) when the lights went out?

PETE: I _____(4) _____(5) someone about the next election.

SUZANNE: Oh? _____(6) _____(7) you _____(8) then?

PETE: I _____(9) _____(10) a cassette recorder with batteries, so we just _____(11) the interview.

SUZANNE: And what about Michael? Where was he _____(12) _____(13) _____(14) _____(15) _____(16)?

PETE: He _____(17) _____(18) his homework at home. When the lights went out, he just _____(19) _____(20) a flashlight and _____(21).

Exercise 3. See Intro. p. viii, Find a word or phrase . . .
Answers: 1. get back 2. found out 3. witnesses 4. took off

Exercise 4. See Intro. p. viii, Warm Up.
Discuss this function in the introductory conversation: Linda wants to end the conversation, so she changes the subject with the phrase *Speaking of . . .* Ask students how they do this in their own languages and in what situations.

Practice A

Study Box. See Intro. p. viii.

Past progressive tense contrasted with simple past tense.

1. Past progressive tense. Explain that the past progressive tense usually describes an action that began before, was in progress at the time of another action and was likely to continue afterward:

Action began before and in progress	when this happened
Linda was visiting Bill at the hospital	when Tom called.

2. Simple past tense. The simple past tense describes an action completed in the past. With the past progressive, the simple past is used to tell about an action at a point in time during the continuing action in the progressive tense.

Give additional practice in forming these tenses. Write in columns:

I	read a book	when	call
you	take a nap		come to visit
he/she	go for a walk		the lights go out
we	wait for a bus		it starts to rain
they			

Have students use these cues and their own ideas to form sentences:

S: They were waiting for a bus when it started to rain.
T: What did they do then?
S: They opened their umbrellas.

Pronunciation point: Point out the blending in *What did Tom do?* /wəṭɪṭtamdu/.
Part 1 of the **Pronunciation** exercises can be used in Practice A to recognize and practice past tense verbs.

Exercise 1. See Intro. p. ix, Look at the pictures.
To ensure that students use the past progressive rather than *be,* elicit the base form of verbs that can be used for each picture and write them on the board: *cook, call, stand in the elevator,* etc.

Exercise 2. See Intro. p. ix, Listening.
**both* Means the two of them.
**on the news* Here, means that Suzanne heard about the blackout from a radio or TV news program.
**flashlight* Draw one on the board or mime looking for something with one.
Answers: 1. were 2. you 3. doing 4. was 5. interviewing 6. What 7. did 8. do 9. was 10. using 11. continued 12. when 13. the 14. lights 15. went 16. out 17. was 18. doing 19. turned 20. on 21. continued

Exercise 3. See Intro. p. ix, Complete the sentences/paragraph.
**coma* Remind students that Bill was unconscious after the car hit him. *He's in a coma* means he's still not conscious.

Answers: 3. was 4. was examining 5. turned on 6. came back 7. continued 8. went on 9. ran 10. was finishing

Optional: Ask students to write freely for a few minutes about the best or worst day they can remember. Then ask them to work in small groups or pairs and talk about the information. Students ask each other questions in the pattern they're studying, e.g.: *What were you doing when it started to rain? What did you do then?* Then individually they write a letter to a new partner as if that day had just ended. Use Alice's letter and some of their experiences to model a letter on the board:

Dear Marisol:

What a terrible day! While I was waiting for the bus, it started to rain. I was wearing my best dress, but I wasn't carrying an umbrella. When the bus came, it splashed me. [Etc.]

Exercise 4. See Intro. p. ix, Ask and answer questions.
best friend Means *closest friend.*

Encourage students to extend the conversation with more questions, e.g.: *What were you wearing that day? What were you thinking about? Where were you working/living then? Was he/she working or living near there?*

3 Alice Thomas was at the hospital when the blackout occurred. Read what she wrote in a letter to her sister and complete it with the simple past tense or the past progressive tense.

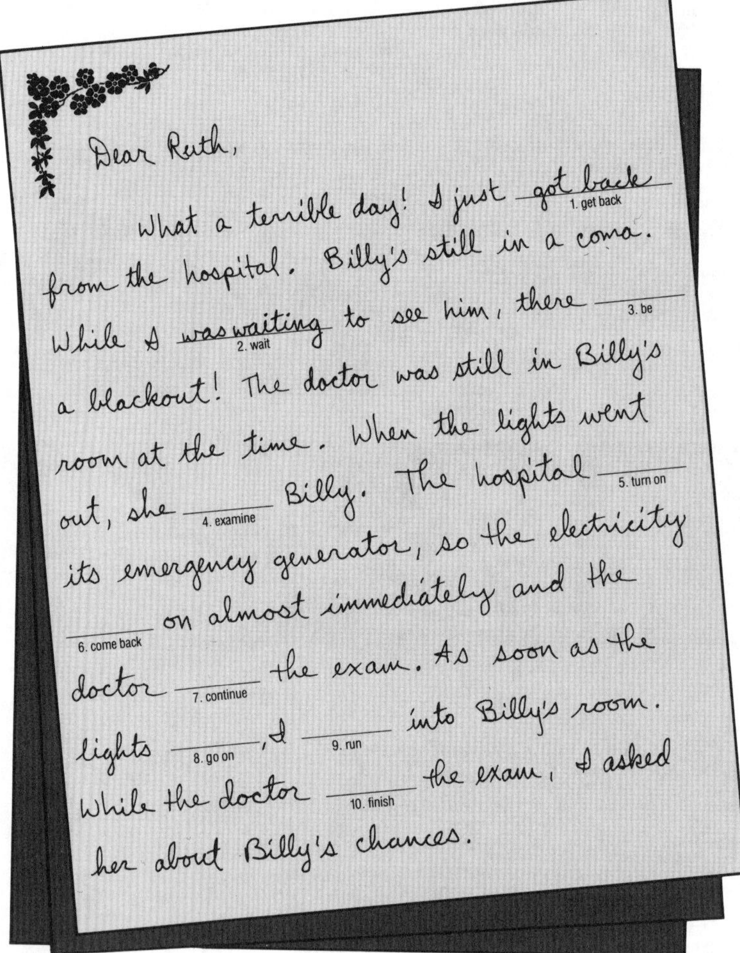
Dear Ruth,

What a terrible day! I just got back (1. get back) from the hospital. Billy's still in a coma. While I was waiting (2. wait) to see him, there ____ (3. be) a blackout! The doctor was still in Billy's room at the time. When the lights went out, she ____ (4. examine) Billy. The hospital ____ (5. turn on) its emergency generator, so the electricity ____ (6. come back) on almost immediately and the doctor ____ (7. continue) the exam. As soon as the lights ____ (8. go on), I ____ (9. run) into Billy's room. While the doctor ____ (10. finish) the exam, I asked her about Billy's chances.

4 Talk about the first time you met someone special.

A: What were you doing the first time you met *your girlfriend?*
B: I was *standing at a bus stop.*
A: What did you do (say)?
B: I *asked her for the time.*

Student A can use these ideas:

best friend *Alicia*	husband
fiancé (fiancée)	wife
boyfriend	

B.

Before her accident, Angela **used to ski,** but now she doesn't.	
Did Angela **use to paint?**	No, she **didn't.**
She **didn't use to paint.**	

1 Find six things in Angela's past that are different from her life now. Talk about them like this:

Angela used to *ski*, but now she *paints.*

2 Can you remember the story? Complete the sentences with *didn't use to* or *used to* + verb.

1. Pete / work on weekends at the Dallas *Star*

Pete didn't use to work on weekends at the Dallas *Star.*

2. Bill / get into trouble a lot
3. Linda / write her stories on a typewriter
4. Angela / live in Toronto
5. Minh / ride a motorcycle in Vietnam
6. Alice Thomas / be married
7. the Houston *Herald* / have computers

3 The Houston *Herald* is an old paper. Use the cues and the chart to ask and answer questions about the *Herald* in 1910 and now.

1910	Now
15 employees	110 employees
reporters used typewriters	reporters use computers
no women	1/2 staff are women
cost 5¢	costs 30¢
10 pages	40 pages
weekly	daily

1. How many people / work there

A: How many people used to work there?
B: Fifteen.
A: How many people work there now?
B: 110.

2. How / reporters / write stories
3. How many women / work there
4. How much / it cost
5. How many pages / it have
6. How often / it come out

Practice B

Study Box. See Intro. p. viii.

Used to.

1. Explain that *used to* + verb describes an activity or a situation that existed in the past but does not exist any longer.

2. Point out that the base form of the verb is used after *used to.*

3. Note that like other regular verbs in the past tense, *used to* drops the final *-d* in negative statements and questions.

Give additional practice. Ask students about things they used to or didn't use to like or do:

T: What foods didn't you use to like as a child?
S: I didn't use to eat vegetables, but now I love them.

They can practice in pairs with these ideas: *What did you use to do during your summer vacations? Did you use to wear a uniform to school? What hobbies did you use to have? Where did you use to live? Did you use to live in the country or in the city?*

Pronunciation point: Point out stress and reduction in:

Did Angela used to paint? /dɪdændʒələyustəpent/

Exercise 1. See Intro. p. ix, Look at the pictures.
Answers: Angela used to live in the suburbs, but now she lives in the city. She used to have long hair, but now she has short hair. She used to have a dog, but now she has a cat. She used to be single, but now she's married. She didn't use to use a cane, but now she does.

Exercise 2. See Intro. p. ix, Make sentences.
get into trouble Here, means have trouble with the law.

Answers: 2. Bill used to get into trouble a lot. 3. Linda used to write her letters on a typewriter. 4. Angela used to live in Toronto. 5. Minh didn't use to ride a motorcycle in Vietnam. 6. Alice Thomas used to be married. 7. The Houston *Herald* didn't use to have computers.

Exercise 3. See Intro. p. ix, Ask and answer questions.
Note that here *staff* takes a plural verb in *Half the staff are women.* Explain that this is because the writer is focusing on the number of women on the staff.
weekly Means every week.

Answers: 2. A: How did the reporters use to write their stories? B: On typewriters. A: How do they write them now? B: On computers. 3. A: How many women used to work there? B: No women. A: How many women work there now? B: Fifty-five. OR Half the staff. 4. A: How much did it use to cost? B: Five cents. A: How much does it cost now? A: Thirty cents. 5. A: How many pages did it use to have? B: Ten. A: How many pages does it have now? B: Forty. 6. A: How often did it use to come out? B: Weekly. A: How often does it come out now? B: Daily.

Exercise 4. See Intro. p. ix, Ask and answer questions.
Elicit some information from students and put it on the board to get the conversations started, e.g.: *What sports did you use to play? Who did you use to see all the time? What jobs did you use to do at home? What kind of clothes did you use to wear? What kind of things did you use to do for entertainment—movies, discos, trips?*

Exercise 5. See Intro. p. ix, Ask and answer questions.
Optional: If students did not use their own photographs for Ex. B1 on Student's Book p. 23, ask them to do so here.

Practice C

Study Box. See Intro. p. viii.

Verb + object = infinitive.
1. Introduce the meaning of the pattern by writing commands on the board, e.g.:

Luis, please shut the door.
Amrita, please turn on the lights.
Students, please open your books.

Then transform these into the pattern:

I wanted Luis to shut the door.
I wanted Amrita to turn on the lights.
I wanted the students to open their books.

2. Review the object pronouns. Write the subject pronouns on the board and elicit object pronouns. Give additional practice with a transformation drill using names of students from the class:

T: I wanted Amrita to turn on the lights.
A: You wanted her to turn on the lights.
T: I wanted all of you to open your books.
B: You wanted us to open our books.
T: I wanted Diego and Nazing to write on the board.
C: You wanted them to write on the board.

Pronunciation point: Point out the stress and reduction in *She wanted him to get the information* /ʃiwãnṭɪdɪmtəgɛ̣tðəinfərmẹʃən/.

Exercise 1. See Intro. p. ix, Listening.
fire commissioner The public official in charge of the fire department.
mayor The elected head of the city.
renovation Here, they are fixing up the museum. Point out that the word means *renew.*
rewrite Means write again to correct mistakes, take out or add material.

Answers: 2. Linda 3. Brad 4. Tom 5. Cathy 6. Minh 7. Minh 8. Tom 9. Linda

Now talk about. . . See Intro. p. ix, Ask and answer questions.

4 Talk about how your life has changed since you moved to this country.

A: Has your life changed a lot since you moved here?
B: Oh, yes. I used to *visit my relatives often, but now I never see them.* How about you?
A: I didn't use to *like American food, but I do now.*

5 Reminisce with a classmate.

A: Who do you remember best from your childhood?
B: *My uncle. He* always used to *tell me stories.*

C.

What did Angela **want Brad to do?**	She **wanted him to get** the information for Linda and **to help** Pete Gómez.

1 Before Angela left for Dallas, she told Brad what she wanted people at the *Herald* to do. Brad made a list. Listen to the conversation and write the name of the person next to each job.

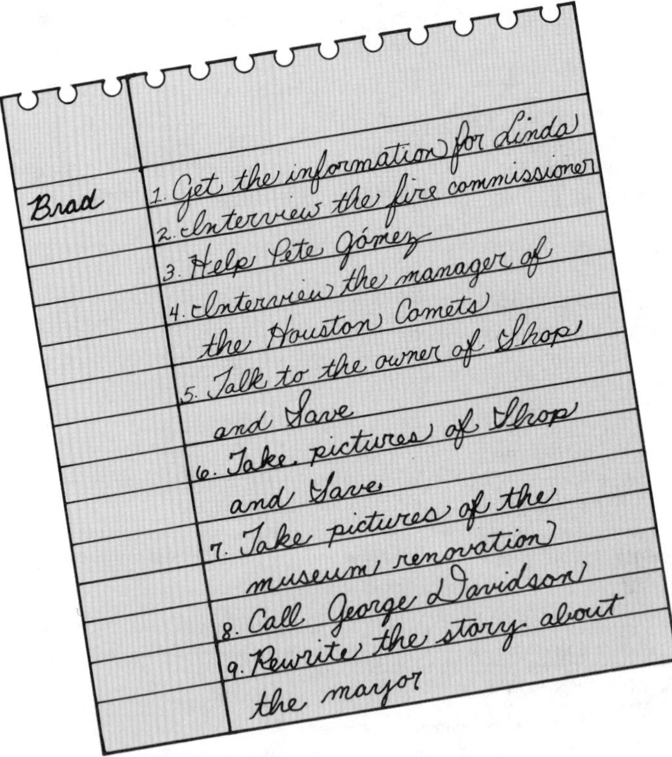

Brad
1. Get the information for Linda
2. Interview the fire commissioner
3. Help Pete Gómez
4. Interview the manager of the Houston Comets
5. Talk to the owner of Shop and Save
6. Take pictures of Shop and Save
7. Take pictures of the museum renovation
8. Call George Davidson
9. Rewrite the story about the mayor

Now talk about what Angela wanted her staff to do.

1. A: What did Angela want Brad to do?
B: She wanted him to get the information for Linda and to help Pete Gómez.

2 Make sentences about the people with the words below each note or picture.

1. Angela wanted Brad to get Linda the information.

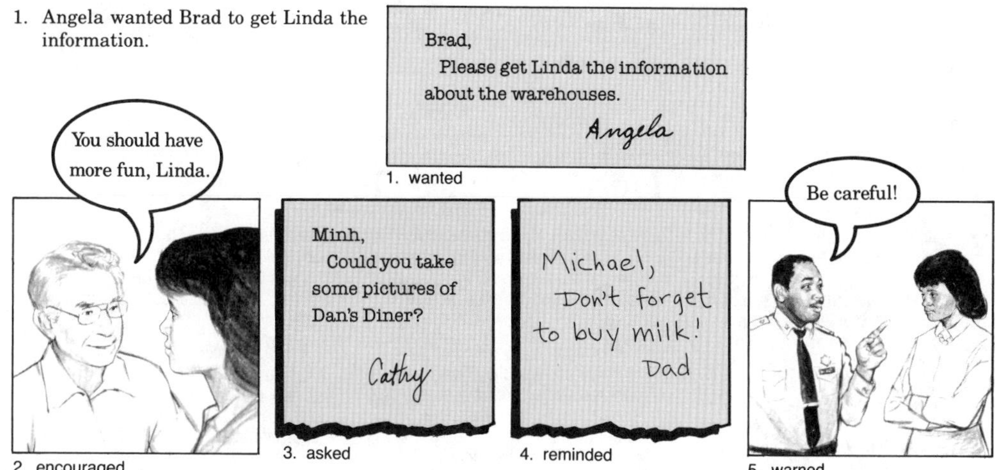

Brad,
Please get Linda the information about the warehouses.
Angela
You should have more fun, Linda.
Minh,
Could you take some pictures of Dan's Diner?
Cathy
Michael,
Don't forget to buy milk!
Dad
Be careful!

1. wanted
2. encouraged
3. asked
4. reminded
5. warned

3 Think of something you asked someone to do this week.

A: I asked *my sister* to *call me at 9:00.*
B: Why did you want *her* to do that?
A: I wanted *her* to *wake me up.*

PUT IT ALL TOGETHER

Bill Thomas has come out of his coma. Officer Brady is asking him some questions. Read the notes below. Then listen to the conversation and choose the notes that Officer Brady made.

1
BT says he didn't start fires and doesn't know who did. Says hit-and-run was definitely an accident. Can describe the driver. Send police artist to see him.

2
BT says he started fires because someone he used to know in prison asked him to. Send police artist to see him. Arrest him when he is ready to leave hospital.

3
BT says someone asked him to start fires. Didn't know man but can describe him. Thinks hit-and-run may not be an accident. Send police artist to see him.

ON YOUR OWN

Think about Tom's feelings about computers and discuss these questions with your classmates.

1 Have you ever used a computer? Do you like them? Why or why not?

2 How have computers changed people's lives? What are some advantages of computers? Disadvantages?

25

Exercise 2. See Intro. p. ix, Look at the pictures.
encourage Refer to the picture. Tom wants Linda to do something she might be afraid to do or she might not want to do. Give more examples: *His co-workers encouraged him to apply for a promotion.*

Answers: 2. Tom encouraged Linda to have more fun. 3. Cathy asked Minh to take some pictures of Dan's Diner. 4. Pete reminded Michael to buy milk. 5. Officer Brady warned Linda to be careful.

Exercise 3. See Intro. p. ix, Ask and answer questions.
Optional: Write some sentence openers on the board and have students write notes to each other using some of them, e.g.:

Would you please . . . Why don't you . . . You should . . . Don't forget to . . . Be careful when you . . .

Then ask students to report what their classmates said. For example, a note might say, *Would you please help me with my homework?* The student who gets the note reports, *Renée asked me to help her with her homework.* Large classes can report in groups.

Put It All Together. See Intro. p. ix, Listening.

Play the cassette (or read the tapescript) several times and discuss with students the reasons for the answer (3).

On Your Own. See Intro. p. xi.

Refer to the Introductory Conversation and elicit Tom's feelings about the computer: *Why does he feel this way? Is he just old-fashioned or are there some good reasons for his feelings?* If students do much writing in their own languages, ask them if they have special conditions, pens or times that make them feel most comfortable when they write.

1. If students have used a computer, ask them about the circumstances: *Did/Do you use it at school, at work or at home? What kinds of work do you do on the computer?* If the answer is no, ask, *Do you want to? Why or why not?*

2. Discuss computerization that students encounter every day: *Have these changes affected you? Do you like these changes or not? Do you feel computers make daily life too impersonal, or is the efficiency worth it?* Groups may also want to discuss the personal computer and the advantages in record keeping and word processing that have been pointed out in the storyline.

Reading

See Intro. p. xi.

Exercise 1.
Elicit the type of article (a current news story). Point out the telegraph style for the headline, and call on students to make a full sentence (Houston was blacked out). Point out the information you can pick up immediately (dateline and reporter's questions—*who, what, when, where, how, why*) in the first paragraph. Go over the instruction line and tell students they will be learning how to work with unfamiliar vocabulary in the exercises, so they should read and guess as many meanings as they can at this point. Since students will be working with strategies for figuring out unfamiliar words, do not preteach unfamiliar vocabulary. As students do Ex. 3, discuss which strategies they used to infer the meanings.

occur Means *happened.* Can be inferred from the sentence.
**turbine* Infer approximate meaning of *a piece of equipment.*
**blew up* Infer from the fact the damage caused a power failure.
**restored* Infer from the next clause: *all areas would have power.*
spokesperson*/repairperson* Infer from *speak* and *repair* and *person.*
massive Infer from the need for extra officers.
traffic lights Infer from the situation.
**affected* Infer from the context—they used emergency generators, so nothing happened to them. *However* in the next sentence also contrasts *not affected* with *unusual events.*
**event* Infer from the two examples that follow.
spectators Infer from the situation—a baseball game in a stadium.
gave birth Infer from *baby girl.*
rescuers Infer that she was waiting for help.
**heavy use of air conditioners* Students might be able to infer the meaning of these unfamiliar words from the spokeperson's comment about *two weeks of extremely hot weather.*
**full blast* Students know *full* from *full-time* and should infer the meaning from the context.

Exercise 2. See Intro. p. xi, Answer the questions.
Answers: 1. At 7:38 P.M. 2. They sent repairpersons to repair the damage. 3. He called in extra police officers to take care of the massive traffic problems. 4. The 38,000 spectators were led out of the stadium in the dark. 5. Sarah Marsden gave birth to a baby girl in the elevator. 6. Heavy use of air conditioners during the day.

Exercise 3.
Elicit answers: 1. *Broken glass* suggests the meaning. 2. *Hand* and *full* with *only* suggests a few people. 3. You can infer that a *modem* is used with a computer. 4. The sentence offers no clue.

Work out a few examples with the whole class. Then have students work on their lists in groups. When they finish, ask them to discuss how they guessed meanings.

Reading

1 Read the article. As you read, make a list of the words you don't know.

The Houston Herald

Houston Blacked Out

HOUSTON—Almost all of Houston stood still last night as the city experienced its biggest power blackout. The blackout occurred at 7:38 P.M. when a turbine at the East Texas Power Plant blew up. Power was restored to most of the city within three hours, and a spokesperson for East Texas Power said all areas would have power by noon.

As soon as the power went out, repairpersons from East Texas Power rushed to the power plant to try to repair the damage. Police Chief Michaelson called in extra police officers to take care of the massive traffic problems that occurred when the traffic lights stopped functioning.

Local hospitals were not affected because they have emergency generators; however, the blackout did cause some other unusual events. The power went out just as the Houston Astros were starting their game, and the 38,000 spectators were led out of the stadium in the dark. In the Conroy Building, Sarah Marsden gave birth to a baby girl in the elevator while she was waiting for rescuers. Both Ms. Marsden and the baby are in good condition.

A spokesperson from East Texas Power said that unusually heavy use of air conditioners during the day probably caused the blackout. "We've had two weeks of extremely hot weather, and everyone's had their air conditioners on full blast all that time. The plant just couldn't take it," she admitted.

2 Comprehension. Answer the questions.

1. When did the blackout happen?
2. What did East Texas Power Company do when the electricity went off?
3. What did the police chief do? Why?
4. What happened at the baseball game?
5. What happened at the Conroy Building?
6. What caused the blackout?

3 Vocabulary building.

1. Sometimes you can figure out what a new word means from the way it is used in the sentence:
   He was cut by the broken glass when he *smashed* the window.
   What is the meaning of *smash?* How did you figure it out?
2. Sometimes a word looks like one you already know:
   Only a *handful* of people came to the party.
   What two words does *handful* contain? What do you think it means?
3. Many times you can only get an approximate meaning, but it is enough to continue reading:
   He bought a *modem* so he could send messages through his computer.
4. Sometimes you cannot figure out the meaning of the word, and it is necessary to the sentence. Then you have to look it up in the dictionary:
   Everyone agrees that the boy is a *genius.*
   Does this sentence make sense, if you don't know the word *genius?*

Now look at your list. Find the words you didn't know in the article.

1. Which new words did you figure out from the way they were used in the article?
2. Which ones did you have to look up in the dictionary?

Writing

Skill: Putting events in order
Task: Writing a story

1 **When you tell a story, it is important to use time markers. They help the reader understand the order of the events of the story. Two of the time markers in the newspaper article on p. 26 are *when* and *after*. What others can you find?**

2 **Read these events from a story and rewrite them as a paragraph. Use the time markers in parentheses to connect them.**

Note: You can write these sentences two ways:

When As soon as After	she finished, she left. OR She left	when as soon as after	she finished.

Note the comma.

1. A man went into the First National Bank.

(while)

2. He was standing in line.
3. A security guard noticed that he seemed nervous.

(when)

4. The man got to the teller's window.
5. He gave the teller a note.

(as soon as)

6. The security guard saw the teller give him a lot of money.
7. The security guard pulled the alarm.

(when)

8. The man tried to leave the bank.
9. The guard tried to stop him.

(as)

10. The man and the guard were fighting.
11. The guard's gun went off and the man was hit.

3 **Now write a story about something unusual that happened to you. Before you write, organize the events of the story. Use time markers to make the order of the events clear.**

For pronunciation exercises for Unit 3, see page 113.

Writing

See Intro. p. xii.

Exercise 1.
Have students reread the newspaper article on Student's Book p. 26 and note the time markers:
as Means *at the same time.*
as soon as Means *immediately after.*
just as Means *at the same point in time.*
while Means *over the same period of time.*

Exercise 2. See Intro, p. ix, Writing sentences.
security guard Here, someone who protects the bank from robberies.
note (n) A short letter.
fight (v) Refer to the context—the guard tried to stop him.
go off Refer to the context—the man was hit.

Answer:

A man went into the First National Bank. While he was standing in line, a security guard noticed that he seemed nervous. When the man got to the teller's window, he gave the teller a note. As soon as the security guard saw the teller give him a lot of money, he pulled the alarm. When the man tried to leave the bank, the guard tried to stop him. As the man and the guard were fighting, the guard's gun went off and the man was hit.

Exercise 3.
Give some types of experiences students can write about, e.g.:
- an accident you saw or experienced
- a time you saw someone do something very brave or very foolish
- a time you learned to take care of yourself
- an experience that made you realize something about the way the police work
- an event that made you realize that you or someone close to you had changed

Elicit some topics from students to give others ideas.

Have students write the steps of their experience in order, then work in pairs and read each others' steps. They can ask questions to clarify any problems. The teacher should circulate at both stages to help out students who need topics.

Before students write, briefly check the students' steps and put a list of time markers on the board, reminding students to use them in their writing.

For **Pronunciation** exercises for Unit 3, see p. 25

UNIT 4

Language Summary

Functions

Asking for and giving information about activities
What have you been doing these days? I've been learning how to drive.
Comparing
Mexico City isn't as modern as Chicago, but it's more exciting.
Describing people
Ellen's too young to go to the movies, but Johnny's old enough.
Making and responding to suggestions
Let's go to the zoo. No, it's too cold. Let's go bowling instead.

Introduction

Vocabulary

air conditioned *adj*
annoy
bored *adj*
budget *n*
could (possibility)
discouraged *n*
elephant
heat wave
inexpensive
instead
opening *n*
return *trans* (= take back)
space (outer space)
zoo

For recognition only
spaceship

Expression

Welcome to . . .

Practice A

Structures

Present perfect progressive tense
What have you been doing these days? I've been working hard.
Present perfect progressive tense contrasted with present perfect tense
Ken has been looking for a job for three months.
He has had two interviews with Getty.

Vocabulary

enroll
how *conj*
journal (= diary)
read *past part*
recently
wallpaper *v*

For recognition only
unemployed
what *rel pron*

Expressions

so far (= up to now)

For recognition only
at least
it takes time
keep busy
so long (= for such a long time)

Practice B

Structures

***Too** * and **enough** (+ infinitive)*
Ellen's too young to go to the movies.
Johnny's old enough to go.

Vocabulary

aggressive
clumsy
dancer
disorganized *adj*
experienced *adj*
graceful
join *trans*
shy
sketch *n*
soldier
stranger *n*
weak

Expression

For recognition only—on cassette
sort of

Practice C

Structure

Comparative of adjectives *(not) as . . . as*
San Francisco isn't as sunny as Los Angeles.

Vocabulary

beet
compare
cosmopolitan
crowded *adj*
cucumber
feather
hectic
huge
king
light *adj* (not heavy)
lion
low
mouse
muggy
neat
peaceful
polluted *adj*
rich
scenic
South Pole
tower *n*

*Structure introduced in Student's Book 2 and reviewed here.

Life Skills

Shopping for clothes

Returning an item and explaining the problem with it
Understanding store refund policies
Understanding sizes
Trying on clothes
Understanding a credit card bill

Vocabulary

exchange *v*	refund *n*	zipper *n*
hole	size *n*	
receipt	stain *n*	

For recognition only

above *adv*	finance charge	policy
allow	following *adj*	previous
average *adj*	inquiry	rate *n*
avoid	minimum *adj*	shown
balance *n*	payment	
credit *n*	periodic	

Expressions

according to . . .

For recognition only

closing date   past due

On Your Own

Vocabulary

For recognition only
unemployment rate

Pronunciation

Pronunciation points

1. Practicing final /ər/
2. Distinguishing reduced *can* and *can't*
3. Distinguishing reduced *to* and *too*

Pronunciation exercises. *The pronunciation exercises for Unit 4 also appear in the Student's Book on p. 113.*

Part 1. *Practicing final /ər/*

Steve Wilson is talking to his friend Bob. Listen to their conversation and complete it.

See Intro. p. xiii, Recognizing and distinguishing sounds 2 and 3

BOB: What's the ______(1)?
STEVE: My ______(2) can't find a job.
BOB: He's a good ______(3). Where's he been looking?
STEVE: He looks in the ______(4) every day.
BOB: I ______(5) when I was unemployed. It's hard, but I'm sure he'll find ______(6) job soon.

Answers: 1. matter 2. brother 3. welder 4. paper 5. remember 6. another

Now listen again and repeat the conversation.

Part 2. *Distinguishing reduced* can *and* can't

Listen to these sentences and complete them with *can* or *can't*.

See Intro. p. xiii, Recognizing and distinguishing sounds 2 and 3

1. We ______ go to the movies.
2. Johnny ______ play outside.
3. You ______ find a job.
4. They ______ stop at the store.
5. The Wilsons ______ spend a lot of money.

Answers: 1. can't 2. can 3. can 4. can't 5. can't

Now listen again and repeat the sentences.

Part 3. *Distinguishing reduced* to *and* too

Listen to these sentences. Notice the difference in pronunciation between stressed *too* and unstressed *to*.

See Intro. p. xiii, Stress and intonation 1 and 4

1. It's too hot to drink.
2. They're too tired to work.
3. She's too young to vote.
4. It's too expensive to buy.
5. I'm too busy to talk.

Now listen again and repeat the sentences.

See p. 139 for the Pronunciation Tapescript.

Teaching Notes

Getting Started

1. Students work in pairs and practice Unit 3, Ex. 4 on Student's Book p. 20. First, review the function (politely changing the subject). Then, have students work with new partners.

2. Students work in pairs and practice Unit 2, Ex. A4 on Student's Book p. 12. First, review time expressions. If time permits, pairs of students can form groups and report, e.g., *Luis has worn glasses for ten years.*

Introduction

 **1. Introductory Conversation.** See Intro. p. vii.

Preteaching

The words defined in Ex. 3 do not appear here.
bored (adj) Someone who is bored has nothing interesting to do.
space Refer to picture 3 on Student's Book p. 28. The Johnson Space Center has a museum that has exhibits about space—the area beyond the earth—and space exploration.
inexpensive Means *cheap.*

Preparation

Remind or elicit from students that Cathy Wilson is the food columnist at the *Herald.* Talk about how Johnny and Ken seem to feel in the pictures—happy or sad? Ask focus questions: *Does Cathy want Johnny to keep watching TV?* (No, she doesn't. She wants him to go outside.) *Is the Johnson Space Center expensive?* (No, it's not.)

Exercise 2. See Intro. p. viii, Say *That' right . . .*
Answers: 1. That's wrong. 2. That's right. 3. That's right. 4. I don't know. 5. That's wrong.

Exercise 3. See Intro. p. viii, Find a word or phrase . . .
Answers: 1. depressed OR discouraged 2. annoy 3. return 4. budget

Exercise 4. See Intro. p. viii, Warm Up.
zoo A place where animals are kept and exhibited. Give an example of the local zoo.
instead Means *in place of.*
elephant Draw one on the board.
could Here, used to make a suggestion, not talk about ability.

Develop Your Vocabulary: Elicit from the students some of their own weekend activities. Review popular sports, e.g.: *tennis, golf, skiing, sailing, hiking.* Mention well-known museums, theaters, etc., in your own city.

Additional ways to accept a suggestion: *Sounds great. That's fine with me.* To reject a suggestion: *Won't it be too cold/hot/crowded?* To suggest an alternative: *We can always . . . I think I'd rather . . .*

UNIT 4 A Heat Wave

1 Houston is having a heat wave. Cathy Wilson and her family are trying to decide what to do on Sunday. Listen to their conversation.

1
CATHY: You've been watching TV for two hours, Johnny. Why don't you go out and play?
JOHNNY: It's too hot to play outside. I want to go to a movie.
CATHY: We can't do that. Your sister isn't old enough. She'll annoy everyone.

2
KEN: What's the matter with Johnny?
CATHY: Nothing, really. He's just bored. Are there any jobs in the paper?
KEN: No. I'm really discouraged. I've been looking for work for three months.
CATHY: Don't worry, Ken. You're a good welder. There'll be an opening soon.

3
KEN: Why don't we go out today, Cathy? I'm too depressed to stay home.
CATHY: OK. But we can't go anywhere expensive. Remember our budget, Ken.
KEN: How about the Johnson Space Center? It's interesting, inexpensive and air conditioned.
CATHY: OK. I hope Johnny thinks it's as exciting as TV. Oh, I forgot. I've got to go to the mall to return that dress I bought.
KEN: That's OK. We can stop on the way.

2 Say *That's right, That's wrong* or *I don't know.*

1. Johnny wants to go outside.
2. Ken's looking for a job.
3. Cathy's worried about money.
4. Johnny likes spaceships.
5. They're going to stop at the store after they go to the space center.

3 Find a word or phrase in the conversation that means:

1. very unhappy
2. bother someone
3. take back
4. a plan of how to spend your money

4 Warm Up

Suggest a plan for the weekend.

A: Let's do something this weekend.
B: OK. *Let's go to the zoo.*
A: No, *it's too cold. Let's go bowling* instead.
OR Yes, that sounds *good. I love the elephants.*

DEVELOP YOUR VOCABULARY

How about *the beach?*
Why don't we . . . ?
We could . . .
. . .

Practice

A.

How long **has** Richie **been watching** TV?	**He's been watching** TV	for two hours. since 9:00.
What **have** you **been doing** these days?	**I've been working** hard.	

1 Talk about the pictures.

1. A: How long has Richie been watching TV?
   B: He's been watching TV for two hours.

1. Richie / two hours

2. Juanita / lunchtime

3. Liz / one hour

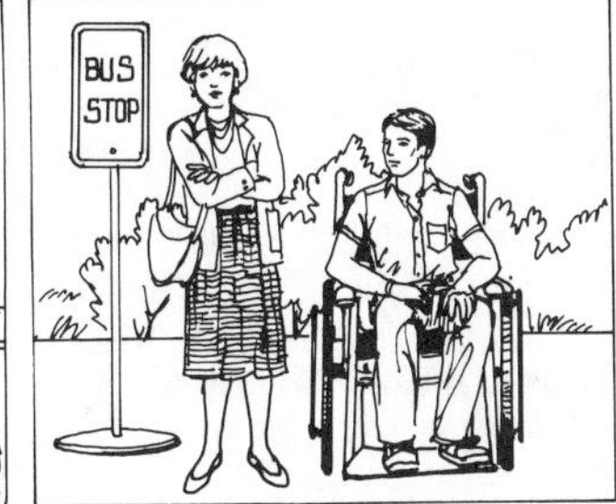

4. Roger and Lois / a long time

5. Ann and Betty / 2:00

2 Ask a classmate what he or she has been doing recently.

A: What have you been doing *these days?*
B: I've been *learning how to drive.*

DEVELOP YOUR VOCABULARY

since you enrolled in this class	lately
for the last month	recently

3 Ask classmates what they've been doing to improve their English.

A: What have you been doing to improve your English?
B: I've been *watching TV.*

Student B can use these ideas:

read the newspaper	keep a journal
talk to neighbors	go to movies

Practice A

Study Box. See Intro. p. viii.

Present perfect progressive tense.

1. Use. Explain that like the present progressive tense, this tense describes an action beginning in the past and continuing to the present. The present perfect progressive stresses the continuity of the action and often refers to an activity that began soon before and continued up to the present time, e.g.: *She's been playing tennis for hours. It's been raining since 2:00.* Unlike the present perfect, this tense can never be used for a completed action. In the above sentences, for example, it is understood that she's still playing tennis and that it's still raining.

2. Form and word order. Point out that this tense is formed with *have/has* + *been* + *-ing* form of the verb, e.g., *have/has been doing* something. Explain that in *yes/no* questions and *wh-* questions, the auxiliary *have* or *has* goes before the subject, while the rest of the phrase *(been doing)* follows it, e.g.:

He has been watching TV.
Has he been watching TV?
How long has he been watching TV?

3. Contractions. Point out that in spoken English, *'ve* and *'s* are almost always used. Elicit and write them on the board:

I've, you've, he's, she's, it's, we've, they've

4. Use of *for* and *since*. Review that *for* is used with a length of time, e.g.: *for an hour, for two months,* and *since* is used with a point in time, including one described with a clause, e.g.: *since 2:00, since I got to this country.*

Pronunciation point: Note reduction: *for two hours* /fətuaʊrz/
What've you been doing? /wəṭəvyubɪnduɪŋ/

Exercise 1. See Intro p. ix, Look at the pictures.
Answers: 2. A: How long has Juanita been typing? B: She's been typing since lunchtime. 3. A: How long has Liz been sleeping? B: She's been sleeping for one hour. 4. A: How long have Roger and Lois been waiting for a bus? B: They've been waiting for a bus for a long time. 5. A: How long have Ann and Betty been swimming? B: They've been swimming since 2:00.

Exercise 2. See Intro. p. ix, Ask and answer questions.
enrolled in Means registered for (a class).
recently Means the same as *lately.*

Develop Your Vocabulary: *this semester, in the last few weeks, since you arrived in (name of city).*

Elicit or suggest more ideas, e.g.: *working a lot of overtime, taking care of my niece, trying to lose/gain some weight.*

Exercise 3. See Intro. p. ix, Ask and answer questions.
Additional ideas are *going to club meetings, writing to a pen pal, exchanging (student's own language) lessons for English lessons.*

Study Box. See Intro. p. viii.

Present perfect progressive tense contrasted with present perfect tense. Remind students that the progressive emphasizes that the action is continuous. The present perfect tense may be used for completed actions, but the present perfect progressive tense always describes action still going on: *He's watched that movie twice. He's been watching that movie for three hours.*

Exercise 4. See Intro. p. ix, Listening.
Answers: 1. wrong 2. right 3. right 4. wrong 5. right 6. wrong

Exercise 5. See Intro. p. ix, Match the sentence with the picture.
Answers: 1. a 2. b 3. a 4. b

Exercise 6. See Intro. p. xi, Complete the sentences.
wallpaper (v) Point out that the noun is often used as a verb in English. Give other examples: *to house, to water, to voice.*
**unemployed* Means doesn't have a job.

Answers: 2. been reading 3. answered 4. been 5. painted 6. wallpapered 7. been doing 8. been

Optional writing exercise: Have students write short letters to each other on the material in Ex. A3. On the board write a format and some suggestions.:

First paragraph: What have you been doing to practice English, e.g.: talking to neighbors, reading the newspaper.

Second paragraph: What you have accomplished, e.g., made friends with the family downstairs, written five pages in your journal, seen (names of movies).

Then model a letter on the board as students make suggestions. Include connecting words. Students then write their own letters and exchange them with classmates. Model letter:

Dear Silvie,

I have been doing a lot of things to improve my English lately. First, I've been talking to neighbors every morning when I leave for work. I've also been reading part of the newspaper during my lunch hour. And I've been keeping a journal about what I do every day.

All these things have helped me a lot. I've already made friends with the family downstairs, and they've invited me to dinner next week. I've found a few interesting columns in the English newspaper, and I really enjoy reading them. So far I've written five pages in my journal.

What have you been doing lately?

Your friend,

Ken **has been looking** for a job for three months.* He **has had** two interviews with Getty.**

*He's still looking. He's not finished yet.
**The two interviews are finished.

4 Linda and Pete are talking. Read the statements below. Then listen to their conversation and say if the statements are right or wrong.

1. Officer Brady just called Linda.
2. Officer Brady already spoke to Bill.
3. Linda doesn't know what Bill told Officer Brady.
4. Linda has talked to Bill.
5. The doctors are examining Bill.
6. Linda wants Pete to help her with the story.

5 Choose the sentence that describes the picture.

1. a. "But you've eaten your dinner."
 b. "But you've been eating your dinner."

2. a. "You've eaten the cake."
 b. "You've been eating the cake."

3. a. "I've ironed your blouse."
 b. "I've been ironing your blouse."

4. a. "I've read a book."
 b. "I've been reading a book."

6 Ken is talking to his brother Steve about looking for work. Read their conversation and complete it with the present perfect tense or the present perfect progressive tense of the verbs. Use the present perfect progressive when you can.

STEVE: How long have you *been looking* (1. look) for work now?

KEN: Almost three months.

STEVE: Have you ______ (2. read) the ads in the paper?

KEN: Oh, yes, I've ______ (3. answer) at least 50 ads by now. I think I've ______ (4. be) to every employment agency in town.

STEVE: Sometimes it just takes time, but I know it's difficult when you have nothing to do.

KEN: Yeah. I try to keep busy. I've already ______ (5. paint) the first floor, and I've ______ (6. wallpaper) our bedroom. I'm almost finished.

STEVE: Say, Ken, how about working as a security guard? I've ______ (7. do) it for six months now and it's not so bad.

KEN: I've ______ (8. be) unemployed so long, I'll take any job.

7 Talk about your work experience in this country.

A: How long have you been living *in the United States?*
B: *Two years.*
A: How many *jobs have you had so far?*
B: I've had *three.*
OR None. I haven't started working yet.

Now continue the conversation.
You can talk about these things:

write a résumé	get a promotion
go on job interviews	take a vacation

B.

Ellen's **too young** to go to the movies. She's **not old enough** to go.
Johnny's **old enough** to go. He's **not too young.**

1 Talk about the pictures. Use *too* or *enough*.

1. Johnny's old enough to see *Superman.*

1. old

2. young

3. small

4. big

5. short

6. tall

Exercise 7. See Intro. p. ix, Ask and answer questions.
Suggest additional ideas, especially ones that can be discussed in the present perfect progressive, e.g.: *make friends at work, learn new skills on your job, use a computer, get along with your boss.*

Practice B

Study Box. See Intro. p. viii.

***Too* and *enough* (+ infinitive).** Point out that *too* goes before the adjective and that *enough* goes after it. When the infinitive is used, it shows the result. In the Study Box sentence, for example, *Ellen's too young to go to the movies* means *She's too young, so she can't go to the movies.*

For additional practice, present students with situations and ask them to make sentences with *too* and *enough,* e.g.:

Why didn't you go to the party? Were you too tired?
Why don't you write with your pencil? Isn't it sharp?
It's very warm. Why don't we go to the park?
This bookbag is really heavy. Can you lift it?

T: Why didn't you buy the book? Was it too expensive?
S: Yes, it was. It was too expensive to buy. OR: No, it wasn't. It was cheap enough, but I didn't have the time.

Pronunciation point: Point out the difference between stressed *too* and unstressed *to: She's too young to go.* /ʃiztuyəŋtəgo/. Part 3 of the **Pronunciation** exercises can be used here.

Exercise 1. See Intro. p. ix, Look at the pictures.
Answers: 2. Johnny's too young to see *Killer Dogs.* 3. Ellen's small enough to play under the table. 4. Johnny's too big to play under the table. 5. Johnny's too short to reach the cookie jar. 6. Cathy's tall enough to reach the cookie jar.

Exercise 2. See Intro. p. ix, Ask and answer questions.
experienced (adj) Brad hasn't worked on the paper long, so he hasn't got much experience.
join (trans) Here, means becomes a member of (a group).

Answers: 2. A: Why doesn't Angela want Brad Kimball to interview the fire commissioner? OR Why does Angela want Linda to interview the fire commissioner? B: Brad's not experienced enough to interview the commissioner. OR Linda's experienced enough to interview the commissioner. 3. A: Why does Pete Gómez want to find a new apartment? B: His apartment's too small. 4. A: Why isn't Tom Kirby going to retire yet? B: He's not old enough to retire. 5. A: Why will Michael Gómez probably join the swimming team? B: He's good enough to join. OR He's not too busy to join. 6. A: Why doesn't Linda go to the movies very often? B: She's too busy to go.

Exercise 3. See Intro. p. ix, Ask and answer questions.
agressive Means *forceful*, not afraid of someone's anger or refusal.
shy Means *timid*, the opposite of *aggressive*.
stranger (n) Means a person you don't know.
dancer Someone who dances professionally.
graceful Means able to move in a charming and pleasing way.
clumsy Means the opposite of *graceful*.
soldier A man or woman in the army.
disorganized (adj) Means the opposite of *efficient;* without any system.

First, elicit some things that a member of each profession must do so the students can complete the conversation, e.g.: *dancer—dance, jump, turn, move quickly; firefighter—carry another person, handle heavy equipment; basketball player—reach the basket; soldier—carry heavy equipment, march long distances, follow directions; secretary—file papers, organize someone else's work, remember someone's schedule.*

Also elicit other professions and the skills needed for them, e.g.: *politician—ambitious/easygoing; construction worker—strong/weak* or *skilled/unskilled.*

Exercise 4. See Intro. p. ix, Listening.
Answer: Sketch b. *Sketch a:* His nose is too big/not small enough. His hair is too dark/not light enough. He's too old/not young enough. *Sketch c:* His hair is too long/not short enough, and it's too dark/not light enough. He's too old/not young enough. His ears are too small/not big enough.

2 Talk about the people in the story. Use the adjectives in the box and *(not) enough* or *too*.

busy	old
experienced	small
good	~~weak~~

1. Bill Thomas can't leave the hospital yet.
   A: Why can't Bill leave the hospital?
   B: He's too weak.
2. Angela doesn't want Brad Kimball to interview the fire commissioner. She wants Linda to do it.
3. Pete Gómez wants to find a new apartment.
4. Tom Kirby isn't going to retire yet.
5. Michael Gómez will probably join the swimming team.
6. Linda doesn't go to the movies very often.

3 Ask a classmate about his or her abilities.

A: Do you think you could be *a newspaper reporter?*
B: Yes. I think so. I'm *aggressive enough to interview people.*
OR No, I don't think so. I'm *too shy to talk to strangers.*

You can use these ideas:

dancer . . . graceful / clumsy
firefighter . . . strong / weak
basketball player . . . tall / short
soldier . . . old / young
secretary . . . efficient / disorganized

4 Bill Thomas is trying to identify the man who asked him to start the fires. Officer Brady is showing him three police sketches. Listen to the conversation and choose the correct sketch. Then talk about it with a classmate like this:

A: I think it's sketch . . .
B: I agree. It can't be sketch . . . His hair's not . . . enough.
OR It can't be sketch . . . His hair's too . . .

a

b

c

C.

Dallas **isn't as hot as** Houston.
It's **as rainy as** Houston.

1 **Everyone is talking about the weather. Look at the weather map and talk about the weather in these cities. Use the words in parentheses.**

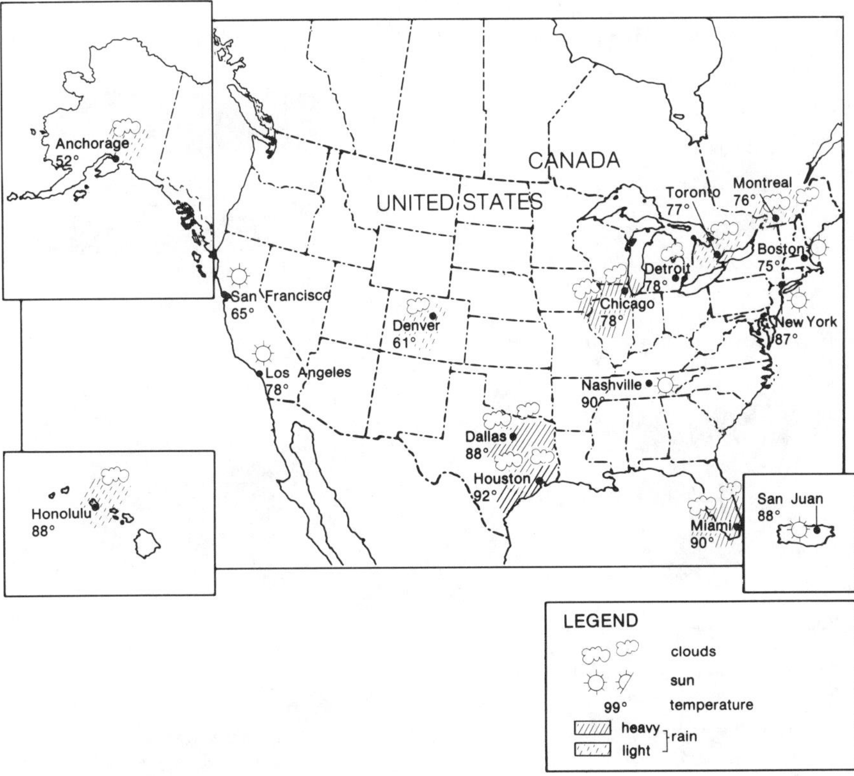

1. Dallas / Houston (hot, rainy)

A: Dallas isn't as hot as Houston.
B: Yes, but it's as rainy as Houston.

2. Honolulu / San Juan (hot, sunny)
3. Toronto / Montreal (cloudy, rainy)
4. San Francisco / Los Angeles (warm, sunny)
5. Miami / Nashville (hot, dry)
6. Detroit / Chicago (cloudy, warm)
7. Denver / Anchorage (cool, cloudy)
8. Boston / New York (hot, sunny)

Practice C

Study Box. See Intro. p. viii.

Comparative of adjectives. Point out the pattern: *(not) as . . . as.*

Give additional practice. Write adjectives on the board and ask students to compare storyline characters: *experienced, hard-working, ambitious, brave, cautious, busy, efficient.* Extend the conversation by asking for their reasons, e.g.:

S: Brad isn't as experienced as Linda.
T: Why do you think that?
S: Because Angela didn't want him to interview the fire commissioner.

Exercise 1. See Intro. p. x, Look at the document.
Go over the symbols. Point out that the United States uses Fahrenheit, not Celsius, for temperatures. Ask students questions about some of the cities, e.g.: *What are people wearing in San Francisco today?* (Light coats or sweaters.) *Imagine it's Sunday. What kind of plans are people in New York making?* (They're planning to go to the beach/park/air-conditioned movies.) *Is Michael riding his bike in Houston today?* (Probably not. It's raining hard.)

Answers: 2. Honolulu is as hot as San Juan, but it isn't as sunny. 3. Toronto is as cloudy as Montreal, and it's as rainy too. 4. San Francisco isn't as warm as Los Angeles, but it's as sunny. 5. Miami is as hot as Nashville, but it isn't as dry. 6. Detroit isn't as cloudy as Chicago, but it's as warm. 7. Denver isn't as cool as Anchorage, but it's as cloudy. 8. Boston isn't as hot as New York, but it's as sunny.

Optional: Ask students to buy the local newspaper and bring it to class. Show them how to use the index to look up the weather page. Point out other terms used: *breezy* (light winds), *partly cloudy, partly sunny, mild* (not too cold, not too hot), *humid* (a lot of moisture in the air). Ask students their preferences. Point out other useful features of the weather page: *daily highs and lows, five-day forecast, temperatures for other cities.*

Exercise 2. See Intro. p. ix, Look at the pictures.
South Pole Point this out on a map, if possible. If not, sketch a globe and point out the North and South Poles.
tower (n) A building that is much taller than it is wide; a building higher than others around it. Refer to the picture.
low Means the opposite of *high.* Not used to describe people.

Answers: 1. b 2. c 3. a 4. d

Optional: Continue the exercise with magazine ads of products of different manufacturers or different vacation spots. Give the exercise a goal—the groups must decide what product they want to buy or where they want to go on vacation. Then elicit a list of appropriate attributes and put them on the board for students to refer to, e.g.: *expensive, efficient, useful, attractive, near, far, cold, rainy, sunny, hot.*

2 Look at the pairs of photographs. Then read the sentences and decide which one is true.

New York City

The South Pole

1. a. The South Pole is not as cold as New York City.
   b. New York City is not as cold as the South Pole.
   c. New York City is as cold as the South Pole.
   d. New York City is not as warm as the South Pole.

Transco Tower

Houston Post Building

2. a. The Transco Tower is as tall as the Houston Post Building.
   b. The Transco Tower is not as tall as the Houston Post Building.
   c. The Houston Post Building is not as tall as the Transco Tower.
   d. The Houston Post Building is not as low as the Transco Tower.

Kodak

Canon

3. a. The Kodak is not as expensive as the Canon.
   b. The Canon is as expensive as the Kodak.
   c. The Canon is not as expensive as the Kodak.
   d. The Kodak is not as inexpensive as the Canon.

Margot

Carine

4. a. Margot is not as young as Carine.
   b. Carine is not as young as Margot.
   c. Margot is not as old as Carıne.
   d. Margot is as old as Carine.

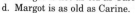

3 **Compare the city or town you come from and the place you are living now.**

A: Tell me about *Mexico City.* How does it compare to *Chicago?*
B: Well, *Mexico City* isn't as *modern* as *Chicago,* but it's *more exciting.*

DEVELOP YOUR VOCABULARY

crowded	muggy
polluted	picturesque
hectic	cosmopolitan
peaceful	scenic
huge	. . .

Just for Fun

4 ***Scrambled similes.*** **An expression which compares two things using *as . . . as* is called a simile. Can you match the words with the pictures to complete these famous English similes?**

1. as quiet as g
2. as cool as ___
3. as hungry as ___
4. as red as ___
5. as neat as ___
6. as light as ___
7. as rich as ___

a. a king

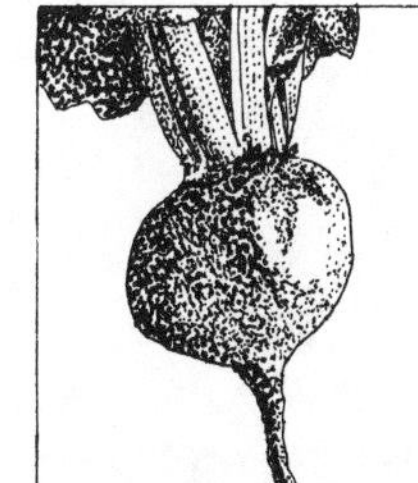
b. a beet

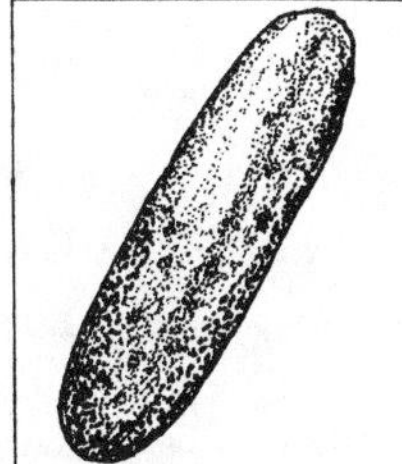
c. a cucumber

d. a feather

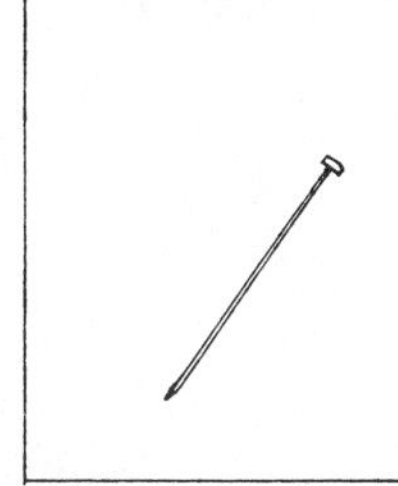
e. a pin

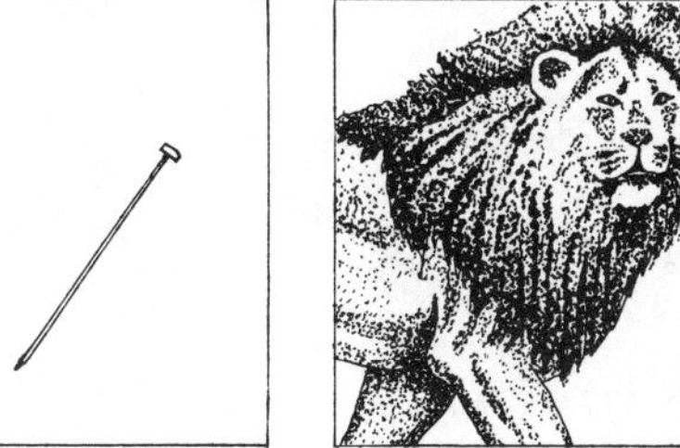
f. a lion

g. a mouse

Now make your own similes. Compare them to your classmates'.

1. As cold as ______________________
2. As depressed as ______________________
3. As old as ______________________
4. As hot as ______________________
5. As happy as ______________________

Exercise 3. See Intro. p. ix, Ask and answer questions.
For these adjectives, ask students to give examples from their own experience living in different places.
crowded Here, means that many people live and/or work there.
polluted Air or water that has become dirty from automobiles, factories or people is polluted.
hectic Means full of excitement and confusion.
peaceful Means *quiet and calm,* the opposite of *hectic.*
huge Means *very large.*
muggy Means unpleasantly hot and humid.
cosmopolitan Means having people from all over the world.
scenic Means having beautiful natural scenery, e.g., mountains or sea.

Develop Your Vocabulary: *fast-paced* (people move quickly; the atmosphere is competitive); *stimulating* (having many interesting features like theater, art museums, colleges and universities); *historic* (having buildings from older periods).

Optional: Encourage students to extend the conversation by giving examples of what they mean, e.g.: *Taipei isn't as peaceful as Toronto, but it's more cosmopolitan. The traffic is very heavy and noisy, but there are people from all over Europe and Asia there.*

Optional: Ask students to continue the exercise by putting together the positive adjectives from their groups and describing an ideal city, e.g.: *as stimulating as Mexico City, as cosmopolitan as Singapore, as scenic as Rio de Janeiro.*

Exercise 4. See Intro. p. xii, Matching.
Refer to the pictures to explain *kind, beet, cucumber, feather, lion* and *mouse.*
neat Means clean and orderly.
light (adj) Means *not heavy.*
rich A rich person has a lot of money.

Answers: 2. c 3. f 4. b 5. e 6. d 7. a

Ask students to add some similes from their own languages and to give examples of how they might use them.

Now make your own similes . . . See Intro. p. ix, Writing sentences.
Optional: Extend the exercise by having students write short paragraphs in which they use their similes as topic sentences, e.g.:

George was hungry as a lion. As soon as he came home, he went to the refrigerator. (Etc.)

Life Skills

In this unit students will learn about store refund and exchange policies, U.S. and metric sizes and billing procedures. They will practice returning an article of clothing, converting from one size system to another and figuring out a monthly credit card statement.

For Your Information. See Intro. p. x.
**policy* Here, means the store's rules for when customers return items.
refund (n) Means money returned to the customer.
exchange (v) When the customer returns an item and gets another item back, not money. Note that some stores will only exchange items; they will not give refunds.

Ask students about their own experiences returning or exchanging items. both in the U.S. or Canada and in their own countries: *Have you ever had a bad experience? Which policies mentioned above do you think are the most fair and under what circumstances (e.g.: damaged items, items that don't fit, items customers have changed their minds about)?* Roleplay asking about store policy. First, explain the word *receipt* by bringing one to class.

A: Can you tell me what your policy is for returning merchandise?
B: The item must be returned within ten days. And, of course, you must show your cash register or credit card receipt.
A: Do you give refunds?
B: Yes, we do. OR No, but you can exchange the item for something else. OR No, we give store credit.

Exercise 1. See Intro. p. ix, Listening.
size (n) Here, means how big the piece of clothing is. Give examples.

Answers: 1. return 2. dress 3. problem 4. take 5. 10 6. too 7. small 8. exchange 9. size 10. prefer 11. refund 12. five 13. money 14. back

Exercise 2. See Intro. p. x, Roleplay.
Students can first ask about the store's policy and then do the roleplay. Write some substitutions on the board:

What seems to be the matter?
What's wrong?
When I got home, I noticed . . .
Would you like to exchange it for another one/another pair?

UNIT 4

Life Skills

Shopping for clothes

For Your Information

Store refund policies
Refund policies are different from store to store, so it is important to check each store's policy before you buy something. At some stores there are no *refunds* or *exchanges.* Some stores only allow exchanges. Other stores only give you *store credit.* This means you have to buy something else at the same store for the same amount as your first item.

1 Cathy is at Peers Department Store. She is talking to a salesperson. Listen and complete their conversation.

CATHY: I'd like to ____(1)____ this ____(2)____.
SALESPERSON: What seems to be the ____(3)____ with it?
CATHY: Well, I usually ____(4)____ a size ____(5)____, but this is ____(6)____ ____(7)____ on me.
SALESPERSON: Would you like to ____(8)____ it for a larger ____(9)____?
CATHY: No, I'd ____(10)____ to get a ____(11)____. I bought it only ____(12)____ days ago.
SALESPERSON: Do you have your receipt?
CATHY: Yes, here it is.
SALESPERSON: OK. We'll be glad to give you your ____(13)____ ____(14)____.

**2 Roleplay a similar situation. You are in a department store.
You want to return one of the items below.
Student A is the customer.
Student B is the salesperson.**

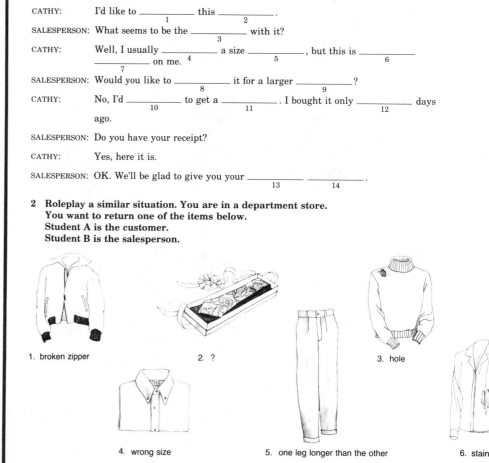

1. broken zipper

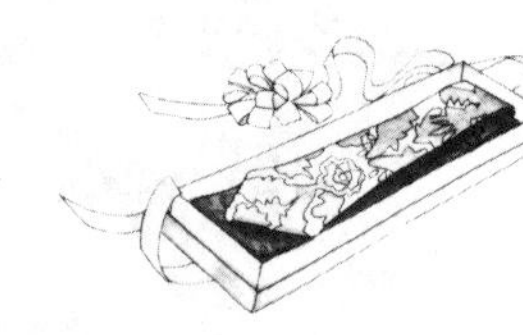
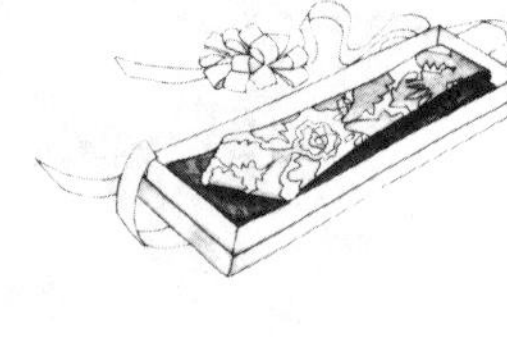
2. ?

3. hole

4. wrong size

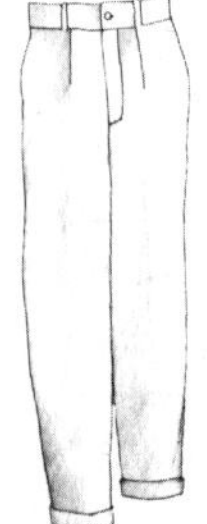
5. one leg longer than the other

6. stain

3 Another customer at Peers is trying to buy a pair of shoes. Read the conversation the customer is having with a salesperson.

CUSTOMER: I'd like to try on *these shoes*, but I'm not sure of my size in this country.
SALESPERSON: What size do you take in your country?
CUSTOMER: In *Italy* I take a size *44*.
SALESPERSON: Well, according to this chart, you take size *11* here.

Roleplay a similar conversation with a classmate. Use the information in the chart to talk about other items of clothing.

Clothing Sizes

Women's

suits, coats, jackets, dresses, blouses and sweaters

U.S.	6	8	10	12	14
Metric	36	38	40	42	44

shoes

U.S.	5	6	7	8	9
Metric	35	36	37	38	39

Men's

suits, coats, jackets

U.S.	34	36	38	40	42	44	46
Metric	44	46	48	50	52	54	56

shirts

U.S.	14	14½	15	15½	16	16½	17
Metric	36	37	38	39	41	42	43

shoes

U.S.	7	8	9	10	11	12
Metric	40	41	42	43	44	45

4 Cathy Wilson has a credit card at Peers. This is part of her last bill. Look at it and then read the statements below. Decide if the statements are right or wrong. If they are wrong, correct them.

ACCOUNT NUMBER	CLOSING DATE	DUE DATE	
214 255605 149	6/4/90	6/29/90	BILL INQUIRY NO. 736-5151

STORE AND REFERENCE NO.	CHARGES	PAYMENTS & CREDITS	DEPT. NO.	DESCRIPTION	DATE
01 32484-2102	25.11		4193	MEN'S SPORTSWEAR	5-27
01 32484-2602	12.35		2106	CHILDREN'S	5-27
01 32864-698	63.00		4388	WOMEN'S	5-27
01 32484-231	15.29		2106	CHILDREN'S	5-31

PREVIOUS BALANCE	TOTAL CHARGES	TOTAL PAYMENTS AND CREDITS	AVERAGE DAILY BALANCE	FINANCE CHARGE	NEW BALANCE	MINIMUM PAYMENT (INCLUDES PAST DUE)
.00	115.75	.00	.00	.00	115.75	14.06

	PERIODIC RATE	APPLIED TO THE FOLLOWING PORTION OF AVERAGE DAILY BALANCE	ANNUAL PERCENTAGE RATE
PEERS Department Store	% % 1.65 %	0.00	% % 19.8 %

1. Cathy bought three items.
2. Cathy bought two items in the same department.
3. Cathy has to pay this bill before June 4, 1990.
4. The bill is for $115.75.
5. Cathy has to pay the balance at one time.
6. If Cathy doesn't pay the new balance at one time, she will have to pay a finance charge next month.
7. Cathy has to pay a finance charge this month.

ON YOUR OWN

Think about Ken's problems and discuss these questions with your classmates.

1 What are some good ways of looking for a job?
2 Is there a high unemployment rate in your country? Can unemployed people receive financial help from your government? If so, how long can they receive it?

For pronunciation exercises for Unit 4, see page 113.

Exercise 3. See Intro. p. x, Roleplay.
according to . . . Here, means the chart shows that . . .

Discuss with the students which system of sizes they are used to.

Optional: Students can extend the conversation by asking about items for other family members. Magazine pictures can be used to stimulate discussions.

A: I think my brother might like this shirt, but I'm not sure of his size in this country.
B: What size does he take/wear in your country?
A: In Spain he wears a size 38.
B: Well, according to this chart, he takes a U.S. size 15.

Exercise 4. See Intro. p. x, Look at the document.
**closing date* Here, means the date the last charge was put on the bill. Things Cathy buys after June 4 will go on the next bill.
**inquiry* Means a *question. Bill Inquiry No.* is the telephone number to call to ask a question about the bill.
**balance (n)* Here, means the amount of money Cathy owes to the store after new charges and payments are counted. **Previous balance* means this amount from last month. **New balance* means the amount with the new charges added.
**finance charge* The amount the store charges when the customer pays only part of the bill.
**minimum payment* The smallest amount Cathy may pay.
**past due* A balance that the customer should have paid before.

Answers: 1. wrong 2. right 3. wrong 4. right 5. wrong 6. right 7. wrong

On Your Own. See Intro. p. xi.

**unemployment rate* The number of people who have not found a job.

1. Discuss what Ken has been doing to get a job—going to employment agencies, answering classified ads in the newspapers, sending out his résumé. Ask students about other ways, e.g.: word of mouth, placing a situation-wanted ad, working for temporary agencies, using school placement services. In small groups, students can talk about their experiences using these or other methods.

2. In the U.S., workers can collect unemployment benefits if they lose their jobs for a reason not their own fault. The amount of money, the length of time they need to have had at a job before they lost it and the length of time they can collect benefits differ from state to state. In Canada, unemployment insurance is a federal program, so the amount of money paid and the length of time it is paid are the same across the country. There is some variation, however, in the length of work time required before collecting benefits.

Students can also talk about whether they feel this type of financial support is a good idea.

For **Pronunciation** exercises for Unit 4, see p. 35.

REVIEW 2

Exercise 1.
2. happened 3. was washing 4. heard 5. went 6. saw 7. was trying 8. saw 9. ran 10. was sitting 11. was bleeding 12. didn't seem 13. was going 14. drove 15. stopped 16. took

Exercise 2.
2. They didn't use to have electric lights. 3. Women used to wear long dresses all the time. 4. They didn't use to use washing machines. 5. They didn't use to wear contact lenses. 6. They used to cook all their meals over a fire. 7. They didn't use to make telephone calls. 8. They used to live shorter lives.

Exercise 3.
2. won 3. used to have 4. made 5. fired 6. used to play 7. named 8. did, fire 9. missed

Exercise 4.
2. a, Pete would like Tom to use a computer. 3. e, Pete encourages Michael to study hard. 4. c, Cathy wants Minh to take some pictures. 5. b, Bill asked Linda to meet him at a factory. 6. f, Angela reminded Brad to get the information to Linda.

REVIEW 2

1 This is part of a letter that Cathy wrote to her sister. Complete the paragraph with the simple past or the past progressive form of the verbs.

Yesterday I *was working* (1. work) in the kitchen when a terrible thing ______ (2. happen). I ______ (3. wash) the dishes when I ______ (4. hear) a crash outside. I ______ (5. go) to the window, and I ______ (6. see) a young boy. His motorcycle was lying on the ground, and he ______ (7. try) to get up. As soon as I ______ (8. see) him, I ______ (9. run) outside to see if I could help. He ______ (10. sit) in the street. His arm ______ (11. bleed), but he ______ (12. seem – *neg.*) too badly hurt. I ______ (13. go) to call an ambulance, when Dr. Nelson ______ (14. drive) by and ______ (15. stop) his car. He ______ (16. take) the boy to the hospital.

2 Make statements about what people *used to* do or *didn't use to* do 100 years ago.

1. travel by horse

They used to travel by horse.

2. have electric lights
3. wear long dresses all the time
4. use washing machines
5. wear contact lenses
6. cook all their meals over a fire
7. make telephone calls
8. live shorter lives

3 Complete this article with the correct form of the verbs. Use *used to* when you can.

The Houston Herald

Cooper Makes Big Mistake

Ed Cooper, head coach of the Houston Cavaliers, *used to be* (1. be) one of the best baseball coaches in the league. In fact, in 1987, he ______ (2. win) "Coach of the Year." He understood the game better than anyone I've ever met, and he ______ (3. have) the confidence of his team. But that has changed.

Last night Ed Cooper ______ (4. make) the biggest mistake of his coaching career. He ______ (5. fire) star hitter, Mike Daniels. Daniels, who ______ (6. play) for the University of Houston, is very popular with the Houston fans. In addition, Daniels's teammates ______ (7. name) him "Most Valuable Player" last year. Why ______ Cooper ______ (8. fire) this excellent player? Because Daniels ______ (9. miss) practice one day. Although it's important that players on a baseball team practice, perhaps Cooper should give Daniels another chance.

4 Match the phrases in columns A and B. Then combine the phrases with *to*.

	A		B
1. *d.*	Officer Brady told Linda	a.	use a computer
2. ____	Pete would like Tom	b.	meet him at a factory
3. ____	Pete encourages Michael	c.	take some pictures
4. ____	Cathy wants Minh	d.	be careful
5. ____	Bill asked Linda	e.	study hard
6. ____	Angela reminded Brad	f.	get the information to Linda

1. Officer Brady told Linda to be careful.

5 What has Ken been doing since he lost his job? Write about his activities. Use the present perfect progressive tense.

1. work around the house

He's been working around the house.

2. do the cooking
3. go to the grocery store
4. answer ads
5. take care of the children
6. drive Cathy to work
7. visit employment agencies

6 Look at the time line of Ken's life. Then read the answers and write questions in the present perfect progressive or present perfect tense. Begin the questions with *How long*.

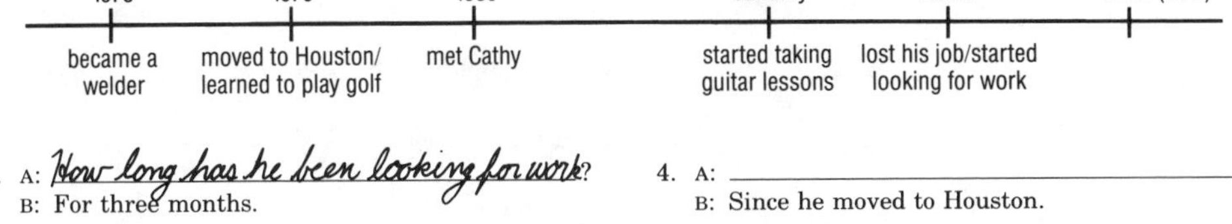

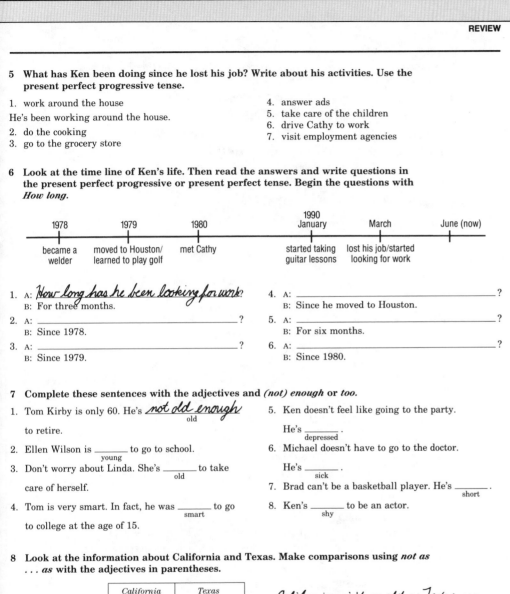

1. A: How long has he been looking for work?
   B: For three months.
2. A: ______?
   B: Since 1978.
3. A: ______?
   B: Since 1979.
4. A: ______?
   B: Since he moved to Houston.
5. A: ______?
   B: For six months.
6. A: ______?
   B: Since 1980.

7 Complete these sentences with the adjectives and *(not) enough* or *too*.

1. Tom Kirby is only 60. He's not old enough (old) to retire.
2. Ellen Wilson is ______ (young) to go to school.
3. Don't worry about Linda. She's ______ (old) to take care of herself.
4. Tom is very smart. In fact, he was ______ (smart) to go to college at the age of 15.
5. Ken doesn't feel like going to the party. He's ______ (depressed).
6. Michael doesn't have to go to the doctor. He's ______ (sick).
7. Brad can't be a basketball player. He's ______ (short).
8. Ken's ______ (shy) to be an actor.

8 Look at the information about California and Texas. Make comparisons using *not as . . . as* with the adjectives in parentheses.

	California	*Texas*
year founded	1769	1682
area	158,693 sq. mi.	267,338 sq. mi.
population density	168.6 people per sq. mi.	62.5 people per sq. mi.
per capita income	$15,255	$13,165
average annual rainfall	14.85″ (Los Angeles)	44.76″ (Houston)

Information as of 1985

1. California isn't as old as Texas. (old)
2. ______ (large)
3. ______ (crowded)
4. ______ (wealthy*)

Now Compare Los Angeles and Houston.

5. ______ (dry)

**wealthy = rich*

39

Exercise 5.

2. He's been doing the cooking. 3. He's been going to the grocery store. 4. He's been answering ads. 5. He's been taking care of the children. 6. He's been driving Cathy to work. 7. He's been visiting employment agencies.

Exercise 6.

2. How long has he been a welder? 3. How long has he lived in Houston? 4. How long has he been playing golf? 5. How long has he been taking guitar lessons? 6. How long has he known Cathy?

Exercise 7.

2. too young 3. old enough 4. smart enough 5. too depressed 6. not sick enough 7. too short 8. too shy

Exercise 8.

2. California isn't as large as Texas. 3. Texas isn't as crowded as California. 4. Texas isn't as wealthy as California. 5. Houston isn't as dry as Los Angeles.

UNIT 5

Language Summary

Functions

Asking for help and responding
Can you help me with my homework later? Sure. I'll be able to help you tonight./Sorry. I have to go to the dentist later.
Expressing hopes
I hope I'll be able to have my own business.
Giving advice
Why doesn't she use the dictionary? Then she'll be able to do it.
Offering encouragement
I'm sure you'll be able to find a job soon.

Introduction

Vocabulary

artist	income tax	refuse *v*
copy *n*	mean *adj*	term paper
discouraging *adj*	myself	type *n* (= kind)

For recognition only
unkind

Expressions

be able to	take a break	Two heads are better than one.
I'm not getting anywhere.	take care of	

Practice A

Structures

Verbal adjectives
Linda's discouraged. Sometimes her work is discouraging.

Vocabulary

annoyed *adj*	frightening *adj*	pleased *adj*
annoying *adj*	interested *adj*	tiring *adj*

For recognition only

activity	embarrassing *adj*	moment
confusing *adj*		

Practice B

Structures

Be able to
Pete was able to find a job in Houston two months after he moved there.
The police haven't been able to catch the arsonist yet.
In three years I'll be able to have my own business.

Vocabulary

beauty salon	crossword puzzle	private *adj*
blackout	destroy	put together
catch *v*	directions	

Expression

For recognition only—on cassette
just a moment

Practice C

Structures

Reflexive pronouns
She can take care of herself.
Reciprocal pronoun *each other*
They take care of each other.

Vocabulary

chase *v*	scratch *v*	stare at
dress *v*		

For recognition only

gotten	protection	scoring *n*

Expressions

enjoy yourself

For recognition only

be in danger	feel sorry for yourself	for a change
drive yourself crazy		make a mistake

Put It All Together

Vocabulary

cast (for a broken bone)	frustrated *adj*	overworked *adj*

For recognition only
without

On Your Own

Vocabulary

For recognition only

academic	common	psychologist
adviser	counselor	social worker
clergy	professional *n*	solve

Reading

Skills

Skimming
Finding the main idea

Vocabulary

create	truly	undergo
major *adj*		

For recognition only

acquire	display *v*	sawing *n*
addition	hammering *n*	shouting *n*
carry	lumber *n*	simply
combine	oilman	sound *n*
complete *adj*	project *n*	whisper *v*

Expressions

no longer

For recognition only

art lover	full of

Writing

Skill

Stating reasons

Task

Writing a paragraph explaining a decision

Vocabulary

capital *n*	hometown	therefore

For recognition only
certain
(= particular)

Pronunciation

Pronunciation points

1. Practicing intervocalic /ṭ/
2. Distinguishing verbal adjectives (*-ing*/*-ed*)
3. Understanding reduced syllables

Pronunciation exercises. *The pronunciation exercises for Unit 5 also appear in the Student's Book on pp. 113–114.*

Part 1. Practicing intervocalic /ṭ/

Listen and complete these sentences.

See Intro. p. xiii, Recognizing and distinguishing sounds 2 and 3

1. I'm not ______ anywhere.
2. Two heads are ______ than one.
3. Johnny's ______ .
4. They're ______ to each other.
5. She can't read the ______ .

Answers: 1. getting 2. better 3. excited 4. writing 5. letter

Now listen again and repeat the sentences.

Part 2. *Distinguishing verbal adjectives (-ing/-ed)*

Listen and complete each sentence with the adjective you hear.

See Intro. p. xiii, Recognizing and distinguishing sounds 2 and 3

1. She's very ____________ . (interesting/interested)
2. He's __________ . (exciting/excited)
3. They're not ____________ . (frightening/frightened)
4. He's ________ . (tiring/tired)
5. Is she ________ ? (boring/bored)

Answers: 1. interesting 2. excited 3. frightened 4. tiring 5. boring

Now listen again and repeat the sentences.

Part 3. *Understanding reduced syllables*

Sometimes an unstressed syllable is reduced so much it disappears. Listen to these sentences and cross out the vowel that you *don't* hear in each underlined word.

Example: The movie was frightening.

See Intro. p. xiii, Stress and intonation 2 and 4

1. I thought the book was interesting.
2. Bill's studying business.
3. Let's do something different.
4. That's Minh's best camera.

Answers: The vowels you don't hear are marked in the sentences above.

Now listen again and repeat the sentences.

See p. 140 for the Pronunciation Tapescript.

(continued on next page)

Teaching Notes

Getting Started

Use Unit 4, Ex. A2 on Student's Book p. 29. Working in pairs with new partners, students practice asking and telling what they've been doing lately. Put some cues on the board, including additional ones elicited when the exercise was done originally.

Introduction

 **1. Introductory Conversation.** See Intro. p. vii.

Preteaching

Two heads are better than one A saying that means it is easier for two people than for one person to solve a problem.
take a break Means stop working for a little while.
type (n) Means *kind.*
discouraging (adj) Linda's work makes her feel *discouraged;* it's *discouraging.*
copy (n) Show an example of a photocopy.
artist Someone who makes art objects such as paintings, drawings and sculpture.
will be able to Means *can* in the future.
take care of myself Linda thinks she can make sure she won't be hurt.

Preparation

Elicit who the characters are (Pete and Linda) and where they are (at the *Herald* and then in a restaurant). Ask how the characters feel. (Linda looks discouraged. Pete looks worried about her.) Ask students to guess who the man in the sketch is. Ask focus questions: *Does Linda want to eat something?* (No, she's too discouraged to eat.) *Does Bill know the man in the sketch?* (No, he doesn't.)

Exercise 2. See Intro. p. viii, Give a reason.
Answers: 1. Because she's been working too hard. 2. Because she's not getting anywhere with the arson story. 3. Because Bill was able to (could) describe him. 4. Because the guy looks mean.

Exercise 3. See Intro. p. viii, Find a word or phrase . . .
**unkind* Means *not kind.*

Answers: 1. refused 2. was able to describe 3. not getting anywhere 4. mean

Exercise 4. See Intro. p. viii, Warm Up.
income taxes If possible, bring in some blank forms. Remind students that *income* means the amount you earn every year.
term paper An essay that a student writes at the end of a semester.

Discuss refusing a favor—who can refuse (perhaps friends and classmates, but not family members) and when (does an exam take precedence over

 (continued on next page)

UNIT 5 Two Heads Are Better Than One

1 Linda and Pete are working late at the office. Listen to their conversation.

1
PETE: You've been working too hard, Linda. Why don't you take a break and get a bite to eat with me?
LINDA: I can't eat. I'm too discouraged. I'm not getting anywhere with this arson story.
PETE: This type of work *can* be discouraging. Why don't you tell me about it? You know what they say—two heads are better than one.
LINDA: OK. Maybe you'll be able to help.

2
PETE: So, what's going on?
LINDA: Well, Bill told the police that a man asked him to start those fires but he refused.
PETE: That's interesting. Did he know the guy?
LINDA: No, but he was able to describe him. Here's a copy of the artist's sketch.

3
PETE: I hope the police will be able to find him soon. He looks mean. You should be very careful, Linda.
LINDA: Don't worry. I can take care of myself.

2 Give a reason for these facts.

1. Pete wants Linda to take a break.
2. Linda feels discouraged.
3. The police artist was able to make a sketch of the man who asked Bill to start the fires.
4. Pete is worried about Linda.

3 Find a word or phrase in the conversation that means:

1. said no
2. could describe
3. not making progress
4. unkind

4 Warm Up

Ask a classmate if he or she can help you with something.

A: Can you help me with *my homework* later?
B: Sure. I'll be able to help you *tonight.*
OR Sorry. I won't be able to help you. *I have to go to the dentist.*

DEVELOP YOUR VOCABULARY

income taxes	application form
report	term paper
. . .	. . .

Practice

A.

Linda is **discouraged** about her work. Sometimes her work is **discouraging.**

1 Use the adjectives to describe the pictures.

1. Linda's discouraged.
   Her work is discouraging.

1. discouraged / discouraging

2. bored / boring

3. annoyed / annoying

4. excited / exciting

5. interested / interesting

2 Linda and Cathy are talking. Read their conversation and complete it with an adjective ending in *-ed* or *-ing*.

LINDA: What's wrong, Cathy?

CATHY: Oh, it's Ken. You know he's been looking for work for three months and he's getting really ________ (1. discourage). I try to be ______ (2. encourage) to him, but even I'm getting ______ (3. depress).

LINDA: I'm sorry. I know that looking for a job can be ______ (4. depress). Believe me, I was ______ (5. please) when I got this job.

3 Listen to the conversations. Then describe these people with an adjective from the box.

1. Johnny is ________.
2. Ellen is ________.
3. The woman is ________.
4. Johnny is ________.
5. Cathy is ________.

annoyed	annoying
discouraged	discouraging
frightened	frightening
~~excited~~	exciting
tired	tiring

4 Talk about your English language experience.

1. What was your most embarrassing moment in trying to speak English?
2. What kinds of classroom language activities do you think are interesting?
3. What kinds of activities do you think are boring?
4. What is the most confusing thing about English?

a request by a family member?). Point out that it's polite to offer an excuse or suggest an alternate time if you must refuse to do a favor by saying, e.g.: *Sorry, I can't. I have to meet someone.* OR *Sorry, I can't tonight. How about tomorrow?*

Practice A

Study Box. See Intro. p. viii.

Verbal adjectives. Give examples with students' names or real events of how the verbal adjectives derive from the verb, e.g.:

The movie *Friday the Thirteenth* frightens children.
The movie *Friday the Thirteenth* is frightening. Children are frightened.
Felipe's job tires him. His job is tiring. He's tired.

Pronunciation point: Part 2 of the **Pronunciation** exercises can be used here to practice distinguishing the *-ed* and *-ing* forms.

Exercise 1. See Intro. p. ix, Look at the pictures. Use the pictures to help explain new vocabulary.

Answers: 2. Cathy is bored. The TV show is boring. 3. Ken is annoyed. Ellen and Johnny are annoying. 4. Johnny is excited. The Johnson Space Center is (rockets are) exciting. 5. Angela is interested. The painting (picture) is interesting.

Optional: Practice additional conversations, and then have students discuss their own situations with the adjectives, e.g.:

A: Do you like your job?
B: Yes, but sometimes my work is discouraging.
A: When is that?
B: I feel discouraged when I don't get anywhere on a project for a long time.

OR

A: In your opinion what's the most interesting TV show?
B: I like the nature shows on Public Broadcasting. I'm interested in animals.
A: I think those shows are boring. I like "Lifestyles of the Rich and Famous." I'm interested in very rich people and how they live.

Exercise 2. See Intro. p. ix, Complete the sentences/paragraph.
pleased (adj) Means *happy.*

Answers: 2. encouraging 3. depressed 4. depressing 5. pleased

Exercise 3. See Intro. p. ix, Listening.
Answers: 2. frightened 3. discouraging 4. annoying 5. tired

Exercise 4. See Intro. p. ix, Ask and answer questions.
**embarrassing moment* A time when you did something (or someone did something to you) that made you feel silly.
**activity* Give examples: *listenings, conversations, pronunciation exercises.*
**confusing (adj)* Means hard to understand.

Practice B

Study Box. See Intro. p. viii.

Be able to. Point out that *be* shows the tense, e.g.: *was/were, has/have been, will be,* while *able to* remains unchanged. The base form of the verb following the phrase is used.

Pronunciation point: Point out the reduction and blending in:

wasn't able to /wəzənebəltə/
hasn't been able to /hæzənbınebəltə/
won't be able to /wonbiyebəltə/

Exercise 1. See Intro. p. ix, Make sentences.
catch (v) Here, means find and arrest someone.
destroy Here, means completely burn down.
blackout What happened as a result of the power failure.

Review the simple past and past perfect tenses—simple past for actions completed in the past, present perfect for actions that began in the past and continue into the present.

Answers: 2. Bill wasn't able to identify the driver of the car after the accident. 3. The police haven't been able to catch the arsonist yet. 4. The firefighters weren't able to put out the fire before it destroyed the factory. 5. Cathy and her family were able to go to the Johnson Space Center last weekend. 6. Pete was able to find a job in Houston two months after he moved there. 7. Angela hasn't been able to ski since her accident. 8. Michael was able to finish his homework during the blackout.

Exercise 2. See Intro. p. ix, Look at the pictures.
Answers: 2. Why doesn't she take lessons? Then she'll be able to skate. 3. Why doesn't he use an adding machine? Then he'll be able to do them. 4. Why doesn't she wear her glasses? Then she'll be able to read it. 5. Why doesn't he read the directions? Then he'll be able to put it together.

Exercise 3. See Intro. p. ix, Listening.
Answer: Message 3.

Optional: Suggest a number of situations and have students practice making telephone calls and writing messages with *be able to*, e.g.:
1. Call your daughter's school and leave a message that you can't meet her that day and she should take the school bus home.
2. Call your friend's office and leave a message for her that you couldn't get the information she wanted.
3. Call your own office and leave a message that you can't come to the meeting later in the day.

B.

He	**was(n't) able to** find a job last month. **has(n't) been able to** find a job yet. **will (won't) be able to** find a job soon.

1 Can you remember the story? Make sentences with *has/have been able to* or *was/were able to.*

1. Ken / find a job yet
Ken hasn't been able to find a job yet.
2. Bill / identify the driver of the car after the accident
3. The police / catch the arsonist yet
4. The firefighters / put out the fire before it destroyed the factory
5. Cathy and her family / go to the Johnson Space Center last weekend
6. Pete / find a job in Houston two months after he moved there
7. Angela / ski since her accident
8. Michael / finish his homework during the blackout

2 Each person in the pictures has a problem. Make a suggestion to help him or her. Use *will be able to.*

1. A: She can't do the crossword puzzle.
B: Why doesn't she use the dictionary? Then she'll be able to do it.

1. She can't do the crossword puzzle.

2. She can't skate.

3. He can't do his taxes.

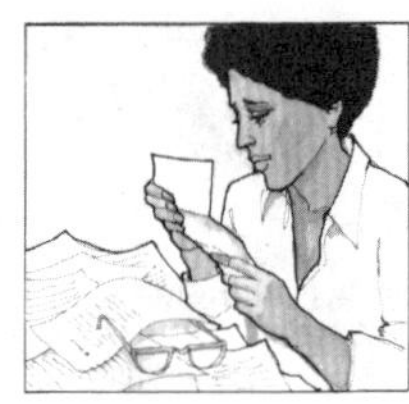
4. She can't read the letter.

5. He can't put the bicycle together.

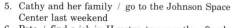

3 Linda is calling the Houston *Herald.* Listen to the conversation and choose the correct message form.

PHONE MESSAGE
to: Pete Gómez
from: Linda Smith
She won't be able to meet you. Please call her at home.

1

PHONE MESSAGE
to: Pete Gómez
from: Linda Smith
She would like to meet with you this morning after she speaks to Officer Brady.

2

PHONE MESSAGE
to: Pete Gómez
from: Linda Smith
She won't be able to meet you. She's gone to see Officer Brady.

3

4 Talk about what you hope you'll be able to do in the future.

A: I hope I'll be able to *speak English really well in three years.*
B: I hope I'll be able to *have my own business.*

You can use these ideas:

buy *a house*
get a job as *a bilingual secretary*
move to *Dallas*
open *a beauty salon*

C.

I		**myself.**
You		**yourself.**
He		**himself.**
She	can take care of	**herself.**
We		**ourselves.**
You		**yourselves.**
They		**themselves.**

1 Describe what the people or animals are doing in the pictures.

1. Pete's looking at himself.

1. look at

2. talk to

3. scratch

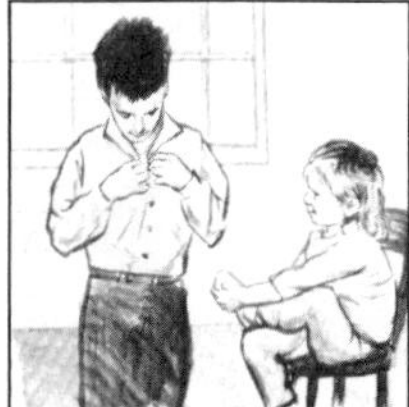
4. dress

Cathy takes care of Ken, and Ken takes care of Cathy.
They take care of **each other.**

5. write

6. stare at

7. chase

Exercise 4.
beauty salon A place where women go to have their hair cut and styled.

Encourage students to extend their conversations by asking questions about their partners' future plans. Write some cues on the board, e.g.: *What are you doing to improve your English? Why do you want to speak really well? What kind of business do you want to open? Do you want to buy a house in the country or the city?*

Practice C

Study Box. See Intro. p. viii.

Reflexive pronouns. Reflexive pronouns usually refer to the subject of the sentence, e.g: *Nieve taught herself to read.* They are sometimes used for emphasis, e.g.: *I paid that bill myself* suggests *I know that bill has been paid because I paid it.*

Pronunciation point: Point out the pronunciation of *selves* /sɛlvz/.

Reciprocal pronoun *each other*. Point out that the same action is done to another person rather than to oneself.

Exercise 1. See Intro. p. ix, Look at the pictures.
stare at Mime and refer to the picture.
chase (v) Means *run after.* Refer to the picture.

Point out that when an animal has a name, *herself* or *himself* would be used.

Answers: 2. Ellen's talking to herself. 3. The dog's scratching itself. 4. Ellen and Johnny are dressing themselves. 5. Suzanne and Pete are writing to each other. 6. Ellen and Johnny are staring at each other. 7. The squirrels are chasing each other.

Optional: Ask students to discuss their answers to the following questions with a partner or small group. They then individually write sentences about themselves and others in the group, using as many of the reflexive pronouns as possible. For example, *Otilia, Felipe and I taught ourselves to swim. Marie and Ruth laugh at themselves when they pronounce words wrong.*

When do you laugh at yourself?
Do you get angry at yourself when you make a mistake in English?
Does it help you to talk to yourself when you do a difficult job?

Exercise 2. See Intro. p. ix, Complete the sentences/paragraph.
**be in danger* Means be in a dangerous situation. Bill might get hurt.
**police protection* When the police make sure someone doesn't get hurt.
enjoy yourself Means *have fun.*
**drive yourself crazy* Here, Linda is making herself very uncomfortable because she's worrying a lot.

Answers: 2. himself 3. himself 4. themselves OR each other 5. yourself 6. myself 7. yourselves 8. herself 9. ourselves

Exercise 3. See Intro. p. ix, Ask and answer questions.
Suggested substitutions are:

your parents/mother/father/boyfriend/girlfriend/visitors
went out to dinner/went to the theater/visited friends/went sightseeing/went to the beach
The show/food was disappointing/The crowds were annoying/The weather was too muggy

Exercise 4.
**feel sorry for yourself* Means feel that you are in a sad situation or have a bad problem you can't do much about. Point out that this is considered to be a negative character trait.
scoring (n) Here, the directions for finding out the results of the test.

Before students do the test, discuss some of the questions and whether these are good or bad traits in the students' own cultures. For instance, some students might be perplexed about the positive score for saying nice things about oneself and feeling good about oneself when meeting new people. If so, point out that these are considered good traits if not exaggerated. One could say, e.g., *I'm doing well in my English class* as a statement of fact and not be considered impolite.

Students can either do the test individually or interview a partner. After they do the test, ask the class to discuss the test with a partner or small group. Encourage them to expand their answers:
1. What do you like to do when you spend time by yourself?
2. What kinds of nice things do you usually say about yourself?
3. What mistakes do you get angry at yourself for? Why did Dr. Cousins' test take points away for this?
4. What do you feel good about when you meet new people?

2 Pete is having lunch with Linda. Complete the conversation with a *-self/-selves* pronoun or *each other.*

PETE: Have you spoken to Bill again?
LINDA: Yes. We spoke to each other (1) yesterday. He's really upset with ______ (2) because of his past. Now he says everyone thinks he's the arsonist.
PETE: Do you think he's gotten ______ (3) into trouble again?
LINDA: No. But I *do* think he's in danger. I'm not sure that Bill and his mother can take care of ______ (4). I think they need police protection.
PETE: And what about *you?* Can you take care of ______ (5)?
LINDA: Oh, I'm not worried about ______ (6).
(Tom enters restaurant)
TOM: You two don't look like you're enjoying ______ (7) very much.
PETE: It's this arson case. Linda is driving ______ (8) crazy over it.
TOM: Maybe we should all go out to a movie after work and try to enjoy ______ (9) for a change.

3 Ask what someone did last weekend.

A: What did *your children* do last weekend?
B: *They went bowling.*
A: Did *they* enjoy *themselves?*
B: Yes, *they* did.
OR No, *they* didn't. *The place was too crowded.*

Just for Fun

4 Read Dr. Cousins's column from the *Herald* and follow the instructions.

Dear Dr. Cousins

Do You Like Yourself?

Take this short test and see for yourself.

	YES	NO
1. Do you enjoy yourself when you are alone?	☐	☐
2. Do you always talk about yourself when you are with other people?	☐	☐
3. Do you say nice things about yourself?	☐	☐
4. Do you look at yourself a lot in the mirror?	☐	☐
5. Do you often feel sorry for yourself?	☐	☐
6. Do you get angry with yourself when you make a mistake?	☐	☐
7. Do you usually feel good about yourself when you meet new people?	☐	☐

Scoring: Give yourself 1 point for a *yes* answer in questions 1,3 and 7. Give yourself 1 point for a *no* answer in questions 2,4,5 and 6. The more points you have, the more you like yourself.

PUT IT ALL TOGETHER

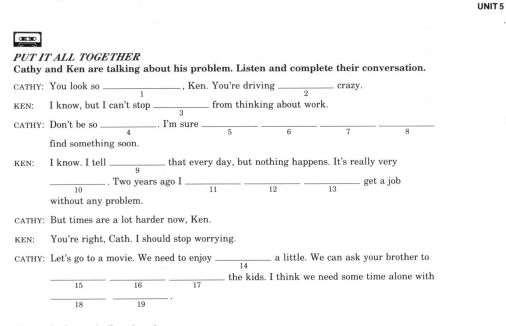

Cathy and Ken are talking about his problem. Listen and complete their conversation.

CATHY: You look so ______(1), Ken. You're driving ______(2) crazy.

KEN: I know, but I can't stop ______(3) from thinking about work.

CATHY: Don't be so ______(4). I'm sure ______(5) ______(6) ______(7) ______(8) find something soon.

KEN: I know. I tell ______(9) that every day, but nothing happens. It's really very ______(10). Two years ago I ______(11) ______(12) ______(13) get a job without any problem.

CATHY: But times are a lot harder now, Ken.

KEN: You're right, Cath. I should stop worrying.

CATHY: Let's go to a movie. We need to enjoy ______(14) a little. We can ask your brother to ______(15) ______(16) ______(17) the kids. I think we need some time alone with ______(18) ______(19).

Now roleplay a similar situation.
Student A has a problem that has no easy solution.
Student B offers encouragement and suggests an activity to take Student A's mind off the problem.

Student A can use these ideas:

You've been looking for an apartment and haven't been able to find one. You are overworked at your job. You broke your arm and will have to wear a cast for six weeks. You've been trying to learn how to use a computer and feel frustrated.

ON YOUR OWN

Discuss these questions with your classmates.

1 Think of a problem you recently had. What did you do to try to solve it? Do you believe "two heads are better than one," or do you usually prefer to solve problems by yourself?

2 Sometimes people with problems get help from professionals (job counselors, academic advisers, psychologists, clergy, social workers). Are these professionals common in your country?

Put It All Together. See Intro. p. ix, Listening.

Answers: 1. depressed 2. yourself 3. myself 4. discouraged 5. you'll 6. be 7. able 8. to 9. myself 10. depressing 11. was 12. able 13. to 14. ourselves 15. take 16. care 17. of 18. each 19. other

Now roleplay a similar situation. See Intro. p. x, Roleplay.
overworked (adj) Means working too hard.
cast Draw one on the board. Explain that it's a kind of bandage that keeps a broken bone from moving.
frustrated (adj) Means angry because you can't do something.

Discuss how to encourage someone in these situations, e.g.: *I'm sure you'll be able to find an apartment/get some time off/play tennis again/figure out your computer/soon.*

On Your Own. See Intro. p. xi.

**solve problems* Means find an answer for problems, figure out what to do.
**professional (n)* A person with special training in psychology or the social sciences who can help people solve personal and job problems.
**job counselor* A professional who gives advice about job problems.
**academic adviser* A professional who helps with school problems.
**clergy* Religious leaders, who often have special training in giving advice.
**social worker* A professional who can help with psychological problems and problems of everyday living. A social worker has special training to help people find support from other professionals—medical, psychological, financial or academic.

1. Discuss some of the advantages of each approach, e.g., getting a different viewpoint, talking to someone not emotionally involved, talking to someone with more experience. A disadvantage might be loss of privacy.

2. If students come from cultures that do not use these professionals much, discuss what kind of alternatives they use for advice and how effective these are, e.g., older relatives and friends or religious leaders.

Reading

See Intro. p. xi.
whisper (v) Demonstrate this.
carry Demonstrate by carrying a book.
sound (n) Means *noise.*
hammering (n) and *sawing (n)* Mime, or draw simple pictures of the tools and tell students the verbs come from these nouns.
shouting (n) Means talk in a loud voice.
simply Means *just* or *only.*
undergo Means to *experience.* Something is happening to the museum.
major (adj) Means very large and important.
acquire Means *get.* The museum probably acquired the paintings in different ways—buying, exchanging for other paintings and receiving them as gifts.
create Means *make.*
display (v) Means *show.*
project (n) Point out that the word refers back to the plan to build the children's room. It means a complicated job with many parts that probably extends over a fairly long period of time.
oilman Someone who owns oil wells.
art lover Someone who loves art and supports it financially.
complete (adj) Means *finished.*
truly Means *really.*

Exercise 1.
Discuss the choices. Except for number 3, all of them refer to only one part of the article. *THE NEW HOUSTON ART MUSEUM: A PLACE FOR ALL* covers all the main points in the article and for that reason appears in the conclusion as well as the headline.

Exercise 2. See Intro. p. xi, Answer the questions.
Answers: 1. The museum is undergoing a renovation. 2. The museum was no longer big enough to hold all the paintings. The restaurant is being added to make the museum more a part of people's lives. The children's room is being built to display art by children and as a place for children to learn how to create art. 3. The Evans Collier Wing, to thank the man who gave the museum the money for the renovation.

Exercise 3.
The exercise can be done individually or in pairs. Discuss the answers with the whole class.

Answers: Paragraph 2: first sentence, lines 19–22. Paragraph 3: first sentence, lines 51–52. Paragraph 4: last sentence, lines 66–69.

Reading

1 Skimming. Sometimes you read an article quickly to find out what it's about. Read this article as quickly as you can. Then choose the best headline from the list below. Discuss why you chose the headline.

1. TEXAS OILMAN GIVES MUSEUM $1 MILLION
2. HOUSTON ART MUSEUM TO OPEN RESTAURANT
3. THE NEW HOUSTON ART MUSEUM: A PLACE FOR ALL
4. AN ART MUSEUM FOR CHILDREN

The Houston Herald

An art museum is usually quiet and peaceful. People generally speak quietly, if they speak at all. The Houston Art Museum, however, isn't as quiet as it used to be. When I visited it two days ago, I saw a very different scene. Instead of art lovers whispering quietly, it was full of workers carrying lumber, bricks and tools. The sound of hammering and sawing combined with shouting made it the noisiest art museum I've ever visited. But don't worry, this is not a new idea in art. The Houston Art Museum is simply undergoing a major renovation.

According to museum director Frank Jordan, there were several reasons for the renovation. First of all, the museum was no longer big enough to hold all the paintings. "We have acquired more than 150 new paintings in the past two years, and we just didn't have room for them," he said. Another reason for the renovation was to add a restaurant and a children's art room. Jordan explained, "We decided to add the restaurant because we wanted to make the art museum more a part of people's lives. We're hoping that people will start saying, 'Let's meet for lunch at the art museum.'" The children's room is a project that is close to Jordan's heart. "We also wanted the art museum to be a place for families, so we decided to create a 'children's room.' We'll use it as a place to display art by children as well as a place for children to learn how to create art. We're one of the first art museums in the country to do this."

And how are they paying for this expensive project? According to Jordan, Texas oilman and art lover Evans Collier gave the museum one million dollars for the renovation. In order to thank him, Jordan says that the new section of the museum will be called the Evans Collier Wing.

When the museum renovation is complete next fall, the museum won't be as small as it was, and with the addition of the children's room it probably won't be as quiet either. However, if Jordan and the museum directors are right, it will truly be a place for all.

2 Comprehension. Reread the article and answer these questions.

1. What is happening at the Houston Art Museum?
2. Why did they decide to make the museum larger? (Give three reasons.)
3. What are they going to name the new section of the museum? Why?

3 Finding the main idea. The main idea of the first paragraph is found in the last sentence (lines 16, 17 and 18):

The Houston Art Museum is simply undergoing a major renovation.

Find the sentences that give the main idea of paragraphs 2, 3 and 4.

Writing

Skill: Stating reasons
Task: Writing a paragraph explaining a decision

1 When we give reasons for things we do, we often use the words *because, so* and *therefore.*

a. *Because* states a reason:

Result	Reason
We stopped for lunch **because** we were hungry.	

Notice there is no comma before *because.*

b. *So* and *therefore* state results:

Reason	Result
We were hungry, **so** we stopped for lunch.	

Notice there is a comma before *so.*

Reason	Result
We were hungry; **therefore,** we stopped for lunch. OR We were hungry. **Therefore,** we stopped for lunch.	

Notice there is a semicolon before *therefore.* Also notice *therefore* can begin a new sentence.

2 Connect each sentence two ways with the words in parentheses.

1. I came to the United States. I wanted a better job. (because) (so)

I came to the United States because I wanted a better job.
I wanted a better job, so I came to the United States.

2. I hated working in the factory. I quit my job. (because) (therefore)
3. My father lost his job at home. He decided to come to the United States. (therefore) (because)
4. My parents don't feel comfortable here. They plan to return home. (so) (because)
5. I wanted my children to have more opportunities than I had. My wife and I decided to move here. (so) (because)
6. There weren't many opportunities in my hometown. I moved to the capital. (because) (therefore)

3 Make a list of the reasons for making an important decision in your life. Some important decisions might include why you:

1. moved to a different city or country.
2. decided to study English.
3. decided (not) to take a certain job.

4 Use your list of reasons to write a paragraph about why you made the important decision. Try to use *because, so* and *therefore.*

For pronunciation exercises for Unit 5, see page 113.

Writing

See Intro. p. xii.

Exercise 1. See Intro. p. viii, Study Box.
Point out that the *because* clause can also begin the sentence but in that case, a comma follows the clause, e.g. *Because we were hungry, we stopped for lunch.*

Exercise 2. See Intro. p. ix, Writing sentences.
Answers: I quit my job because I hated working in the factory. I hated working in the factory; therefore, I quit my job. OR I hated working in the factory. Therefore, I quit my job. 3. My father lost his job at home; therefore, he decided to come to the United States. OR My father lost his job at home. Therefore, he decided to come to the United States. My father decided to come to the United States because he lost his job at home. 4. My parents don't feel comfortable here, so they plan to return home. My parents plan to return home because they don't feel comfortable here. 5. I wanted my children to have more opportunities than I had, so my wife and I decided to move here. My wife and I decided to move here because I wanted my children to have more opportunities than I had. 6. I moved to the capital because there weren't many opportunities in my hometown. There weren't many opportunities in my hometown; therefore, I moved to the capital. OR There weren't many opportunities in my hometown. Therefore, I moved to the capital.

Exercise 3.
Additional ideas are *decided to major in a certain field, change careers, see a particular movie, play a sport, have a hobby.*

After students make their lists individually, ask them to work in pairs to read each other's lists and ask questions.

Exercise 4.
Ask students to reread the second paragraph of the reading selection on Student's Book p. 46 and work in pairs to answer these questions:

Which is the topic sentence? (The first one.)

How does this sentence predict what is to follow? (By the phrase *there were several reasons . . .*)

What connecting words and phrases does the writer use to connect the three reasons? *(First of all, Another reason, also.)*

After the class discusses the questions, ask students to use that paragraph as a model for their own writing.

Optional: Students can write this paragraph in the form of a letter to a classmate explaining the reason for their decision.

For **Pronunciation** exercises for Unit 5, see p. 49.

UNIT 6

Language Summary

Functions

Expressing feelings
I really miss my hometown. I know what you mean.
Giving advice
I'm worried about my sister. She has a terrible rash.
Hmm, she'd better see a dermatologist.
Predicting
If Pete finds a bigger apartment, he'll move.
Talking about likes and dislikes
I really like cooking, but I don't like doing the dishes.

Introduction

Vocabulary

anonymous	special delivery	urgent
immediately	threatening *adj*	

For recognition only

celebration	possession

Expression

had better

Practice A

Structure

Conditional—future with *if*

If Pete finds a bigger apartment, he'll move.

Vocabulary

fly *v*	lose	relax
hard *adv*	protection	

For recognition only—on cassette
threaten

Expression

for a while

Practice B

Structure

Had better
Linda had better call Officer Brady.

Vocabulary

anxiety	fallen arch	orthopedist
blurred vision	ingrown toenail	podiatrist
case (= matter)	insomnia	psychologist
consider	internist	rash *n*
depression	investigate	sore *adj*
dermatologist	kidney stone	speed limit
double vision	ophthalmologist	ulcer

For recognition only

clear up *intrans*	pack *v*	run away

Expressions

For recognition only
leave town

For recognition only—on cassette
Thank you for returning my call.

Practice C

Structure

Verb + gerund
Pete enjoys working in Houston.

Vocabulary

avoid	deny	suggest
continue (= keep)		

For recognition only

belong to	downtown

Expressions

have trouble

For recognition only
Well, yes and no.

Life Skills

Telephone calls
Taking messages
Calling directory assistance
Understanding recorded messages

Vocabulary

beep *n* — hold on — listing *n*
dial *v*

For recognition only
answering machine — directory assistance

For recognition only—on cassette
brief *adj*

Expressions

Speaking. — That's quite all right.

Pronunciation

Pronunciation points

1. Understanding initial and medial /ər/
2. Practicing intonation of *if-* clauses
3. Practicing intonation of *yes/no* and *wh-* questions

Pronunciation exercises. *The pronunciation exercises for Unit 6 also appear in the Student's Book on p. 114.*

Part 1. *Understanding initial and medial* /ər/

Pete and Tom are talking about Linda. Listen to their conversation and complete it.

See Intro. p. xiii, Recognizing and distinguishing sounds 2 and 3

PETE: I'm really ______ (1) about Linda.
TOM: I know. She always ______ (2) too hard.
PETE: No, it's not that. I'm ______ (3) about that letter she got when she ______ (4) to the office today.
TOM: Oh, I ______ (5) about that. What does Officer Brady think?
PETE: I don't know. But I'm ______ (6). I don't want Linda to get ______ (7).

Answers: 1. concerned 2. works 3. worried 4. returned 5. heard 6. nervous 7. hurt

Now listen again and repeat the conversation.

Part 2. *Practicing intonation of* if- *clauses*

Listen to these sentences. Notice how the voice rises and then falls in the *if-* clause.

See Intro. p. xiii, Stress and intonation 1 and 4

1. If Pete finds an apartment, he'll move.
2. If Ken gets a job, he'll be happy.
3. If Michael doesn't study, he won't pass.
4. If Cathy calls, I'll tell you.
5. If Linda isn't careful, she'll get hurt.

Now listen again and repeat the sentences.

Part 3. *Practicing intonation of* yes/no *and* wh- *questions*

A. Listen and repeat these *yes/no* questions. Remember that your voice goes up at the end.

See Intro. p. xiii, Stress and intonation 4

1. Have you seen Linda?
2. Are you enjoying working in Houston?
3. Can I take a message?
4. Could I have the day off?

B. Now listen and repeat these *wh-* questions. Remember that your voice goes down at the end.

See Intro. p. xiii, Stress and intonation 4

1. Who sent it?
2. What's it about?
3. What's the matter?
4. Where's Linda?

See p. 141 for the Pronunciation Tapescript.

Teaching Notes

Getting Started

1. Use Unit 5, Ex. B4 on Student's Book p. 43. Pairs of students practice talking about what they hope they'll be able to do in the future. Write cues on the board to encourage students to extend their conversations with *wh-* questions, e.g.:

Where do you want to buy a house?
Why did you decide to become a bilingual secretary?
Who will help you open your beauty salon?

2. Use Unit 4, Ex. B3 on Student's Book p. 32. Review the vocabulary and write on the board some of the words elicited when the class did this exercise the first time. This exercise can also be done as a continuation of 1 above:

A: Why did you decide to become a bilingual secretary?
B: My English and my Spanish are good enough for the job. And I'm efficient enough to be a good secretary.

Introduction

1. Introductory Conversation. See Intro. p. vii.

Preteaching

special delivery A special service from the post office. Linda's letter did not go with the regular delivery of mail but was delivered as soon as it arrived at the post office.
threatening letter The writer says that Linda must do something or she will get hurt.
immediately Means *right away.*

Preparation

Discuss who the characters are and elicit the storyline. Linda has been feeling discouraged about the arson story. Pete just moved to Houston. Brad is Angela's assistant. Ask focus questions: *Why's Brad looking for Linda?* (To give her a special delivery letter.) *Is Officer Brady in his office?* (No, he's not.)

Exercise 2. See Intro. p. viii, Say *That's right . . .*
Answers: 1. That's right. 2. That's wrong. 3. I don't know. 4. That's wrong. 5. That's wrong.

Exercise 3. See Intro. p. viii, Find a word or phrase . . .
Answers: 1. anonymous 2. you'd better 3. urgent 4. kept

Exercise 4. See Intro. p. viii, Warm Up.
holiday celebrations Give examples students know about, e.g.: *Christmas, Chanukah, Easter,* and include some of the foods served. Then elicit examples from students and ask for some details of the celebration.
possessions Means things you own. If possible, give an example of a possession that has meaning for you.

Before the class breaks into groups, elicit some examples from individual students, e.g.: types of food, favorite restaurants, outing or vacation spots, schools. Ask individuals to describe them: *What were they like? What do you miss about them?* Practice the conversation as a group, using some of the examples elicited from students. If time allows, encourage students working in pairs or groups to extend their conversations by asking partners to describe the things they're talking about.

UNIT 6 A Special Delivery Letter

1 Brad is looking for Linda. He has something to give her. Listen to the conversation.

1

BRAD: Pete, have you seen Linda? A special delivery letter just came for her.
PETE: No. But if I see her, I'll tell her.
BRAD: Thanks. By the way, are you enjoying working in Houston?
PETE: Yes. But I miss Dallas sometimes.

2

LINDA: Hi, guys. I just finished talking to Bill. What's happening here?
BRAD: This just came for you.
LINDA: I don't believe it! It's a threatening letter!
BRAD: What? Who sent it? What's it about?
LINDA: I don't know who sent it. It's anonymous. But it's about my arson stories.
PETE: I kept warning you this could be dangerous.
BRAD: You'd better call the police.
PETE: Yes. This is serious. If *you* don't call, *I* will!

3

LINDA: Can I speak to Officer Brady, please?
CLERK: Sorry, but he's not here now. Can I take a message?
LINDA: Yes. Please tell him that Linda Smith from the *Herald* called. I have to speak to him immediately. It's urgent!

2 Say *That's right, That's wrong* or *I don't know.*

1. Linda received a letter.
2. Pete doesn't like working in Houston.
3. Pete misses working at the Dallas *Star.*
4. Linda knows who sent the letter.
5. Linda spoke to Officer Brady on the phone.

3 Find a word or phrase in the conversation that means:

1. without a name
2. you should
3. very important
4. continued

4 Warm Up

Tell a classmate about something you miss.

A: I really miss *my hometown.*
B: I know what you mean. I miss *my friends.*

You can use these ideas:

types of food	certain places
holiday celebrations	possessions

Practice

A.

If Pete **finds** a bigger apartment, he'**ll move.**
If he **doesn't find** one, he **won't move.**

1 What will happen if . . . ? Match the possible events in column A with their correct results in column B. Give a reason for your choices like this:

1. If Pete finds a bigger apartment, he'll move because he needs more room.

	A		B
1.	d. If Pete finds a bigger apartment, he	a.	will get sick.
2.	___ If Ken finds a job, he	b.	will move to Houston.
3.	___ If Michael doesn't study hard, he	c.	will celebrate.
4.	___ If the police don't catch the hit-and-run driver, Bill	d.	will move.
5.	___ If Linda doesn't relax more, she	e.	won't feel safe.
6.	___ If the lights go out again, Tom	f.	won't pass his test.
7.	___ If Suzanne gets a job at the *Herald*, she	g.	won't lose the story he's working on.

2 Linda is talking to Cathy. Listen to their conversation and find out what Linda will do if she gets another threatening letter.

1. Stop working on the arson story.
2. Work harder on the arson story. ✓
3. Write about the letter in the newspaper.
4. Tell Alice Thomas.
5. Call Officer Brady.
6. Ask for police protection.
7. Go live with Cathy for a while.
8. Ask Angela for help.

3 Complete these sentences with information about yourself. Then tell a classmate.

1. If I study hard, . . .
2. If I don't speak English every day, . . .
3. I'll ask the teacher if . . .
4. I won't be happy if . . .

4 It's a busy day at the newsroom. Say what will or won't happen if . . .

If Tom doesn't close the window, the papers will fly out.

Practice A

Study Box. See Intro. p. viii.

Conditional—future with *if*. Discuss the meaning of the Study Box sentences: Pete must find a bigger apartment first, and then he can move. Point out that the present tense is used in the *if-* clause, the future tense in the main clause. Point out that the *if-* clause can also follow the main clause. In this case, there is no comma: *Pete will move if he finds a bigger apartment.*

Pronunciation point: Point out the rising and falling intonation for *if-* clauses:

If Pete finds a bigger apartment, he'll move.

Part 2 of the **Pronunciation** exercises can be used here to practice this intonation pattern.

Optional: Give additional practice. Write some conditions on the board and ask students to say what they'll do in these situations, e.g.:
It rains on Saturday./My car breaks down./I get a promotion.
If it rains on Saturday, I'll stay home.

Exercise 1. See Intro. p. xii, Matching.
hard (adv) Give other examples: *work hard, play hard, run hard.* Explain that it means to do something with a lot of effort.
relax Means *rest,* have more leisure time.
lose Mime looking for something. Explain that *lose* means be unable to find something. Teach the past form, *lost.*

Answers: 2. c 3. f 4. e 5. a 6. g 7. b

Exercise 2. See Intro. p. ix, Listening.
protection Teach *protect,* which means keep safe.
**threaten* Remind students about the threatening letter that Linda received. The writer threatened her—said he or she would harm her if she didn't do what the writer asked.

Answers: 2, 5, 8

Exercise 3. See Intro. p. ix, Writing sentences.
Give some examples of negatives and clauses in the third person singular: *If I don't speak English every day, I won't improve very fast. I won't be happy if my wife doesn't find a job soon.*

Exercise 4. See Intro. p. ix, Look at the pictures.
Teach: *Look where you're going, watch out, be careful.*

Some possible answers: If Minh doesn't pay attention, he'll miss his phone call. If Cathy isn't careful, she'll knock over her flowers. If Linda and Pete don't watch where they're going, they'll bump into each other/Linda will spill her coffee. If Brad doesn't watch out, he'll fall down.

Exercise 5.
Start with the whole class. Go around the room having students read the example sentences. When you get to E, have the student finish the sentence, and go on to the next few students until it is clear they all have the idea. Then break into groups of five or six.

Optional: Bring in copies of a very short news item about an issue that touches students' lives. Read it with the class and then write the problem or situation on the board, e.g., *Computer services are growing, and many companies now need employees with computer training.* Ask students to work in pairs and write two or three sentences with *if-* clauses that could logically follow that sentence, e.g.:

Computer services are growing, and many companies now need employees with computer training. If your company starts using computers, you will be able to get this training at your job. If you already know how to use a computer, it will be easier to find work in the next few years.

Practice B

Study Box. See Intro. p. viii.

Had better. *Had better* is stronger than *should,* and it often implies a warning, e.g.: *You'd better carry your umbrella today (or you'll get wet).* The contracted form, *'d better,* is usually used in spoken English.

investigate Means study to find the reason for something.

Optional Give additional practice. Write situations on the board, using different personal pronouns. Call on students to form sentences with *had better* and *had better not,* e.g.:

We have a test tomorrow. (We'd better study. We'd better not go to the movies.)
Maria has a fever.
The students in the back can't hear the teacher.

Exercise 1. See Intro p. ix, Look at the pictures.
Answers: You'd better study harder. 3. You'd better not hit her. 4. You'd better not forget your helmut. 5. You'd better come to work on time.

Just for Fun

THE CHAIN GAME

5 One student says a sentence with *if* or *will.* The next student uses part of that sentence to say a new sentence. Continue around the class and see how many ideas you can think of. Look at the example and use your imagination.

A: If I stay home, I'll get bored.
B: If I get bored, I'll call my friend.
C: If I call my friend, we'll talk for hours.
D: If we talk for hours, I'll get a big phone bill.
E: If I get a big phone bill, . . .

B.

Linda's in danger.
Linda **had better** call Officer Brady.
She**'d better not** investigate the case anymore.

she'd better = she had better

Note: We don't use *had better* in affirmative questions.

1 What are the people saying? Use *had better* or *had better not.*

You'd better
call the police.
1. call

2. study

3. hit

4. forget

5. come

2 **Officer Brady is returning Linda's phone call. Listen to their conversation. Then choose the letter Linda received.**

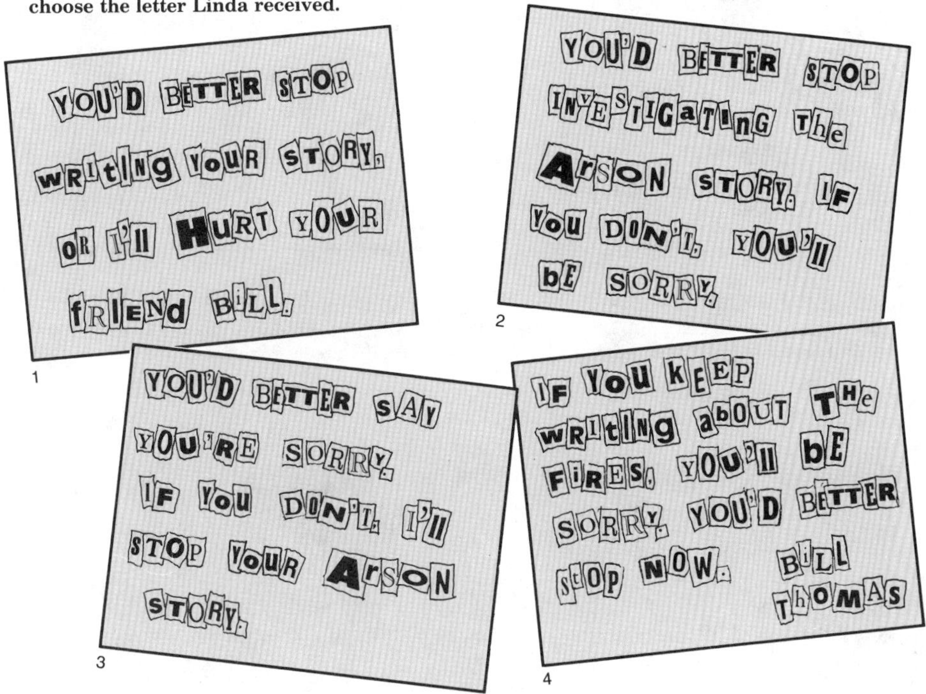

3 **Officer Brady is at the *Herald* talking to Linda and Angela. Complete their conversation with *had better* or *had better not.***

BRADY: I think you'd better not work (1. work) on this case anymore. You're making someone nervous. And you ________ (2. tell) me everything you know.

ANGELA: In fact, Linda, maybe you ________ (3. consider) leaving town for a while.

LINDA: I can't just run away.

ANGELA: Well, you ________ (4. stay) with someone then. Why don't you come stay with me until this is cleared up?

BRADY: That's a good idea.

LINDA: OK. I'll go home and pack some things.

BRADY: Wait for me. I ________ (5. drive) you. Oh, and you ________ (6. tell) anyone else about this letter. I ________ (7. read) about it in the *Herald.*

ANGELA: Don't worry, Officer. I'll make sure that no one here says anything. In fact, I ________ (8. do) that now. And I think I ________ (9. tell) everyone that Linda has stopped investigating the case.

Exercise 2. See Intro. p. ix, Listening.
**Thank you for returning my call.* Means *Thank you for calling me back.*

Elicit or explain the appearance of the letters—the writer cut the letters from books or newspapers. He or she did this because the police can often identify a typewriter that has been used.

Answer: Letter 2.

Exercise 3. See Intro. p. ix, Complete the sentences/paragraph.
**this is cleared up* Means the problem is ended.
**pack some things* Means put things in a suitcase.

Answers: 2. 'd better tell 3. 'd better consider 4. 'd better stay 5. 'd better drive 6. 'd better not tell 7. 'd better not read 8. 'd better do 9. 'd better tell

Optional: Ask students their opinions about Linda's situation. What had she better do—stay with someone or leave town? Stop covering the story or keep investigating?

Optional: After the discussion, have students write a short paragraph explaining their opinions. Remind them about the sentence patterns they have learned recently: *if-* clauses, *had better,* sentences with *so, because* and *therefore,* and sentences with *but* and *however.* Model some on the board:

> I think Linda had better stay with Angela, but she should not stop working on the case. If Linda stops investigating the story, the arsonists will keep setting fires. They are frightened because Linda has discovered something important.

Exercise 4. See Intro. p. ix, Match the sentence with the picture. Write on the board and discuss *you'd better, you should* and *please.* Remind students that *you'd better* often suggests a warning, so it's often used by people with authority. *You should* also gives advice but is not as strong. *Please* and other polite requests are used to address those in authority.

Answers: 1. b 2. c 3. a 4. a

Exercise 5. See Intro. p. ix, Ask and answer questions.
Teach *specialist*—a doctor who has special training in one branch of medicine. Explain that all the words in the left column of the Develop Your Vocabulary box are names of specialists and the conditions in the right column are problems they would treat. Give explanations in English, but have students check their dictionaries.
dermatologist Specializes in diseases of the skin.
rash An eruption (bumps or spots) on the skin.
internist Specializes in problems of the internal organs, e.g., stomach, liver, lungs.
ulcer A sore on the skin or inside the body, e.g., in the stomach, which may bleed.
orthopedist Specializes in problems of the bones.
podiatrist Specializes in the care and treatment of the feet.
ingrown toenail When the toenail grows into the toe.
fallen arches When the curved bones under the foot flatten out.
ophthalmologist Specializes in the eye. This specialist is a medical doctor who can treat all diseases of the eye. Teach also *optometrist,* who prescribes lenses for glasses but not drugs or treatment, and *optician,* who makes or sells lenses.
psychologist Not a medical doctor, but a specialist trained in helping people with emotional problems. Teach also *psychiatrist,* a medical doctor who can also prescribe medication.
anxiety A feeling of fear that is often too great for the problem that is causing it. People with anxiety often doubt their ability to handle the situation that causes this fear.
depression An illness that causes sadness and problems with sleep and concentration.

Develop Your Vocabulary. Add:
pediatrician Specializes in treating babies and children.
chicken pox A childhood disease marked by low fever and spots.
mumps A childhood disease causing fever and swelling on the neck and near the mouth. It can also occur in adults, at which time it is more serious.
measles An often serious childhood disease causing fever and spots.
family practitioner Specializes in general medicine and can treat common conditions for all family members.

4 Decide what the people should say in the situations.

1. a. "Would you please obey the speed limit?"
   b. "You'd better obey the speed limit."
   c. "It's a good idea to obey the speed limit."

2. a. "You'd better buy me some ice cream."
   b. "You should buy me some ice cream."
   c. "Please buy me some ice cream."

3. a. "Could I have the day off?"
   b. "You'd better give me the day off."
   c. "You should give me the day off."

4. a. "You should see this movie."
   b. "You'd better see this movie."
   c. "Would you please see this movie?"

5 Give a classmate advice about a health problem that you or someone you know has.

A: What's the matter?
B: I'm worried about *my sister. She has a terrible rash.*
A: Hmm. That sounds serious. *She*'d better see *a dermatologist.*

DEVELOP YOUR VOCABULARY

internist	ulcer, kidney stones
orthopedist	sore *arm,* back problems
podiatrist	ingrown toenail, fallen arches
ophthalmologist	double vision, blurred vision
psychologist	anxiety, depression, insomnia
. . .	. . .

C.

Pete enjoys **working** in Houston, but he misses **seeing** his girlfriend.

Some other verbs that are followed by the verb + *-ing* (the gerund):

avoid	deny	keep	start
consider	dislike	practice	stop
continue	have trouble	remember	suggest

1 Can you remember the story? Ask questions with the phrases below. Then ask your classmates.

1. Who / enjoys / work in Houston

A: Who enjoys working in Houston?
B: Pete does.

2. Who denied / start the fires
3. Who's having trouble / find a job
4. Who enjoys / paint
5. Who dislikes / work on a computer
6. Who just started / study computer programming
7. Who misses / see his girlfriend
8. Who's avoided / ask for help
9. Who suggested / call the police

Bill · Angela · Pete · Tom · Linda · Brad · Ken

2 Linda is at Angela's apartment. Complete their conversation with the gerund.

LINDA: What beautiful paintings, Angela! Are they yours?

ANGELA: No, I enjoy painting (1. paint), but I'm not *that* good. These belong to the art museum. We're just keeping them until they finish ______ (2. do) the renovation.

LINDA: You're lucky to have them.

ANGELA: Well, yes and no. I don't even enjoy ______ (3. go) out anymore. I'm too nervous about the paintings.

LINDA: Do you have all the museum's paintings here?

ANGELA: Oh, no! We avoided ______ (4. bring) the most valuable ones here. They're in a warehouse downtown.

3 Talk about your likes and dislikes.

A: I really like cooking, but I don't like *doing the dishes.*
B: I like *reading,* but I don't like *looking up words in the dictionary.*

4 Talk about your childhood.

1. What did you enjoy doing when you were a child?
2. What did you dislike doing?
3. Was there anything you had trouble doing?
4. Was there anything you had to practice doing?

Practice C

Study Box. See Intro. p. viii.

Verb + gerund. Explain that the *-ing* form of the verb is used after certain verbs in English. There is no general rule for these; they must be learned.

avoid Means *try not to.* Give an example: *Tom avoids using a computer* means he doesn't like to use one and tries not to.
continue Means *keep.* Linda will continue investigating the arson story.
deny Means say something is not true. Give an example: *Bill denied knowing the hit-and-run driver* means he said he didn't know him.
suggest Give an example: *Tom suggested seeing a movie* means that Tom told Linda it was a good movie to see.
have trouble Give an example: *Brad has trouble coming to work on time* means it's not easy for him to come to work on time.

Exercise 1. See Intro. p. ix, Ask and answer questions.
Answers: 2. A: Who denied starting the fires? B: Bill did. 3. A: Who's having trouble finding a job? B: Ken is. 4. A: Who enjoys painting? B: Angela does. 5. A: Who dislikes working on a computer? B: Tom does. 6. A: Who just started studying computer programming? B: Bill did. 7. A: Who misses seeing his girlfriend? B: Pete does. 8. A: Who's avoided asking for help? B: Linda has. 9. A: Who suggested calling the police? B: Brad did.

Exercise 2. See Intro. p. ix, Complete the sentences/paragraph.
**belong to* Means *be the property of.* The museum owns the paintings.
**downtown* Means in the main part of town.

Answers: 2. doing 3. going 4. bringing

Exercise 3. See Intro. p. ix, Ask and answer questions.
Other verbs students can use are *enjoy, miss/don't miss, have trouble, avoid, dislike, e.g.:*

I enjoy driving, but I have trouble reading a map.
I miss going to school, but I don't miss studying late at night.

Elicit some activities students enjoy and the negative aspects of them, and write them on the board as cues.

Exercise 4. See Intro. p. ix, Ask and answer questions.
Write some categories on the board to help students in their discussion, e.g.: *schoolwork, housework* and *family responsibilities, musical instruments, hobbies* and *sports.* Elicit a few examples before students work in groups.

Give the past forms of irregular verbs: *had trouble, kept.* Remind the class of *used to: I used to dislike going to my math class.*

Life Skills

This unit will give students practice in taking telephone messages and understanding a telephone answering machine message. Students will also learn how to ask for directory assistance and practice asking for a number.

Exercise 1. See Intro. p. ix, Listening.
Go over the message form with students. Point out that *of* asks for the caller's business. Remind them that *urgent* means *very important* and *returned your call* means *called back*. Tell them we generally write the messages in a shortened style because the subject is understood, e.g.: *Will be in Houston next week. Wants to see you.*

Answer: To: Cathy Wilson / Ms. Dupont / Of French Café / 525–9110
Message: Enjoyed meeting you last night. Will call again if she finishes work before 10:00 P.M.

Exercise 2. See Intro. p. ix, Listening.
**directory assistance* A *directory* is a list of names and numbers. *Directory assistance* is the service that looks up the number for the caller. Tell students that to find out someone's telephone number in the United States or Canada, you dial:
1. 1 + the area code + 555–1212 if you are calling from a different area code from the telephone number you want. (Teachers in the U.S. and Canada should give some examples from their own areas.)
2. 411 or 555–1212 if you are calling from the same area code as the number you need.

After students hear the listening exercise, point out that after you tell the operator the name, a recording will often give the number.

Answers: 1. number 2. Baretta 3. spell 4. last 5. name 6. B-A-R-E-T-T-A 7. V 8. Victor 9. B 10. Bob 11. address 12. 25 13. number 14. 271–9830 15. 271–9830

Life Skills

Telephone calls

1 Cathy Wilson received a phone call while she was away from her desk. Listen to the call and then complete the message. Use today's date and the correct time.

IMPORTANT MESSAGE
TO ______
DATE ______ TIME ______ A.M. / P.M.
WHILE YOU WERE OUT
M ______
OF ______
Area Code & Exchange ______

TELEPHONED		WILL CALL AGAIN	
CALLED TO SEE YOU		URGENT	
WANTS TO SEE YOU		RETURNED YOUR CALL	
PLEASE CALL			

Message ______

2 Pete Gómez is calling directory assistance to ask for someone's phone number. Listen to the conversation and complete it.

OPERATOR: Hello. Mrs. Ketcham.
PETE: Hello. Can I have the ____(1) of John ____(2)?
OPERATOR: Can you ____(3) the ____(4) ____(5), please?
PETE: It's _-_-_-_-_-_-_(6).
OPERATOR: ____(7) as in ____(8)?
PETE: No, ____(9) as in ____(10).
OPERATOR: And do you know the ____(11)?
PETE: Yes, ____(12) Grove Street.
OPERATOR: The ____(13) is ____(14).
PETE: ____(15)?
OPERATOR: Yes, that's right.
PETE: Thank you.

3 Now roleplay a similar situation.
Student A calls directory assistance and asks for the number of someone from the list on the left.
Student B is the operator and uses the information from the phone book. If Student B can't find the number, he or she will say, "There's no listing."

```
Jeff Groman, 1836 Wood
Ann Grometstein, 39 Kane Street
John Gromek, 3162 Lamar
Melinda Gromit, 29 Maple
Karl Gromis, 10713 Winkler
Edith Gromm, 1403 University Blvd
Arthur Grombach, 8210 Memorial Dr.
Robert Gromek, 115 West Main
Bob Gromet, 3816 Broadway
Maria Grondski, 2136 Hamilton
```

Groman Jeff 1836 Wood 287-2356
Grombach A 8210 Memorial Dr 533-9876
Gromek Bob 115 West Main 877-8284
Gromet Bob 2164 Lamar 982-9394
Gromet Bob 3816 Broadway 227-6200
Grometstein Ann 39 Kane 561-3836
Gromick John 20 Picnic Dr 798-1243
Gromis Joseph 1134 Beechnut 267-7546
Gromis Karl 10713 Winkler 228-4362
Gromm Edith 1403 University Blvd 871-3298
Grondski Maria 2136 Hamilton 836-0209

4 Pete is calling John Baretta. He is not there. Listen to John's answering machine and choose the message Pete left for him.

1. "Mr. Baretta, please call me back at 928–2413. Thank you."
2. "This is Pete Gómez. It's 5:00. Please call me at 6:00."
3. "This is Pete Gómez from the Houston *Herald* calling at 5:00 P.M. Please call me back at 928–2413."

5 Match the sentences in columns A and B to make short conversations.

A	B
1. Can I speak to Monica, please?	a. That's quite all right.
2. I'm sorry. I dialed the wrong number.	b. Speaking.
3. Can I leave a message?	c. This is Vilma Ortiz at 928–1873. Please return my call before 5:00.
4. At the sound of the beep, please leave a short message.	d. Could you spell the last name, please?
5. I'd like the number of Edward Ulin, please.	e. Sure. Please hold on while I get a pen.

ON YOUR OWN
Discuss these questions with your classmates.

1 Do you prefer to talk to someone on the phone or in person? Why?
2 How do you feel about speaking English on the phone? Why?
3 Are telephone answering machines common in your country? If so, who has them? (businesses? homes?) How do you feel about leaving a message on one?

For pronunciation exercises for Unit 6, see page 114.

Exercise 3. See Intro. p. x, Roleplay.
There's no listing. Means that the person's name and number are not in the directory.

Review the abbreviations: *Dr* for *Drive*, *Blvd* for *Boulevard*. Remind students that street numbers are said like the time: *one fifteen Winkler*, *eighteen thirty-six Wood*. *Zero* is said as *oh*—*fourteen oh three University Boulevard*.

After they do the exercise, students should actually call directory assistance for a number.

Exercise 4. See Intro. p. ix, Listening.
**answering machine* A machine that automatically answers the telephone and gives instructions about leaving a message. Point out that many times these instructions will give the number you have reached but not the name of the person.
**beep* Mimic the sound.
brief Means *short*.

If possible, after students do the exercise, they should call and leave a number on a telephone answering machine.

Answer: Message 3. Discuss the answer and elicit or point out that the message asks callers to leave their name, time and a message.

Exercise 5. See Intro. p. xii, Matching.
Speaking. Means *I am the person you asked for.*
hold on Means *Don't hang up.*

Answers: 1. b 2. a 3. e 4. c 5. d

On Your Own. See Intro. p. xi.

1 and **2.** Students can discuss why face-to-face conversation is useful—facial expressions, gestures and body language can convey information that help you understand what a speaker is saying. Elicit some situations where students would prefer to use the telephone or face-to-face conversation and ask them to discuss why they have this preference.

3. Suggest examples of who might find answering machines useful and elicit other examples from students, e.g.: working parents who can't be reached by telephone but who have children in day care or people who run small businesses. Ask students if they have machines and why. Discuss why people feel embarrassed about leaving messages—many don't like "talking to a machine." Others feel embarrassed about a foreign accent.

For **Pronunciation** exercises for Unit 6, see p. 59 .

REVIEW 3

Exercise 1.
2. tired 3. boring 4. interesting 5. excited 6. encouraging
7. depressed 8. frightening 9. embarrassed 10. disappointed
11. disappointed 12. pleased

Exercise 2.
2. was not (wasn't) able to 3. will ('ll) be able to 4. were able to
5. have not (haven't) been able to 6. were not (weren't) able to
7. will ('ll) be able to 8. was able to

Exercise 3.
2. themselves 3. she 4. himself 5. ourselves 6. you 7. yourself

Exercise 4.
B's answers will vary. 2. each other 3. each other 4. yourself
5. himself 6. herself

REVIEW 3

1 Michael is talking to Pete about his schoolwork. Complete their conversation with the *-ed* or *-ing* form of the words.

MICHAEL: Dad, I'm still discouraged (1. discourage) about my bad grades. I'm really ______ (2. tire) of studying hard and not doing well.

PETE: What's the problem? Are your classes ______ (3. bore)?

MICHAEL: No. They're very ______ (4. interest), and I'm really ______ (5. excite) about my science project.

PETE: What does your teacher say?

MICHAEL: She's really ______ (6. encourage) to me. She says I shouldn't get ______ (7. depress) about things and that I should keep trying.

PETE: That's true. Starting a new school is often hard, you know, and a little ______ (8. frighten). It's nothing to feel ______ (9. embarrass) about.

MICHAEL: I know, Dad. It's just that I never had trouble before and I feel ______ (10. disappoint). I really want to do well.

PETE: I know you're ______ (11. disappoint), Michael. But I'm ______ (12. please) with your attitude, and I'm sure you'll do better soon.

2 Can you remember the story? Complete these sentences with the correct form of *be able to.*

1. Pete is very friendly. He has been able to make a lot of new friends since he moved to Houston.
2. Tom ______ go to the movies last night. He had too much work.
3. Suzanne ______ move to Houston if she gets a job.
4. The doctors ______ help Bill after he was hit by the car.
5. The police ______ catch the arsonist yet.
6. The firefighters tried, but they ______ put out the fire.
7. Pete hopes that he ______ find a bigger apartment.
8. A few years ago Ken ______ find a job without any problem.

3 Complete this chart.

1. myself	I		5. ______	we
2. ______	they		6. yourselves	______
3. herself	______		7. ______	you
4. ______	he			

4 Complete these questions with a reflexive pronoun or *each other.* Then answer them.

1. A: How do you enjoy yourself?
   B: ______.
2. A: What do you and your friends talk to ______ about?
   B: ______.
3. A: How often do you and your friends speak to ______ in English?
   B: ______.
4. A: When you were a child, did you ever hurt ______? How?
   B: ______.
5. A: Why's Michael Gómez disappointed with ______?
   B: ______.
6. A: Do you think Linda can take care of ______?
   B: ______.

5 Match the phrases in columns A and B. Then combine them with *if* and *will / won't.*

	A		B
1.	d you don't study	a.	be late
2.	___ he works too hard	b.	make a lot of money
3.	___ she is successful	c.	gain weight
4.	___ I drive too fast	d.	not pass
5.	___ we don't leave soon	e.	get sick
6.	___ you don't exercise	f.	have an accident

1. If you don't study, you won't pass.

6 Read these situations. Then write what each person *had better* or *had better not* do.

1. Tom's flying to Los Angeles this morning. It's 10:00, and his plane leaves at 10:20. He isn't at the airport yet.

He'd better hurry.

2. Cathy has been feeling sick for the last few days.
3. Ken would like to buy a new car, but he knows that he doesn't have the money now.
4. Linda hasn't spoken to her parents for two months.
5. Bill would like to go back to work, but the doctor has told him not to.

7 Make sentences with these words.

1. Tom / enjoys / go to movies

Tom enjoys going to movies.

2. Ken / keeps / look for a job
3. Bill / denied / start the fires
4. Michael / has trouble / get good grades
5. Pete / misses / see Suzanne
6. The police / haven't stopped / look for the arsonist
7. Angela / suggested / take a break
8. Brad / practices / play tennis

8 Match the sentences in column A and B. Then combine them with *therefore.*

	A		B
1.	d Linda words too hard.	a.	The police suspected him of arson.
2.	___ Tom doesn't like computers.	b.	He feels discouraged.
3.	___ Angela had a bad accident.	c.	He uses a typewriter.
4.	___ Cathy writes restaurant reviews.	d.	She's always tired.
5.	___ Bill used to get into trouble.	e.	He calls her a lot.
6.	___ Pete misses Suzanne.	f.	She often eats out.
7.	___ Ken can't find a job.	g.	She walks with a cane.

1. Linda words too hard; therefore, she's always tired.

Now rewrite the sentences with *because.*

1. Because Linda works too hard, she's always tired.
   OR Linda's always tired because she works too hard.

Exercise 5.

2. e, If he works too hard, he'll get sick. 3. b, If she is successful, she'll make a lot of money. 4. f, If I drive too fast, I'll have an accident. 5. a, If we don't leave soon, we'll be late. 6. c, If you don't exercise, you'll gain weight.

Exercise 6.

Answers may vary. 2. She'd better go to the doctor. 3. He'd better not buy a new car. He'd better wait. 4. She'd better call them. 5. He'd better listen to the doctor. OR He'd better not go back to work. OR He'd better stay home.

Exercise 7.

2. Ken keeps looking for a job. 3. Bill denied starting the fires. 4. Michael has trouble getting good grades. 5. Pete misses seeing Suzanne. 6. The police haven't stopped looking for the arsonist. 7. Angela suggested taking a break. 8. Brad practices playing tennis.

Exercise 8.

2. c, Tom doesn't like computers; therefore, he uses a typewriter. 3. g, Angela had a bad accident; therefore, she walks with a cane. 4. f, Cathy writes restaurant reviews; therefore, she often eats out. 5. a, Bill used to get into trouble; therefore, the police suspected him of arson. 6. e, Pete misses Suzanne; therefore, he calls her a lot. 7. b, Ken can't find a job; therefore, he feels discouraged.

Now rewrite the sentences. . .

2. Because Tom doesn't like computers, he uses a typewriter. OR Tom uses a typewriter because he doesn't like computers. 3. Because Angela had a bad accident, she walks with a cane. OR Angela walks with a cane because she had a bad accident. 4. Because Cathy writes restaurant reviews, she often eats out. OR Cathy often eats out because she writes restaurant reviews. 5. Because Bill used to get into trouble, the police suspected him of arson. OR The police suspected Bill of arson because he used to get into trouble. 6. Because Pete misses Suzanne, he calls her a lot. OR Pete calls Suzanne a lot because he misses her. 7. Because Ken can't find a job, he feels discouraged. OR Ken feels discouraged because he can't find a job.

UNIT 7

Language Summary

Functions

Asking for and giving information
Is rice grown in Thailand? Yes, it is.
Expressing wishes
I'd like to be a flight attendant.
Talking about likes and dislikes
What's your favorite pastime? Taking long walks. What about you?

Introduction

Vocabulary

astronaut	flight attendant	overheard *s past*
bartender	hairdresser	paramedic
comedian	mention *v*	social worker
court reporter	overhear	
crime		

For recognition only

accidentally	heard *s past*

Practice A

Structures

Gerund as subject and after prepositions
Reading is Linda's favorite pastime.
She's good at writing about crime and politics.

Vocabulary

keep on (= continue)	pastime

For recognition only

act *v*	temporary

signs of the zodiac

Aries	Leo	Sagittarius
Taurus	Virgo	Capricorn
Gemini	Libra	Aquarius
Cancer	Scorpio	Pisces

Expressions

be good at	look forward to

For recognition only

be thankful to	come over

Practice B

Structure

Passive voice—present tense
Where is corn grown?

Vocabulary

coal	grown	pineapple
collect	kept *past part*	produce *v*
corn (food)	lock *v*	set *v*
dairy product	meter (measuring machine)	steel *n*
deduct	mine *n*	street light
evaluation	paid *past part*	take out (= deduct)
garbage	patrol *v*	taken
give out *trans*		turn on *trans*
given		wheat
grape *n*		

For recognition only

area	especially	night shift
break in *trans* (enter illegally)		

Expressions

All you have to do is . . .	because of	make *your* rounds

Put It All Together

Vocabulary

For recognition only

alarm box	security	worker
main *adj*	side *n*	

Expression

For recognition only
all set

Reading

Skills

Predicting
Putting steps in order

Vocabulary

For recognition only

among	national	saying *n*
appropriate *adj*	nutmeg	slice *n* and *v*
cinnamon	oven	spice
classified *adj*	peel *trans*	steam *n*
core *v*	pie crust	tart *adj*
cover *v*	pie plate	top *adj*
dot *v*	preheat	traditional

ending *n*	prick	tribute
fill	ready-made	unbaked *adj*
flavor *n*	recipe	
line *v*	reduce	

Expressions

à la mode	It's as American as apple pie.	the red, white and blue
all-American		tried and true

Writing

Skill

Writing steps in a process

Task

Writing Instructions

Vocabulary

avocado	hold *v*	remove
face *v*	iced tea	side *n*
flat *adj*	place *v*	toothpick
hang	recording *n*	

For recognition only

edge	plant *n*	wide
indoor	rest *trans*	

Expression

in half

Pronunciation

Pronunciation points

1. Understanding /r/
2. Understanding reduced *and* and *or*
3. Distinguishing statements and questions by intonation

Pronunciation exercises. *The pronunciation exercises for Unit 7 also appear in the Student's Book on pp. 114–115.*

Part 1. *Understanding* /r/

Listen and complete these sentences.

See Intro. p. xiii, Recognizing and distinguishing sounds 2 and 3

1. Linda's ________ a special ________ .
2. ________ is ________ .
3. Linda's ________ isn't always ________ .
4. She ________ a ________ letter.
5. Angela doesn't ________ mentioning the ________ .

Answers: 1. writing, story 2. Reporting, routine 3. work, interesting 4. received, threatening 5. remember, report

Now listen again and repeat the sentences.

Part 2. *Understanding reduced* and *and* or

A. When we speak quickly, the word *and* is sometimes pronounced *n* and the word *or* is sometimes pronounced *er*. Listen and repeat these phrases.

See Intro. p. xiii, Stress and intonation 4

1. Linda and Carol
2. Cathy and Ken
3. writing about politics and investigating crimes
4. a couple of people at the paper and the police
5. an editor or a social worker
6. painting or reading
7. Wisconsin or Kansas
8. oranges or grapes

B. Now listen to these sentences and complete them with *and* or *or*.

See Intro. p. xiii, Stress and intonation 3 and 4

1. She writes about politics ________ crime.
2. We can celebrate tomorrow ________ Saturday.
3. Let's invite Frank ________ Angela.
4. Cathy likes jogging ________ bicycling.
5. I think corn is grown in Kansas ________ Illinois.
6. I'd like apple pie ________ ice cream, please.

Answers: 1. or 2. and 3. and 4. or 5. and 6. or

Now listen again and repeat the sentences.

Part 3. *Distinguishing statements and questions by intonation*

Listen to these sentences. Put a period after each statement and a question mark after each question.

1. a. She's here ____	b. She's here ____
2. a. Routine____	b. Routine ____
3. a. They're eating ____	b. They're eating ____
4. a. It's 10 o'clock ____	b. It's 10 o'clock ____
5. a. He's not sure ____	b. He's not sure ____

Answers: The answers are marked in the sentences above.

Now listen again and repeat the sentences.

See p. 142 for the Pronunciation Tapescript.

Teaching Notes

Getting Started

Use Unit 6, Ex. A5, the Chain Game, on Student's Book p. 50. Divide the class into groups of four or five. Review the game by having one group read the example sentences, and then continue. Give other starting sentences, e.g.:

If it rains tomorrow . . .
If I get a raise . . .
If I get married this year . . .

Introduction

 **1. Introductory Conversation.** See Intro. p. vii.

Preteaching

a couple of Point out that this may mean either *two* or *a few*. Here, it means *a few*.

Preparation

Elicit the storyline: *Where's Linda now?* (Staying with Angela and Frank.) *Why's she there?* (She got a threatening letter.) *Who's at the dinner table?* (Angela, Frank, Linda and Frank's assistant.) Discuss how people are feeling: *How does Angela feel in the second picture?* (Surprised, puzzled.) *How does Cathy feel in the third picture?* (Happy, excited.) Ask focus questions: *What does Carol want Linda to talk about?* (Linda's job.) *Why did Cathy call Linda?* (To tell her about Ken's new job.)

Exercise 2. See Intro. p. viii, Say *That's right . . .*
Answers: 1. That's wrong. 2. I don't know. 3. That's wrong. 4. That's wrong. 5. That's right.

Exercise 3. See Intro. p. viii, Find a word or phrase . . .
**heard/overheard* Past tense of *hear* and *overhear*.
**accidentally* Carol didn't mean to hear it; she just happened to be close to the people talking.

Answers: 1. overheard 2. joining us 3. mention it

Exercise 4. See Intro. p. viii, Warm Up.
flight attendant Means *steward* or *stewardess*, the worker on an airplane who takes care of the passengers during a flight.
astronaut The scientist or pilot who flies a spaceship.
bartender Someone who makes drinks in a bar.
comedian A professional entertainer who tells stories and jokes and makes comments that make people laugh.
court reporter Someone trained to make a shorthand record of what happens at court.
hairdresser Someone who is trained to cut, style, dye, etc., hair.
paramedic A trained worker in the health field who assists a doctor or gives first aid. *Parademics* often work on ambulances.
social worker A professional who assists people in obtaining various services, e.g., medical, economic, legal, psychiatric.

Elicit students' opinions of these professions and put additional adjectives on the board: *boring, dangerous, frightening, stressful* (causes worry and tension), *interesting, satisfying, creative*. Students can also talk about a friend's or relative's ambitions.

UNIT 7 Not Just Routine

1 Linda, Angela, her husband Frank and Frank's assistant are having dinner at Angela's. Listen to their conversation.

1

CAROL: Being a newspaper reporter sounds so exciting, Linda. Writing about politics and investigating crimes is just so interesting. I want to hear all about your work.
LINDA: Well, most of it's done at my desk—like any office job. It's really just routine.
CAROL: Routine? Getting threatening letters isn't just routine.

2

ANGELA: What? How did you hear about that? Only a couple of people at the paper and the police know.
CAROL: Didn't someone here just mention it?
FRANK: *I* don't remember talking about threatening letters.
CAROL: Well, maybe I overheard it at the museum. I'm not sure now . . .

3

ANGELA: Linda, it's for you. It's Cathy.
CATHY: Guess what! Ken's brother Steve just got him a job! How about joining us for dinner tomorrow night? We feel like celebrating.

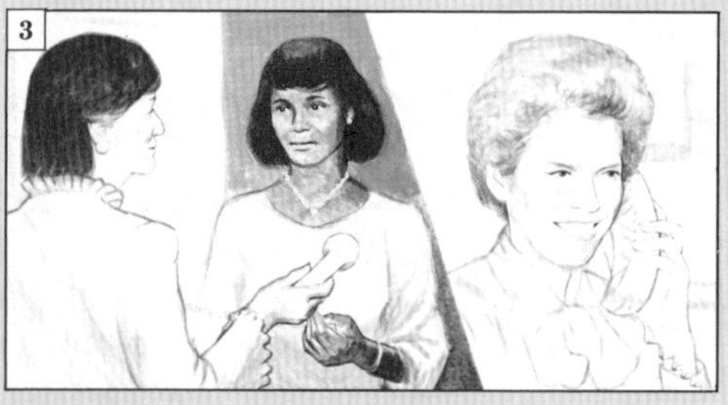

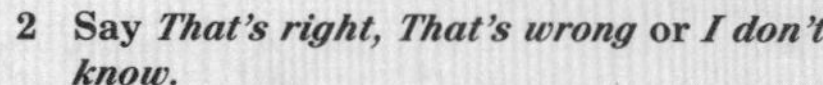

2 Say *That's right, That's wrong* or *I don't know*.

1. Linda and Carol are close friends.
2. Carol doesn't like her job.
3. Linda thinks her job is always exciting.
4. Frank told Carol about the letter.
5. Cathy and Ken are happy about his new job.

4 Warm Up

Talk about a job you'd like to have.

A: I'd like to be *a flight attendant*.
B: I wouldn't. It's too *tiring*.
OR So would I. It's very *exciting*.

3 Find a word or phrase in the conversation that means:

1. heard accidentally
2. coming with us
3. say something about it

DEVELOP YOUR VOCABULARY

astronaut	hairdresser
bartender	paramedic
comedian	social worker
court reporter	. . .

Practice

A.

Reading is Linda's favorite pastime.
She's good at **writing** about crime and politics. She'll keep on **covering** the arson story.

1 Say what each person's favorite pastime is.

1. Reading is Linda's favorite pastime.

1. Linda

2. Minh

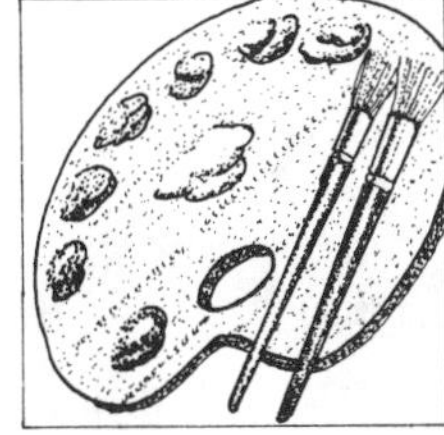
3. Angela

4. Pete

5. Tom

6. Cathy

2 Linda's having dinner with Ken and Cathy. Listen and complete their conversation.

LINDA: Are you excited about starting (1) your new job, Ken?

KEN: Well, I'm certainly looking forward to _____ (2) again. I'm really tired of _____ (3) home.

CATHY: Ken's going to keep on _____ (4) for a job as a welder. _____ (5) a security guard is just temporary.

LINDA: I understand. It's better to have a job at something you're good at _____ (6).

KEN: Yes, but I'm thankful to my brother for _____ (7) me this job. It's great to be able to read the paper without _____ (8) depressed.

CATHY: Talking about _____ (9) depressed, Linda, how do you feel about _____ (10) at Angela's? You probably miss _____ (11) at home.

LINDA: Oh, it's OK. Last night, her husband's assistant, Carol Fullerton, came over for dinner.

CATHY: How was that? Is she nice?

LINDA: A little strange. She was *very* interested in _____ (12) all about the arson story.

Practice A

Study Box. See Intro. p. viii.

1. Gerund as subject. Point out that the *-ing* form of the verb can be used as a noun and can, therefore, function as a subject or object, e.g.: *Flying small airplanes is her hobby. She likes flying.*

Optional: After going over the Study Box sentences, give additional practice. Write a number of phrases with gerunds on the board and ask students to make sentences using a gerund as subject:

smoking in an elevator	reading the newspaper
waiting for a bus in the rain	going to the dentist
not keeping a promise	offering to help

2. Gerund as object of preposition. Tell students that the *-ing* form is often used after expressions with prepositions. Give a list of some of these expressions:

dream about	keep on	be excited about	be thankful for
feel about	look forward to	be good at	be tired of
insist on	worry about	be interested in	be worried about

Give some examples from the story and call on students to do the same: *Linda insisted on working on the arson story. She's dreaming about covering a big story for the paper. She didn't worry about getting hurt.*

Optional: Give additional practice. With students making suggestions, write a number of questions on the board using these expressions, e.g.:

What do you dream about doing in the next five years?
How do you feel about living in (your city)?
What TV program does your daughter/son/wife/husband insist on watching?
Do you ever keep on working or studying when you're too tired?
What are you worried about when you read the newspaper?
What kind of movies are you tired of?

Have pairs of students interview each other.

Exercise 1. See Intro. p. ix, Look at the pictures.
Answers: 2. Taking pictures is Minh's favorite pastime. 3. Painting is Angela's favorite pastime. 4. Cooking is Pete's favorite pastime. 5. Going to the movies is Tom's favorite pastime. 6. Jogging/Running is Cathy's favorite pastime.

Exercise 2. See Intro p. ix, Listening.
**be thankful to* Point out the root *thank* and ask students to infer the meaning.
**come over* Means go to someone's house for a visit.

Answers: 2. working 3. staying 4. looking 5. Being 6. doing 7. finding 8. getting 9. being 10. staying 11. being 12. hearing

Exercise 3. See Intro. p. ix, Ask and answer questions. Remind students of the activities in Ex. 1. Elicit and list other types of activities. Other possibilities are *knitting, sewing, cooking ethnic foods, programming a personal computer, making things in a woodworking shop, doing volunteer* (unpaid) *work.*

Exercise 4. See Intro. p. ix, Complete the sentences/paragraph. The zodiac is an imaginary strip in space 18 degrees wide through which all the planets (except Pluto) travel. It is divided into twelve constellations or signs. The year is divided by these signs, and some people think that they influence personalities and events.

If possible bring in a map of the constellations for students to see how they are represented. The symbols of the constellations are: Aries–Ram, Taurus–Bull, Gemini–Twins, Cancer–Crab, Leo–Lion, Virgo–Virgin, Libra–Balance (scales), Scorpio–Scorpion, Sagittarius–Archer, Capricorn–Goat, Aquarius–Water Bearer, Pisces–Fishes.

Bring in the horoscope from a newspaper or magazine. Have students work in pairs to read each others' horoscopes and discuss whether the predictions actually apply to their own lives. Then have them work together to do the exercise and write each other's horoscopes. While the students write, go around the room to help them with vocabulary.

Optional: Discuss systems other cultures use. If possible, ask students to bring in pictures of the symbols and discuss how and when people use this system.

Optional: Discuss other ways of predicting or establishing good luck, e.g., fortune telling, palm reading, geomancy, and how prevalent they are.

3 Ask a classmate about his or her favorite pastime or sport.

A: What's your favorite *pastime?*
B: *Taking long walks.* What about you?
A: Oh, I always look forward to *playing cards with my friends.*

Just for Fun

4 Complete these horoscopes. Use a gerund (verb + *ing*) and any other words you need. Then tell a classmate his or her horoscope.

The Houston Herald

Your Horoscope

♈ Aries (March 21–April 19) Spend time *doing things* with a good friend. Avoid ________ at night. Don't worry about ________.

♉ Taurus (April 20–May 20) Enjoy ________ alone. Don't think a lot about ________. ________ money is a bad idea.

♊ Gemini (May 21–June 20) Keep on ________. You can look forward to ________ something interesting. ________ every day is a good idea.

♋ Cancer (June 21–July 22) Avoid ________ too much. You're good at ________, so do more of that. ________ is a good idea.

♌ Leo (July 23–August 22) Don't be too interested in ________ with your family. You can enjoy ________ alone.

♍ Virgo (August 23–September 22) You'd better act now if you are interested in ________. Start ________ before it's too late.

♎ Libra (September 23–October 22) Stop ________ to your friends. If you feel like ________, that's fine.

♏ Scorpio (October 23–November 21) Worry more about ________ every day. You should enjoy ________ with a good friend.

♐ Sagittarius (November 22–December 21) If you want to be successful, keep on ________. Don't feel sorry for ________ last month.

♑ Capricorn (December 22–January 19) A great day for ________. Avoid ________ before you have more information. ________ is dangerous.

♒ Aquarius (January 20–February 18) You're bored with ________. Try to get excited about ________. Avoid ________.

♓ Pisces (February 19–March 20) Think about ________ something new next weekend. How about ________ with a new friend?

B.

Where do they grow corn?	OR	Where **is** corn **grown?**
They grow corn in Kansas.	OR	Corn **is grown** in Kansas.
Where do they make cars?	OR	Where **are** cars **made?**
They make cars in Michigan.	OR	Cars **are made** in Michigan.

1 Pete's helping Michael study for a geography test. Ask questions in the passive voice. Then look at the map and answer the questions.

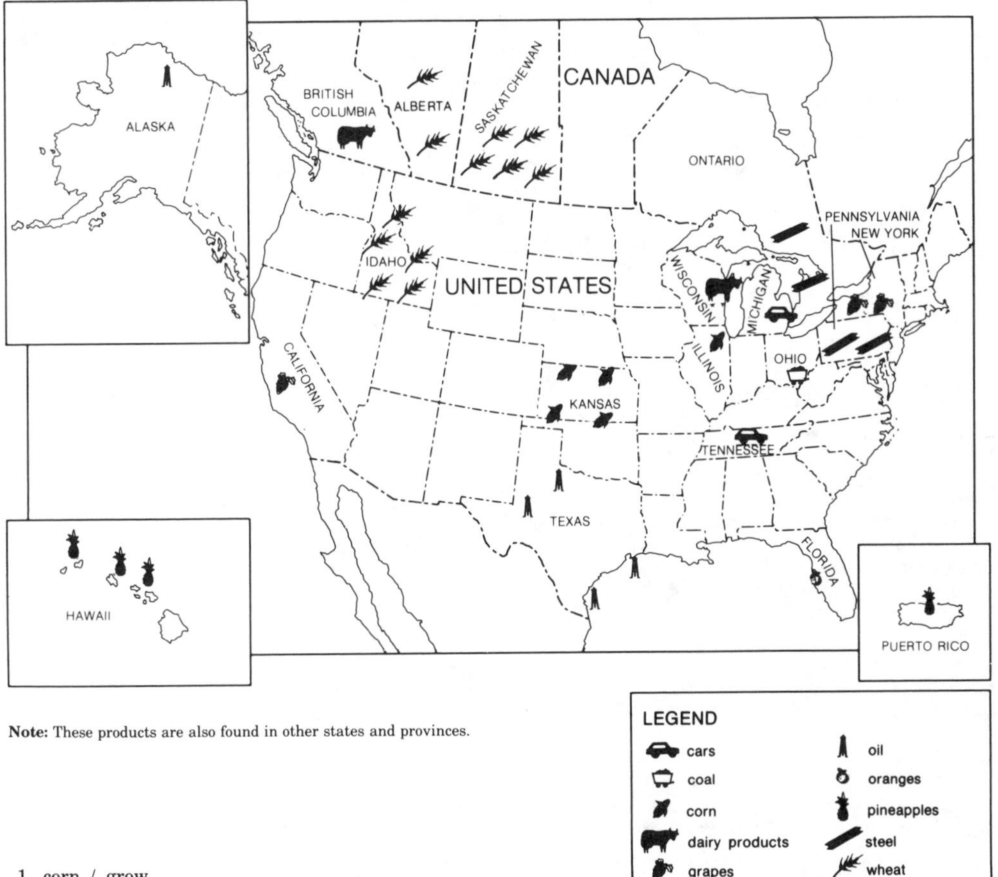

Note: These products are also found in other states and provinces.

1. corn / grow

PETE: Where's corn grown?
MICHAEL: Corn's grown in Illinois.

2. oil / find
3. cars / make
4. coal / mine
5. grapes / grow
6. steel / manufacture
7. oranges / grow
8. dairy products / produce
9. wheat / grow
10. pineapples / grow

Practice B

Study Box. See Intro. p. viii.

Passive voice—present tense.

1. Use. Ask the class, *Do you know who grows corn?* (No. And it's not important here.) Tell the students that the passive voice is often used when the subject of the sentence is vague or not as important as the object, as in the Study Box sentences. In the passive voice, the object of the action becomes the subject of the sentence.

2. Form. Point out that the passive voice is formed with *be* and the past participle of the verb. For the negative, place *not* between *be* and the past participle, e.g., *It's not grown in Alaska.*

3. Contractions. Tell students that the contracted form is usually used in spoken English for the singular, e.g.: *Where's corn grown? Corn's grown in Illinois.*

Pronunciation point: Note the reduction in *Where are cars made?* /wɛ̇ərəkȧrzmėd/ and *Cars are made* . . . /kȧrzəmėd/.

Optional: Give additional practice and preparation by discussing products that are *found, produced* and *manufactured* in your area.

Exercise 1. See Intro. p. x, Look at the document.
Explain the map symbols. Ask students about other places in Canada and the U.S. where these products are grown or made.
corn Bring in a picture or refer to the map symbol.
grown Past participle of *grow;* used for farm products.
grape Bring in a picture or refer to the map symbol.
mine (n) Means take a mineral, e.g., gold, out of the ground.
steel (n) A form of iron used for heavy construction.
dairy products Cheese, butter, buttermilk and other milk products.
produce (v) Means *make.*
pineapple Bring in a picture or refer to the map symbol.

Answers: 2. A: Where's oil found? B: Oil's found in Alaska and Texas. 3. A: Where are cars made? B: Cars are made in Tennessee and Michigan. 4. A: Where's coal mined? B: Coal's mined in Ohio. 5. A: Where are grapes grown? B: Grapes are grown in New York and California. 6. A: Where's steel manufactured? B: Steel's manufactured in Pennsylvania and Ontario. 7. A: Where are oranges grown? B: Oranges are grown in Florida. 8. A: Where are dairy products produced? B: Dairy products are produced in British Columbia and Wisconsin. 9. A: Where's wheat grown? B: Wheat's grown in Idaho, Kansas, Alberta and Saskatchewan. 10. A: Where are pineapples grown? B: Pineapples are grown in Hawaii and Puerto Rico.

Optional: Divide the class into teams and either assign each team a region to research or ask teams to choose one. Ask each group to look up the region in a simple encyclopedia and report their findings to the class. They can mention what goods are manufactured, produced and grown there.

Exercise 2. See Intro. p. ix, Ask and answer questions.
Optional: Bring in a map of the world and ask: *Where's corn grown? Where are good watches manufactured? Where are electronic goods produced?*

Optional: Students can also talk about possessions, e.g.: *My watch was made in Switzerland. Was your sweater made in China?*

Exercise 3. See Intro. p. ix, Complete the sentences/paragraph.
Remind students about the list of irregular verbs on Student's Book p. 117.
set (v) Here, it means make the alarms ready to go off.
patrol (v) Means walk through an area to make sure nothing is wrong. Point out the spelling rule: the *l* is doubled *(patrolled)* because the stress is on the last syllable. It is not doubled for words like *traveled,* in which the stress is on a previous syllable.

Answers: 2. are set 3. is kept 4. is patrolled 5. are paid 6. are given out 7. are taken out

Exercise 4. See Intro. p. ix, Ask and answer questions.
job evaluation When the employer studies and discusses with the employee how well he or she is doing the job.
deduct Means take away a part from the total; here, means *take out.*
Teach *weekly, monthly, annually, once a week, once a month* and *once a year.*

Answers: 2. Are checks mailed or given out? 3. Are taxes deducted? 4. How often are raises given? 5. Are job evaluations done? 6. How often are promotions given?

Exercise 5. See Intro. p. ix, Ask and answer questions.
garbage collected Means *garbage picked up.*
meter (n) A machine to measure how much electricity or gas is used.

2 Now ask and answer questions about your classmates' countries.

A: Is *rice grown* in *Thailand?*
B: Yes, *it is. It's grown* in . . .
OR No, *it isn't.*

3 Ken, Steve and Cathy are talking about Ken's new job. Read their conversation and complete it.

STEVE: Don't worry about the job. It's really easy. The doors are locked (1. lock) when the warehouse closes at 6:00. Then the alarms ______ (2. set). All you have to do is make your rounds.

KEN: It sounds like an easy job.

CATHY: I'm nervous about him working there. Especially at night.

STEVE: Don't worry, Cathy. Nothing valuable ______ (3. keep) in that warehouse. No one will want to break in. And now the area ______ (4. patrol) all night by the police because of all the fires.

KEN: And I'll make more money working on the night shift. How often ______ we ______ (5. pay)?

STEVE: Checks ______ (6. give out) every week. After your taxes ______ (7. take out), you'll get about $160.00.

4 Find out about someone's job.

1. How often / pay

A: How often are you paid?
OR How often is your sister paid?
B: Once a month.
OR I don't know.

2. checks / mail or give out
3. taxes / deduct
4. How often / raises give
5. job evaluations / do
6. How often / promotions give

5 Talk about neighborhood services.

A: When *is the mail delivered* in your neighborhood?
B: *It's delivered in the morning.*

Student A can use these ideas:

garbage collected	street lights turned on
streets cleaned	electric meters read

PUT IT ALL TOGETHER

Two men are talking. Listen and complete their conversation.

LUKE: Well, is everything all set for Saturday night?

PHIL: Yes. We'll meet you at 1:00 A.M.

LUKE: Which warehouse (1) is it?

PHIL: Number ____ (2). It's on the west side of Palmer Road, south of Warehouse 6.

LUKE: What do you know about the ____ (3)?

PHIL: There are ____ (4) doors. The main ____ (5) is on the south side. The doors ____ (6) ____ (7) when the workers go home at 6:00.

LUKE: What about ____ (8)?

PHIL: There are two on the east side and ____ (9) on the west side.

LUKE: ____ (10) they all protected ____ (11) alarms?

PHIL: Yes, they are. The alarm box ____ (12) located on the right side of the main door.

LUKE: What other security is there?

PHIL: Well, there's a ____ (13). His desk is to the left of the main door.

Now read the conversation and match the numbers on the diagram with these places:

10 Palmer Road
____ Warehouse 6
____ main door
____ windows on the east
____ windows on the west
____ security guard's desk
____ alarm box

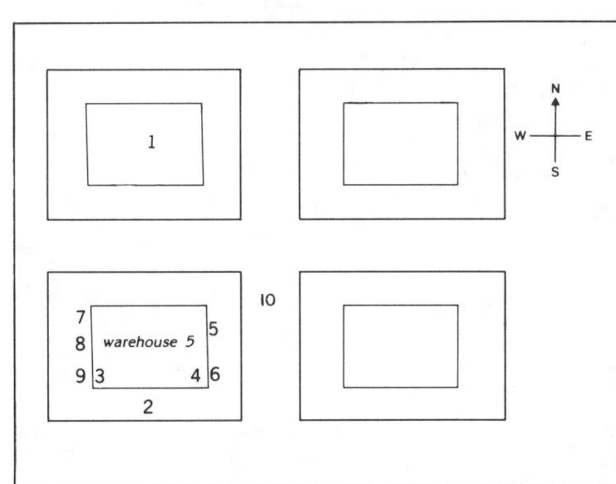

ON YOUR OWN

Think about Angela's dinner party at the beginning of the unit and discuss these questions with your classmates.

1 Do you like inviting people to dinner at your home? At a restaurant?

2 If you go to someone's home for dinner, do you usually bring him or her something? If so, what? Do you usually arrive early, late or exactly on time? What about in your country?

Put It All Together. See Intro. p. ix, Listening.

**all set* Here, means *completely ready.*
**security* Here, a system for guarding the building.
**side (n)* Refer to the diagram to show sides of the street.
**worker* Means *employee.*
**alarm box* Means the switch that turns the alarm on and shuts it off.

Answers: 2. five 3. security 4. two 5. door 6. are 7. locked 8. the windows 9. three 10. Are 11. by 12. is 13. guard

Now read the conversation . . . See Intro. p. xii, Matching.
Answers: 1–Warehouse 6 2–main door 5, 6–windows on the east 7, 8, 9–windows on the west 3–security guard's desk 4–alarm box

On Your Own. See Intro. p. xi.

1. Students can also discuss typical occasions for dinner parties and whether the home or a restaurant is more appropriate for each. Ask students in groups to discuss particular events that they enjoyed or didn't enjoy and why.

2. North Americans sometimes bring flowers, wine or dessert. The host or hostess will usually open the gift and use it at the dinner. American and Canadian custom is to arrive approximately on time—never early, and not more than half an hour late.

Reading

See Intro. p. xi.

Exercise 1.
Students should look at the article quickly—the illustration, the title—and quickly skim the two columns.

Bring in the home section of the newspaper. Point out other articles, e.g., on decorating, child rearing and nutrition.

Answer: 2

Exercise 2.
saying (n) A traditional statement.
flavor (n) Something that gives a food a certain taste. Give some examples of ice cream flavors.
ending (n) Ask students to infer the meaning.
recipe Instructions for making something to eat.
tried and true Here, Cathy has tried this recipe and found that it works.
appropriate (adj) Means right for this occasion.
tribute Means a gift or celebration that shows respect for someone or something.
tart Means *sour.*
cinnamon and *nutmeg* Spices (flavorings) for apple pie.
preheat the oven Means turn on the oven before beginning the recipe.
oven The inside of the stove where food is baked. Also teach *burners,* on top of the stove.
unbaked (adj) Here, the crusts are not baked yet.
ready-made crusts Crusts that you buy already made.
core (v), peel (v) and *slice (v)* Means remove the inner part and the peel, and cut into thin pieces.
line a pie plate Means cover the bottom of the plate.
dot (v) Mime this action.
cover it with the top crust Refer to the picture.
prick . . . to allow steam . . . Refer to the picture.
reduce Means make less.

Point out that the Fourth of July is the U.S. Independence Day, a national holiday celebrating July 4, 1776, when the American colonists signed the Declaration of Independence from the British. That is why Cathy uses the headline *All-American* and why this traditional recipe is appropriate for this holiday. Ask students about their own traditional national dishes and on what occasions they are eaten.

Exercise 3. See Intro. p. viii, Say *That's right . . .*
Answers: 1. That's right. 2. That's right. 3. That's wrong. 4. That's wrong. 5. That's wrong.

Exercise 4. See Intro. p. xii, Put the sentences in the right order.
Answers: a. 4 b. 3 c. 8 d. 1 e. 6 f. 2 g. 5 h. 7

Reading

1 Predicting. The Houston *Herald,* like other newspapers, has sections on different subjects. Look at the article. Which of these sections do you think it came from?

1. Local News
2. Home
3. Business
4. Classified Ads
5. Sports

2 Read this article about apple pie.

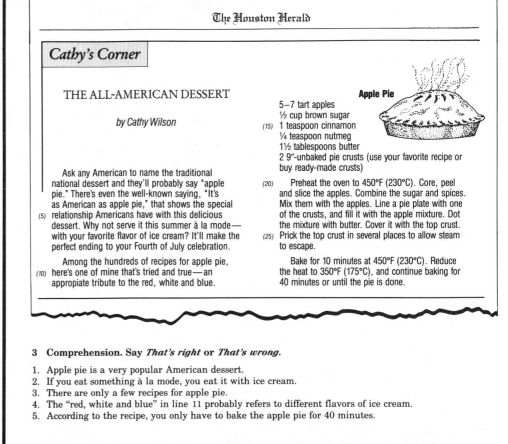

The Houston Herald

Cathy's Corner

THE ALL-AMERICAN DESSERT

by Cathy Wilson

Ask any American to name the traditional national dessert and they'll probably say "apple pie." There's even the well-known saying, "It's as American as apple pie," that shows the special relationship Americans have with this delicious dessert. Why not serve it this summer à la mode—with your favorite flavor of ice cream? It'll make the perfect ending to your Fourth of July celebration.

Among the hundreds of recipes for apple pie, here's one of mine that's tried and true—an appropiate tribute to the red, white and blue.

Apple Pie

5–7 tart apples
½ cup brown sugar
1 teaspoon cinnamon
¼ teaspoon nutmeg
1½ tablespoons butter
2 9"-unbaked pie crusts (use your favorite recipe or buy ready-made crusts)

Preheat the oven to 450°F (230°C). Core, peel and slice the apples. Combine the sugar and spices. Mix them with the apples. Line a pie plate with one of the crusts, and fill it with the apple mixture. Dot the mixture with butter. Cover it with the top crust. Prick the top crust in several places to allow steam to escape.

Bake for 10 minutes at 450°F (230°C). Reduce the heat to 350°F (175°C), and continue baking for 40 minutes or until the pie is done.

3 Comprehension. Say *That's right* or *That's wrong.*

1. Apple pie is a very popular American dessert.
2. If you eat something à la mode, you eat it with ice cream.
3. There are only a few recipes for apple pie.
4. The "red, white and blue" in line 11 probably refers to different flavors of ice cream.
5. According to the recipe, you only have to bake the apple pie for 40 minutes.

4 Putting steps in order. Read these steps for making apple pie. Then put them in the correct order.

a. ____ Fill the pie crust with the apple mixture.
b. ____ Mix the apples with sugar and spices.
c. ____ Turn the oven to 350°F (175°C).
d. __1__ Turn the oven to 450°F (230°C).
e. ____ Cover the mixture with the top crust.
f. ____ Cut the apples into slices.
g. ____ Dot the mixture with butter.
h. ____ Put the pie in the oven.

Writing

Skill: Writing steps in a process
Task: Writing instructions

1 Look at the pictures. They show how to grow an avocado plant. Then read the sentences and put them in the correct order according to the pictures.

1

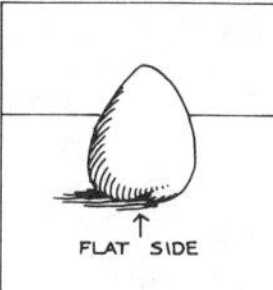

2

3

4

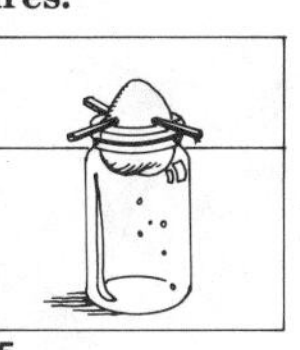
5

6

a. ____ Put three or four toothpicks into the sides of the seed.
b. ____ Cut the avocado in half and remove the seed.
c. ____ Put the jar in a sunny place.
d. ____ Hold the avocado seed so that the flat side is facing down.
e. ____ Fill the jar with water.
f. ____ Place the seed with the toothpicks into the jar.

2 Now read the instructions for growing an avocado plant and complete them by adding the six steps in Exercise 1. Notice how the sequencing words—*first, next, then, after that* and *finally*—help show the order of events.

AVOCADO PLANTS

It's not hard to grow an avocado plant. You will need an avocado, a jar about 7 inches tall and 4 inches wide, and some toothpicks. First, ____________. Next ____________. Then ____________. After that, ____________. Next ____________, resting the toothpicks on the edge of the jar so that only the bottom of the seed is covered by water. Finally, ____________.

You won't get avocados from an indoor avocado plant, but you will have a pretty plant to look at.

3 Now write a paragraph explaining how to do something. First, choose one of these topics or a topic of your own.

How to:	
make a glass of iced tea	change a tire
make a cassette recording	hang a picture

Next, list the steps in the correct order. Finally, write your instructions in paragraph form. Be sure to use sequencing words to help indicate the order of events.

For pronunciation exercises for Unit 7, see page 114.

Writing

See Intro. p. xii.
Tell students they are going to practice writing the steps in a process. This is a very common type of writing task. Point out that the reading selection is an example of this kind of writing, and if possible, bring in the "Best Sellers" column of your newspaper and point out the number of "how-to" books, e.g., on diet, nutrition and exercise, real estate and other investments and rearing children.

Exercise 1. See Intro. p. xii, Put the sentences in the right order.
avocado Refer to the picture.
hold (v) Mime this by holding something in your hand.
flat (adj) Refer to the picture, the desk top or other flat surfaces.
place (v) Means *put.*

Answers: a. 3 b. 1 c. 6 d. 2 e. 4 f. 5

Exercise 2. See Intro. p. ix, Writing sentences.
Answers: First, cut the avocado in half and remove the seed. Next hold the avocado seed so that the flat side is facing down. Then put three or four toothpicks into the sides of the seed. After that, fill the jar with water. Next place the seed with the toothpicks into the jar. Finally, place the jar in a sunny place.

Exercise 3.
Point out that the model paragraph and Cathy's article both have topic sentences—statements that come before the directions and give some general idea about the process, e.g.: *It's not hard to grow . . .* or *Ask any American to name the traditional national dessert . . .*

Additional ideas are *write a résumé, print with your computer, lose five pounds safely, cook (your favorite dish), start a car on a cold morning, give a dog a bath, quit smoking, talk with your teacher on a crowded elevator, plan a party.*

After students choose a topic and list the steps, check quickly to make sure they have not missed any important steps. After they write the paragraph, have them exchange papers and read each other's paragraphs, answering the following questions: *Are the steps in order? What sequencing words does the writer use? Could you follow these directions?*

For **Pronunciation** exercises for Unit 7, see p. 71.

UNIT 8

Language Summary

Functions

Complaining
It's hard being unemployed.
Making deductions
Cathy must be worried about Ken.
Sympathizing
I'm sorry to hear that. I hope your friend gets well soon.
Talking about plans
When are you going to buy a car? As soon as I get my driver's license.

Introduction

Vocabulary

fire department
hire
luckily
mortgage
must (deduction)
night shift
punch out *intrans*
salary
smell *trans*
without

Expressions

I can sympathize with you.
I know how you feel.
I know what it's like.
make ends meet
on fire
You'd better believe it.

Practice A

Structures

Present tense after *when, as soon as, after* and *before*
I'll be ready to go as soon as I punch out.

Practice B

Structures

Passive Voice
past tense
The firefighters were called to the scene.
+ *by* + agent
The police suspect that the fire was started by an arsonist.

Vocabulary

demote
injure
mug *v* (= assault)
rush *trans*

For recognition only
blaze *n*
burning *adj*
cheer up *trans*
churn *n*
costly
dedicate
flame
igloo
injury
same *adj*
sand *n*
satisfactory
suspect *v*
trivia
unable
worth *prep*

For recognition only—on cassette
release *v*

Expressions

be laid off
by fire
That's a shame.

For recognition only
get-well note
Get well soon.
in addition to
on duty

For recognition only—on cassette
You know, . . .

Practice C

Structure

***Must* (deduction)**
Cathy must be worried about Ken.

Vocabulary

captain
chosen *past part*
elect
president
promote
relaxed *adj*
relieved *adj*
scholarship
team

Expressions

be allergic to

For recognition only
make a deduction

Life Skills

Shopping for food
Asking for and giving the location of products in a supermarket
Comparative shopping
Understanding coupons

Vocabulary

aisle	cleaning supplies	ounce
baby food	detergent	pancake
baking needs	dozen	paper towel
bran	egg	price *n*
buy *n*	fresh	salad dressing
canned *adj*	(in good	shoe polish
catsup	condition)	spinach
cereal	frozen food	toilet paper
chopped meat		

For recognition only

coupon	oz. (= ounce)	roll *n*
limit *n*	purchase *v*	thru (= through)
manufacturer	rigatoni	

Expression

the same as

Pronunciation

Pronunciation points

1. Understanding /ʃ/
2. Distinguishing *is/isn't, are/aren't* and *was/wasn't*
3. Practicing intonation of time clauses with *when, as soon as, after* and *before*

Pronunciation exercises. *The pronunciation exercises for Unit 8 also appear in the Student's Book on p. 115.*

Part 1. *Understanding /ʃ/*

A. Listen and complete these sentences.

See Intro. p. xiii, Recognizing and distinguishing sounds 2 and 3

1. Ken works the night ________ .
2. Are you ________ ?
3. Don't ________ this to anyone.
4. You ________ go alone.
5. Can you repeat the ________ ?
6. Rob has to go to ________ and Save.

Answers: 1. shift 2. sure 3. mention 4. shouldn't 5. conversation 6. Stop

Now listen again and repeat the sentences.

B. Listen to this tongue twister and repeat it as fast as you can. How many times can you say it without making a mistake?

See Intro. p. xiii, Recognizing and distinguishing sounds 3

She sells seashells by the seashore.

Part 2. *Distinguishing* is/isn't, are/aren't *and* was/wasn't

Listen and complete each sentence with the verb you hear.

See Intro. p. xiii, Recognizing and distinguishing sounds 2 and 3

1. Ken ________ (was/wasn't) hired after Christmas.
2. Bill ________ (was/wasn't) arrested last year.
3. The doors ________ (are/aren't) locked at 6:00.
4. Rice ______ (is/isn't) grown in Arkansas.
5. Paychecks ________ (are/aren't) given out every week.

Answers: 1. wasn't 2. wasn't 3. are 4. is 5. aren't

Now listen again and repeat the sentences.

Part 3. *Practicing intonation of time clauses with* when, as soon as, after *and* before

Listen to these sentences. Notice the rising and then the falling intonation in the clause with the time expression *(when, as soon as, after* or *before).*

See Intro. p. xiii, Stress and intonation 1 and 4

1. When Rob leaves, he'll go home.
2. As soon as I know, I'll tell you.
3. After Pete's done, he'll call Suzanne.
4. Before Linda has dinner, she'll visit Bill.
5. When I get my license, I'll buy a car.

Now listen again and repeat the sentences.

See p. 143 for the Pronunciation Tapescript.

Teaching Notes

Getting Started

Use Unit 7, Practice A, second optional exercise on p. 73 of this Teacher's Manual, for practicing gerunds after prepositions. Students interview each other using these expressions. Use the questions elicited when the class first did the exercise and have students work with a different partner.

Introduction

 **1. Introductory Conversation.** See Intro. p. vii.

Preteaching

Words in the Introductory Conversation that are explained in Ex. 3 need not be pretaught. Ask students to infer their meanings as they do the exercise. The past tense of the passive voice and the tense sequence with *before* and *as soon as* also need not be pretaught. They will be taught in the grammar sections, but the meaning can be inferred here.
punch out Refer to the picture. The time clock records the time the employee arrives at and leaves work. Its use is common in blue-collar but not in white-collar jobs.
without Ken has not had a job for three months.
must Rob means *You're probably glad to have a job again.*
You'd better believe it. Means *That's very true.*
mortgage Means the loan you get to buy a house.
luckily Means *It's a good thing that . . .*
be on fire Means *be burning.*

Preparation

Elicit the storyline: Ken's brother has helped him find this job as a security guard. This is Ken's first night on the job. Ask focus questions: *When did Rob get this job?* (Right after Christmas last year.) *Why does Ken go to Warehouse 5?* (To find Steve.)

Exercise 2. See Intro. p. viii, Give a reason.
Answers: 1. He hasn't had a job for three months. 2. It's hard to make ends meet on his salary. 3. They need the money because they've got two kids and a mortgage. 4. He smells smoke.

Exercise 3. See Intro. p. viii, Find a word or phrase . . .
Answers: 1. shift 2. It's hard to make ends meet. 3. hired 4. salary

Exercise 4. See Intro. p. viii, Warm Up.
Point out that all the expressions for Student B indicate that the speaker understands how unpleasant the situation is for Student A.

Develop Your Vocabulary: Other expressions for A are *Being unemployed is getting on my nerves./I hate being unemployed.* Other expressions for B are *That would drive me crazy too./That's too bad.*

Other ideas are *being divorced/a single parent/a foreigner, living away from home, having two jobs, working nights, raising children today/in a big city, choosing presents, learning a new language, working and going to school at the same time.*

UNIT 8 Do You Smell Smoke?

1 Ken has just gotten to work. He is talking to Rob, another security guard. Listen to their conversation.

1

KEN: How are things tonight, Rob?
ROB: Very quiet. I'll be ready to go as soon as I punch out. So, how do you like working the night shift?
KEN: It's fine. After three months without a job, any shift is OK with me.
ROB: I know what you mean. You must be glad to have a job again.
KEN: You'd better believe it. How long have you worked here, Rob?
ROB: I was hired right before Christmas last year. The job's not difficult, but I'd like to find something better. It's hard to make ends meet on this salary.

2

KEN: I know. We've got two kids and a mortgage. Luckily, my wife works too. The bad thing is she leaves for work right after I get home.
ROB: Oh, that reminds me. *My* wife asked me to get some things at the Stop and Save. I'd better go now. They close at midnight.

3

KEN: Hey, do you smell smoke?
ROB: Warehouse 5 must be on fire!
KEN: Warehouse 5! My brother Steve's working there. Call the fire department! I'm going to find him!

2 Give a reason for each statement.

1. Ken's happy to have this job.
2. Rob would like to find another job.
3. Ken's glad Cathy works.
4. Rob thinks Warehouse 5 is on fire.

3 Find a word or phrase in the conversation that means:

1. hours you work
2. It's difficult to pay all my bills.
3. given a job
4. money you get for work

4 Warm Up

Complain to a classmate. He or she will sympathize with you.

A: It's hard *being unemployed.*
B: *I know what you mean. Being unemployed is terrible.*

DEVELOP YOUR VOCABULARY

(Student B)
I can sympathize with you.
I know what it's like.
I know how you feel.
. . .

Practice

A.

When As soon as After	Rob **punches out,** he'll leave.	OR	Rob will leave	when as soon as after	he **punches out.**
Before	Rob **leaves,** he'll punch out.	OR	Rob will punch out	**before**	he **leaves.**

1 What do you think the characters will do later? Make sentences by combining columns A and B. Be sure to change the form of the verbs.

1. As soon as Rob punches out, he'll leave the warehouse.

A	B
1. As soon as Rob (punch) out, he	a. (go) to baseball practice.
2. After he (finish) his test, Michael	b. (go) to the movies tonight.
3. Tom (write) another story before he	c. (get) home.
4. When Linda (leave) the office this evening, she	d. (leave) the warehouse.
5. This afternoon Ken (leave) for work as soon as Cathy	e. (visit) Bill.
6. After Pete (get) home today, he	f. (call) Suzanne.

2 Minh is talking to his wife, Lan, about their plans for the future. Listen to their conversation and put the pictures in the right order.

____ moving

____ getting raise

____ mother arriving

_1_ talking to Angela

____ looking at beds

3 Tell a classmate about something you'd like to buy.

A: I'd like to buy *a car.*
B: When are you going to buy *one?*
A: As soon as *I get my driver's license.*

Student A can use these ideas:

As soon as *I* get:
a promotion / raise / job / credit card / loan
my income tax refund

As soon as *I*:
save enough money
win the lottery

Practice A

Study Box. See Intro. p. viii.

Present tense after *when, as soon as, after* and *before.* Point out the tense sequence: future tense in the main clause, simple present tense in the clause with the time words.

Pronunciation point: Point out the rising, then falling intonation at the end of the adverbial clause:

When Rob punches out, he'll leave.

Part 3 of the **Pronunciation** exercises can be used here.

Optional: Give additional practice. Write simple sentences on the board:

I go to sleep.
Dinner is cooked.
Summer arrives, and it gets hot.
They call and tell me they're at the airport.

Ask students to add adverbial clauses and use the proper verb tenses. Give some examples:

After I read this chapter, I'll go to sleep.
As soon as dinner is cooked, we'll eat.

Students can work individually or in pairs. Call on volunteers to say their sentences.

Exercise 1. See Intro. p. ix, Make sentences.
Answers: 2. After he finishes his test, Michael will go to baseball practice. 3. Tom will write another story before he goes to the movies tonight. 4. When Linda leaves the office this evening, she'll visit Bill. 5. This afternoon Ken will leave for work as soon as Cathy gets home. 6. After Pete gets home today, he'll call Suzanne.

Exercise 2. See Intro. p. ix, Listening.
Answers: 3–moving 2–getting raise 5–mother arriving 4–looking at beds

Exercise 3. See Intro. p. ix, Ask and answer questions.
Optional: Have students use magazine advertisements as cues. Expand by having students work in small groups and make up stories, using time clauses, about interesting magazine pictures, e.g.:

After she buys those expensive shoes, the woman will leave the store and wait for a bus. As soon as the bus comes, she'll remember she left her purse in the shop. She'll run back to the shop . . . (Etc.)

Optional: Have students work with the same partners they worked with for Getting Started on p. 81 of this Teacher's Manual. They can use the information they elicited for that exercise in this conversation, e.g.:

A: I'd like to start my own business.
B: When can you do that?
A: After my brother comes to this country, we'll start a small import-export company.

Practice B

Study Box. See Intro. p. viii.

1. Passive voice—past tense. Remind students how to form the passive: *be (was/were)* + past participle.

2. *By*. The *by-* phrase shows who or what performed the action. It is only used when it is important to know this, and it is often omitted in the passive voice.

Pronunciation point: Part 2 of the **Pronunciation** exercises can be used here to practice distinguishing between *is/isn't, are/aren't, was/wasn't* and *were/weren't* in passive constructions.

Optional: Give additional oral practice. Write the following sentences on the board and ask students to transform them to passive:

Some students watered the plants last night.
The waiters served lunch late.
Pavlik and Fuchs wrote this book in 1987.
Mr. Brendan taught us to read in the second grade.
A tailor made this suit in Hong Kong.
Your boss told you to be at work at 8:00.
A friend typed my term paper.

Optional: Give additional writing practice. Have students work in pairs and choose one of the storyline characters. Ask them to write a biography of the character using some of the following passive verbs: *was educated at, hired by, married to, promoted, encouraged to, warned not to, advised to.*

Exercise 1. See Intro. p. ix, Complete the sentences/paragraph.
rush (trans) Means take someone somewhere in a hurry.
**flames* and *blaze* Both mean *fire.*
**were unable to* Means *couldn't.*
**suspect (v)* Means *believe.*
**same (adj)* Here, means only one person set all the fires.
**burning (adj)* Ask students to infer the meaning from context.
**satisfactory condition* Ken and Steve were not seriously hurt.
**most costly* Means caused the most damage to people and property.
**injury* Means *hurt* or *harm.*

Answers: 2. was called 3. was started 4. were burned down 5. was injured 6. were found 7. were rushed 8. were listed 9. were destroyed 10. were owned

Exercise 2. See Intro. p. ix, Listening.
**release (v)* Here, means send home from the hospital.
**cheer up (trans)* Means make someone feel happier.

Answer: Get-well note 2

B.

Another warehouse **was destroyed**	**by** an arsonist. **by** fire.
The firefighters **were called** to the scene.	

1 **Read this article from the Houston *Herald* and complete it with the correct forms of the verbs.**

The Houston Herald

4th Warehouse Destroyed Security Guards Injured

HOUSTON—Last night another warehouse in the downtown area of Houston *was destroyed* (1. destroy) by fire. The fire department ________ (2. call) to the scene at 11:00 P.M. Although they arrived only five minutes later, they were unable to put out the flames. The police suspect that the fire ________ (3. start) by an arsonist. Last month three buildings ________ (4. burn down) in the area, and police believe that this was the work of the same person. This, however, is the first time that anyone ________ (5. injure) in the blaze. Two brothers, Ken and Steven Wilson, both security guards on duty at the time, ________ (6. find) unconscious outside the burning building. They ________ (7. rush) to City Hospital, where both ________ (8. list) in satisfactory condition.

This fire is the most costly so far. In addition to the injuries of the Wilson brothers, valuable paintings worth millions of dollars ________ (9. destroy) in the fire. The paintings, which ________ (10. own) by the Houston Art Museum, were going to be returned to the museum next week.

2 **Angela and her husband, Frank, are talking about what happened to Ken Wilson. Listen and choose the get-well note they sent Ken in the hospital.**

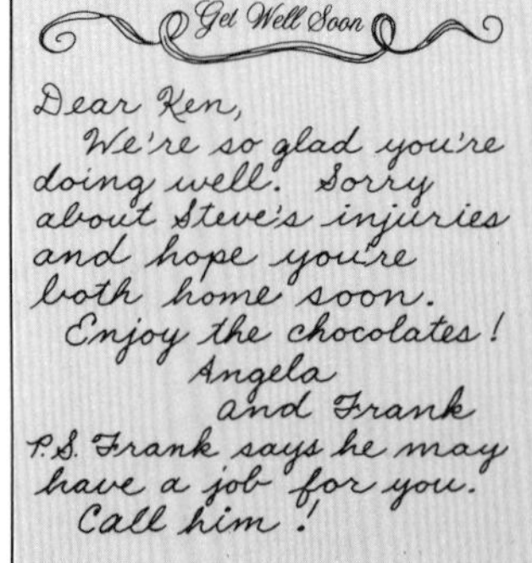
Get Well Soon
Dear Ken,
We're so glad you're doing well. Sorry about Steve's injuries and hope you're both home soon.
Enjoy the chocolates!
Angela and Frank
P.S. Frank says he may have a job for you. Call him!

1

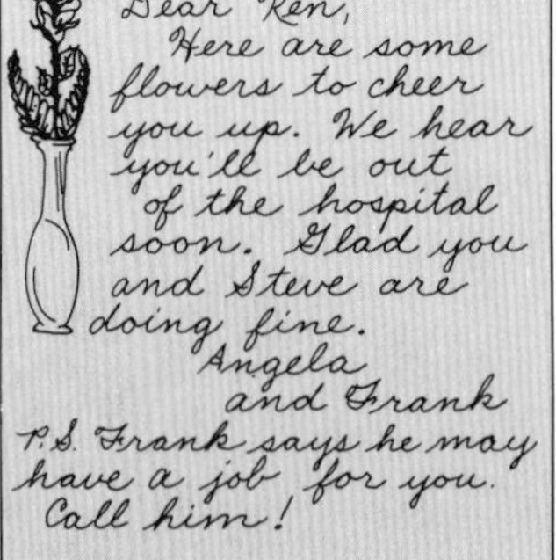
Dear Ken,
Here are some flowers to cheer you up. We hear you'll be out of the hospital soon. Glad you and Steve are doing fine.
Angela and Frank
P.S. Frank says he may have a job for you. Call him!

2

Dear Ken,
Sorry you and Steve are feeling so bad. We wanted to send you some flowers, but Cathy says you are allergic to them.
Get well soon!
Angela and Frank
P.S. Frank says he may have a job for you. Call him!

3

3 Tell a classmate some bad news. He or she will express sympathy.

A: Hey, *Marta*, you look upset. What's the matter?
B: I just got some bad news. *A friend of mine was injured in a car accident.*
A: *I'm sorry to hear that. I hope your friend gets well soon.*
OR *Was your friend badly hurt?*

Student B can use these ideas:

was/were:	
fired	mugged
laid off	robbed
demoted	hurt

DEVELOP YOUR VOCABULARY

(Student A)
That's:
terrible
awful
a shame
. . .

Just for Fun

4

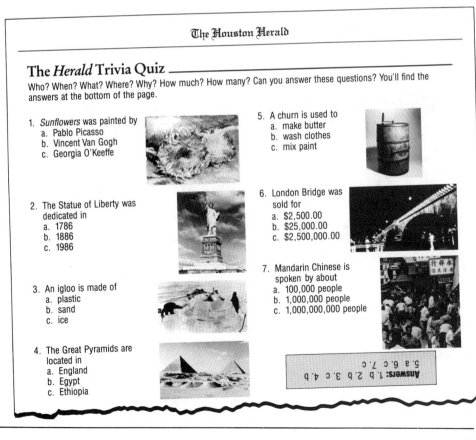

The Houston Herald

The *Herald* Trivia Quiz

Who? When? What? Where? Why? How much? How many? Can you answer these questions? You'll find the answers at the bottom of the page.

1. *Sunflowers* was painted by
   a. Pablo Picasso
   b. Vincent Van Gogh
   c. Georgia O'Keeffe

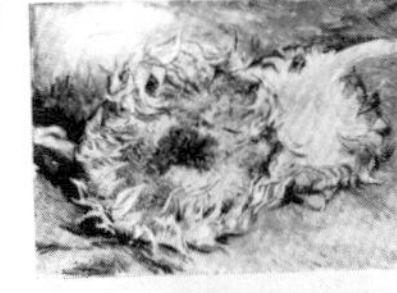

2. The Statue of Liberty was dedicated in
   a. 1786
   b. 1886
   c. 1986

3. An igloo is made of
   a. plastic
   b. sand
   c. ice

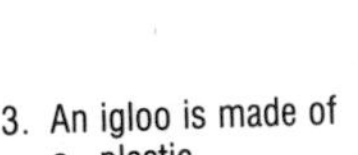

4. The Great Pyramids are located in
   a. England
   b. Egypt
   c. Ethiopia

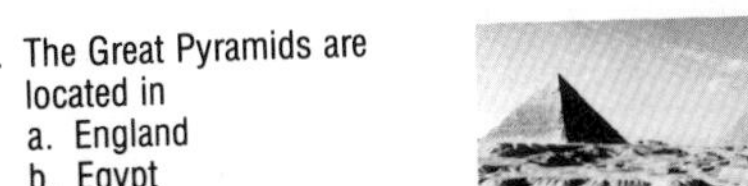

5. A churn is used to
   a. make butter
   b. wash clothes
   c. mix paint

6. London Bridge was sold for
   a. $2,500.00
   b. $25,000.00
   c. $2,500,000.00

7. Mandarin Chinese is spoken by about
   a. 100,000 people
   b. 1,000,000 people
   c. 1,000,000,000 people

Answers: 1. b 2. b 3. c 4. b 5. a 6. c 7. c

Exercise 3. See Intro. p. ix, Ask and answer questions.
injured Means *hurt.*
demoted Means given a lower-level job; the opposite of *promoted.*
mugged Means robbed with force.

Develop Your Vocabulary: Other responses are *Can your friend find/ Is your friend looking for another job? Did your friend call the police? Can I do anything to help?*

Other ideas are *was hurt/injured at work, flunked out of school* (had to leave school because of bad grades).

Exercise 4.
**trivia* Small details and facts; unimportant information. Teach *trivial* (unimportant).
**dedicated* Refers to the ceremony when the statue was finished and opened to visitors.
**igloo* Refer to the picture.
**sand* The soil on the beach or in a desert.
**churn (n)* Refer to the picture.

Answers: 1. b 2. b 3. c 4. b 5. a 6. c 7. c

Optional: Use Longman's ESL book *Talk about Trivia* or have students make up their own trivia questions. Divide the class into teams and play like a quiz show.

Optional: Use a collegiate dictionary to write questions. Divide the class into teams to answer questions with teams using dictionaries to look up key words. Point out the geography and biography sections. Some examples of questions:

1. The telephone was invented by:
   a. Edison
   b. Rembrandt
   c. Bell
2. The kangaroo is found in:
   a. Australia
   b. Africa
   c. Alabama

Optional: Write the following passage on the board and ask students to rewrite it by turning the active verbs into passive. Vague subjects, e.g., *this,* can be left out.

Her boss fired my friend Suzy last year. At first, this upset her. She turned on the TV all day at her house and was very depressed. Then a TV commercial changed her mood. One talk show advertised a school for hairdressers. This interested Suzy, so she forgot her depression. Today she's a successful hairdresser.

My friend Suzy was fired by her boss last year. At first, she was upset. The TV was turned on all day at her house, and she was very depressed. Then her attitude was changed by a TV commercial. A school for hairdressers was advertised by a talk show. Suzy was interested, so her depression was forgotten. Today she's a successful hairdresser.

Practice C

Study Box. See Intro. p. viii.

Must **(deduction).** Explain that *must* in the Study Box sentences means *probably* but is a little stronger. The speaker is saying, *The evidence shows me, or it's logical to believe, that Cathy is worried about Ken.*

Pronunciation point: Point out the intonation pattern and reduction:

She must be worried about Ken. /ʃiməsbi/

Optional: Give additional practice. Write on the board or read the following statements and ask students to make deductions with *must* or *must not:*

Ann wears something blue every day. (She must like the color blue.)
Jaimie is sneezing. (He must have a cold.)
Laura just had a soda, and now she wants a glass of water.
Maria didn't eat breakfast or lunch today.
There's a long line for that movie.
Luis yawned all through the concert.

Exercise 1. See Intro. p. ix, Look at the pictures.
**make a deduction* Means come to a conclusion after looking at some evidence.
relaxed (adj) Means *calm, comfortable.*
be allergic to Means have an allergy; be sensitive to.
relieved (adj) Means not feeling worried any more.

Answers: 2. Pete must miss Suzanne. He must not be very happy. 3. Suzanne must not be at home. She must be out. 4. Linda must be allergic to flowers. She must be in Ken's room. 5. Michael must be relieved. Pete must be proud.

Exercise 2. See Intro. p. ix, Ask and answer questions.
scholarship Money to pay for school expenses; usually given to good students who need money to attend school.
elect Means choose by voting.
promote Means give someone a promotion.
president A leader of a group, chosen by election.
chosen Past participle of *choose.*
captain Leader of an athletic team or a military group.
team A group of players.

C.

Cathy **must be** worried about Ken. She **must not feel** very relaxed.

Note: We do not contract *must not* when we use it to make a deduction.

1 Make deductions by using the words below each picture.

1. Cathy must be worried about Ken.
   She must not feel very relaxed.

1. Cathy / be worried about Ken
   She / feel relaxed

2. Pete / miss Suzanne
   He / be happy

3. Suzanne / be at home
   She / be out

4. Linda / be allergic to flowers
   She / be in Ken's room

5. Michael / be relieved
   Pete / be proud

2 Tell a classmate some good news.

A: I have *good* news. *My sister was given a scholarship.*
B: Oh, that's *wonderful. She* must *be* very *proud.*

Student A can use these ideas:

was:
given a raise
promoted
elected *class president*
chosen *as captain of her volleyball team*

3 Listen to these people. Then make a deduction about each one. Use *must be* and an adjective.

1. He . . .
2. She . . .
3. He . . .
4. She . . .
5. He . . .
6. She . . .
7. He . . .

Just for Fun

4 What deductions can you make about the person who lives in this room? Use *must* and *must not*.

This person must *play baseball*.

Now think about the characters in the story. Whose room do you think this is?

It must be ______________'s room.

Exercise 3. See Intro. p. ix, Listening.
Answers: 1. He must be sick. 2. She must be sad/unhappy. 3. He must be angry. 4. She must be excited/happy. 5. He must be tired. 6. She must be frightened/scared. 7. He must be happy.

Exercise 4. See Intro. p. ix, Look at the pictures.
Some possible answers: He must have a dog/be a student/like (play) baseball/like rock music/play the guitar/not water his plant/have tropical fish/like animals/not have much time to clean his room. It must be Michael's room.

Optional: Have students work in pairs and take turns reading the following sentences and making deductions:

I've been calling Linda all day. No one answers. (She must be out of town./She must not be home.)
Alain has to present some plans to his boss today at work.
There's been loud rock music playing upstairs all night.
My daughter didn't eat any dinner at all last night.
Victor is going home to Guatemala for a vacation this year.
Ann Marie won't talk to me or return my phone calls.

Optional: Have students work in pairs. Each student tells a story about someone he or she knows who is accomplishing something very difficult. The other student listens and makes deductions, e.g.:

A: My friend Fern is a single parent with three children. She hasn't had much money at all since she became single. Her two older sons have taken part-time jobs while they go to high school. Fern started working as a substitute teacher. She also goes to college part time. Her school has weekend classes. She wants to become a social worker. It'll take her five years to get her degree and even longer to find a good job. Her children are all applying for scholarships to college.
B: She must work very hard. She must worry about money. She must realize she needs a better job. She must feel proud of her kids. (Etc.)

Life Skills

In this unit students will learn where to find items in a supermarket. They will compare the prices and sizes of common supermarket items and decide which items are better buys. Finally, they will learn about the advantages and restrictions of coupons. You should bring in a family magazine and the coupon section of the newspaper to illustrate new vocabulary.

Exercise 1. See Intro. p. ix, Listening.
aisle Means *row.* Refer to the floor plan.
Use the magazine and coupon illustrations to help you explain food vocabulary.
spinach A green, leafy vegetable. Refer to the picture in Ex. 2.
chopped meat The meat used for hamburgers; also *ground meat.*
bran The woody, outer portion of a grain, often added to cereals and breads.
cereal Wheat, rice, oats, corn, for example. A typical American breakfast food is cereal in some form, e.g., cornflakes, puffed rice.
detergent Refer to the picture in Ex. 2.
frozen food Refer to the picture in Ex. 2.
cleaning supplies Like laundry detergent, things used to wash clothes or do housecleaning.
catsup Also *ketchup.* A tomato sauce used on hamburgers.
canned Refer to the picture of canned peas in Ex. 2.
fresh Means *in good condition,* not frozen or canned.

Answers: 1. paper 2. towels 3. 2 4. left 5. cleaning

Exercise 2. See Intro. p. ix, Ask and answer questions.
better buy Means you get more of the product for the same price.
price (n) Means *cost.*
ounce A unit of measure. There are 16 ounces to a pound.
oz. The abbreviation for *ounce.*

Better buys: 2. 2 for 97¢ 3. Stop & Save peas for 41¢ 4. 64 fl. oz. for $2.69 5. 72 sq. ft. for $0.99

Ask students why they chose their answers and explain or elicit that often the store brand is a better buy. Also, two of the same item are often—but not always—a few cents cheaper per unit.

UNIT 8

Life Skills

Food

1 **Rob, Ken Wilson's co-worker, is at Stop and Save. He is having trouble finding some of the things on his shopping list. Listen and complete his conversation with a clerk.**

ROB: Excuse me. Where can I find ______(1) ______(2)?
CLERK: In aisle ______(3), ______(4) side, right across from the ______(5) supplies.
ROB: OK. Thanks a lot.

Now look at Rob's shopping list and the floor plan of Stop and Save. Practice asking and giving directions.

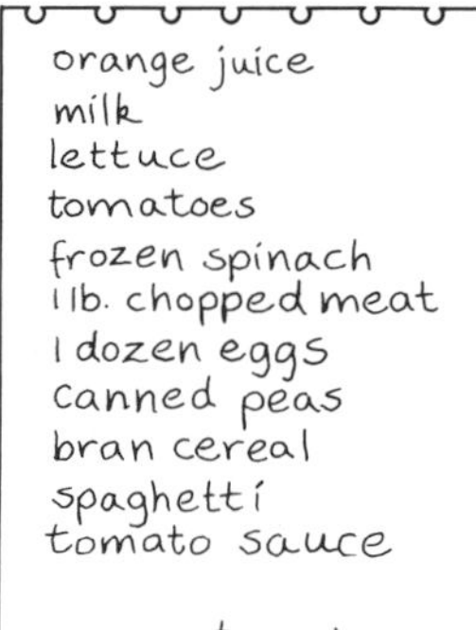

Ice Cream	①	Candy	Paper Products	②	Cleaning Supplies	Pancake Flour	③	Salad Dressing	Canned Fruit	④	Spaghetti	Eggs	⑤	Fresh Fruits and Vegetables
Frozen Food		Baby Food				Cereal		Catsup	Juices		Tomato Sauces	Dairy Products		
Meats		Baking Needs	Detergent		Shoe Polish	Sugar		Pickles	Canned Vegetables		Soup			

2 **Rob is deciding which products to buy. Look at the products and discuss if one is a better buy than the other. Give a reason for your opinion.**

1. A: I think Marvel detergent is a better buy. The bottle is bigger, and the price is the same as Wonder.
   B: But Wonder has 64 ounces of detergent, and Marvel has only 57 ounces.
   OR I agree.

1. $4.59

$4.59

2. 55¢

2 for 97¢

3. 41¢

47¢

4. $2.69

$1.39

5. $0.99

$2.07

3 Rob has several coupons. Look at them. Then read each statement and say *That's right, That's wrong* or *I don't know*.

1. a. Rob can only use this coupon in Stop and Save stores.
   b. He can buy as many rolls as he wants with this coupon.
   c. He can use this coupon next year.
   d. He saves 10¢ a roll when he uses this coupon.

STOP & SAVE
PAPER TOWELS
TOUGHY
58¢
With Coupon
Limit 4
Coupon Good thru Dec. 30, 1990

2. a. Rob can only save on Miller's brand spaghetti.
   b. If he uses this coupon, he'll get one pound of spaghetti.
   c. He can only buy two packages of spaghetti with this coupon.
   d. He can use this coupon next year.

MILLER'S SPAGHETTI
MILLER'S SPAGHETTI or RIGATONI
2 1 LB. PKGS. 89¢

3. a. Rob can only use this coupon in Stop and Save stores.
   b. He has to use this coupon before 1991.
   c. He'll save 25¢ if he uses this coupon.
   d. If he buys two bottles of Rosa's spaghetti sauce, he'll save 50¢.

MANUFACTURER'S COUPON
NO EXPIRATION DATE
Save 25¢
On Any Rosa's Spaghetti Sauce
Limit one Rosa Food Coupon per Rosa product purchased
ROSA'S

ON YOUR OWN

Discuss these questions with your classmates.

1 Where do you shop for food? In a large supermarket? In small stores? At a street market? What are some advantages and disadvantages of supermarkets?

2 Do you ever use coupons? Do you think coupons really save you money?

3 Where can people buy food in your country? When are the stores or markets open? Do people use coupons?

For pronunciation exercises for Unit 8, see page 115.

Exercise 3. See Intro. p. viii, Say *That's right . . .*

**coupon* Refer to the pictures and bring in additional samples. Explain that there are two types of coupons you can use to save money when you go shopping. Store coupons can be used only in a specific store. Manufacturers' coupons can be used in all stores that sell the product and that accept coupons. You can find coupons in newspapers, magazines and supermarkets.

**roll (n)* Refer to the pictures of paper towels.

**thru* A short form for *through,* used mostly in advertising.

**purchasing (v)* Means *buy.*

Answers: 1. a. That's right. b. That's wrong. c. *Answer will vary depending on the current year.* d. I don't know. 2. a. That's right. b. That's wrong. c. That's right. d. I don't know. 3. a. That's wrong. b. That's wrong. c. That's right. d. That's wrong.

On Your Own. See Intro. p. xi.

1. Some advantages of supermarkets are brought out by the story: They are often open late at night. They carry many different kinds of products. They are usually cheaper than small stores. However, they won't offer credit the way a small neighborhood store will. Their fruits and vegetables are usually trucked long distances and are not as fresh as those at street markets or small stores. They are very impersonal.

2. Sometimes people feel impelled to buy a product they wouldn't ordinarily buy because they have a coupon. Sometimes the product sold with the coupon is not the best product.

REVIEW 4

Exercise 1.
2. Playing 3. hitting 4. Becoming 5. being able to 6. learning 7. practicing 8. winning 9. Having 10. Getting

Exercise 2.
2. Televisions are produced in Japan. 3. Gold is mined in the Soviet Union. 4. Leather products are made in Italy. 5. Shoes are manufactured in Brazil. 6. Diamonds are mined in South Africa. 7. Steel is manufactured in South Korea. 8. Cars are produced in Yugoslavia. 9. Pineapples are grown in Thailand.

Exercise 3.
2. are sent 3. are cut 4. are put 5. keep 6. sent 7. choose 8. is 9. means

Exercise 4.
Answers will vary.

REVIEW 4

1 Complete this conversation with gerunds.

A: Do you enjoy playing (1. play) tennis?

B: Yes. ________ (2. play) tennis is really a lot of fun. Unfortunately, I'm not very good at ________ (3. hit) the ball.

A: Be patient. ________ (4. become) good at a sport takes time.

B: I know. But I look forward to ________ (5. be able to) play a good game one day. Do you play?

A: No, but I'm interest in ________ (6. learn).

B: Well, how do you feel about ________ (7. practice) with me?

A: Sounds like a good idea. As long as I don't have to worry about ________ (8. win).

B: Don't worry. ________ (9. have) fun is the most important thing.

A: ________ (10. get) in shape will be good for us too.

2 Rewrite these sentences in the passive voice.

1. They grow rice in India.

Rice is grown in India.

2. They produce televisions in Japan.
3. They mine gold in the Soviet Union.
4. They make leather products in Italy.
5. They manufacture shoes in Brazil.
6. They mine diamonds in South Africa.
7. They manufacture steel in South Korea.
8. They produce cars in Yugoslavia.
9. They grow pineapples in Thailand.

3 Complete this magazine article with the active or passive form of the verbs.

Have you ever wondered where Christmas trees come from? Many of them are grown (1. grow) on Christmas tree farms in New England. From there, they ______ (2. send) all over the United States. Often they ______ (3. cut) two or even three months before Christmas. Then they ______ (4. put) in water so they won't dry out. Growers sometimes even ______ (5. keep) them in lakes or ponds until they're ______ (6. send) to customers. Therefore, you must be very careful when you ______ (7. choose) your tree. Look at the trunk. If it ______ (8. be) black near the bottom, that ______ (9. mean) it was cut a while ago and it may dry out quickly.

4 Complete each sentence with your own information.

1. I'll stop studying English as soon as ______ .
2. Before I ______, I'll have to save more money.
3. After ______, I'll have dinner.
4. I'll be glad when ______ .
5. As soon as ______, I'll buy another one.

5 Complete this conversation between Rob and his wife, Liz. Use the passive form of the verbs.

ROB: Hi, Liz. Sorry I'm late, but there was another fire in one of the warehouses.

LIZ: Oh, no! Was (1. hurt) anyone hurt?

ROB: Yes. The new guard, Ken, and his brother ________ (2. hurt).

LIZ: How? What happened?

ROB: I'm not sure. While I was calling the fire department, Ken rushed to the warehouse to rescue his brother. Later, both men ________ (3. find) unconscious in front of the building. Then they ________ (4. take) to the hospital. That's all I know.

LIZ: ________ their families ________ (5. tell)?

ROB: I'm sure they were.

LIZ: And what happened to the warehouse?

ROB: It ________ (6. destroy) by the fire.

6 Can you remember the story? According to the story, these statements are wrong. Correct them using the passive.

1. The fire destroyed a restaurant.

A restaurant wasn't destroyed. A warehouse was.

2. Steve started the fire.

The fire wasn't started by Steve. It was started by the arsonist.

3. The police found Rob unconscious.
4. The security guards put the fire out.
5. The police rushed the arsonist to the hospital.
6. The fire destroyed some valuable furniture.
7. Cathy wrote the newspaper article about the fire.

7 Make deductions with *must* or *must not.* Use the word or phrase in parentheses.

1. He's carrying a guidebook and has a camera around his neck. (tourist)

He must be a tourist.

2. She's only fifteen, and she's in college. (smart)
3. I smell smoke, and I can hear a fire engine. (fire)
4. He's had five accidents in the past four months. (good driver)
5. He's still in the hospital. (well)
6. She buys the newspaper every day and looks at the employment ads. (new job)
7. Everyone is wearing sweaters and jackets outside. (cool)
8. No one finished reading that book. (interesting)

8 Put these words in the correct order.

1. frightening fires be must fighting

Fighting fires must be frightening.

2. I go as as to I'll store finish letter this the soon
3. leave you'll before have to you out punch
4. guard reported fire was security by the the

Exercise 5.

2. were hurt 3. were found 4. were taken 5. Were, told 6. was destroyed

Exercise 6.

3. Rob wasn't found unconscious. Ken and Steve were. 4. The fire wasn't put out by the security guards. It was put out by the firefighters. 5. The arsonist wasn't rushed to the hospital. The injured men were. 6. Valuable furniture wasn't destroyed. Valuable paintings were. 7. The article wasn't written by Cathy. It was written by Linda.

Exercise 7

2. She must be smart. 3. There must be a fire. 4. He must not be a good driver. 5. He must not be well. 6. She must be looking for (must need/want) a new job. 7. It must be cool. 8. It must not be interesting.

Exercise 8.

2. I'll go to the store as soon as I finish this letter. 3. Before you leave, you'll have to punch out. OR You'll have to punch out before you leave. 4. The fire was reported by the security guard.

UNIT 9

Language Summary

Functions

Comparing
Michael writes more neatly than Cindy.
Expressing obligation
Ken must get a lot of rest.
Expressing wishes
I wish I could type fast.
Prohibiting
Ken mustn't get involved.
Thanking and responding to thanks
Thanks for helping me with my homework. I really appreciate it. You're welcome. I was glad to do it.

Introduction

Vocabulary

easily
involved *adj*
make out *trans* (= understand)
must (obligation)
positive (= sure)
smoky
what *rel pron*
where *conj*

Expressions

Anytime.
Begin at the beginning.
by *ourselves*
Go on. (= Continue.)
Sure thing.
The next thing I knew, . . .

Practice A

Structure

Adverbs of manner
It all happened so quickly.

Vocabulary

beautifully
capable
capably
complete *adj*
courageous
courageously
fast *adv*
fluently
guilty
happily
immediate
impolite
impolitely
incorrect
quick
responsible
responsibly
sloppily
sloppy
slow
slowly

For recognition only
investigation

Expression

For recognition only
Do it yourself.

Practice B

Structures
Comparison of adverbs
Michael writes more neatly than Cindy.
He works harder than her.

Vocabulary

accurately grammatically neatly creatively

For recognition only
bush
dreamt *s past*
outer space
planet
playground
reference
Saturn
saw *s past*
woods

For recognition only—on cassette
attend
regularly
unreliable

Practice C

Structures
Infinitive after question words
Ken didn't know where to begin his story.
He didn't know what to do.

Vocabulary

complain
how much *pron*
ingredient
sink *n*
sister-in-law

For recognition only—on cassette
righthand
put in (= insert)

Expression

For recognition only—on cassette
I've got that. (= I understand.)

Practice D

Structures
Must* (obligation), *must not* (prohibition) and *(not) have to
Ken must get a lot of rest.
He must not go back to work yet.
He doesn't have to stay in bed.

Vocabulary

bleach *v*
checkup
dry *v*
dry clean
lay
medium *adj*
rest *n*

For recognition only
garment
ironing *n*

For recognition only—on cassette

active	office hours

Expressions

inside out

For recognition only

permanent press

For recognition only—on cassette

Take it easy.

Put It All Together

Vocabulary

spoke *s past*

For recognition only

candlelight	homemade	reservation
dining *n*	require	setting *n*

On Your Own

Vocabulary

For recognition only

foreigner

Reading

Skills

Skimming

Guessing the meaning from context

Vocabulary

absence	Diner's Club	self-service	Visa
American Express	eatery	spicy	well-stocked
cuisine	flavor *n*	typical	
decor	MasterCard	usual	

For recognition only

accessible	comfort	jalapeño	review *n*
alpine	crabmeat	moderate	reviewer
atmosphere	diet *v*	mozzarella	spot *n*
burger (= hamburger)	facility	much *adv*	swiss cheese
cheery	handicapped *n*	mushroom	Szechuan
chili-pepper	haven	palace	visit *n*
	heartily	regional	

Expressions

For recognition only

in spite of	It leaves much to be desired.

Writing

Skill

Describing

Task

Writing a review

Vocabulary

For recognition only

decorate	empty *adj*	sterile

Pronunciation

Pronunciation points

1. Understanding /θ/ and /ð/
2. Distinguishing *must* and *mustn't*

Pronunciation exercises. *The pronunciation exercises for Unit 9 also appear in the Student's Book on p. 115.*

Part 1. *Understanding /θ/ and /ð/*

Officer Brady is talking to Ken again. Listen to their conversation and complete it.

See Intro. p. xiii, Recognizing and distinguishing sounds 2 and 3

BRADY: ______ (1) for coming again, Mr. Wilson.

KEN: Sure ______ (2), Officer Brady. I want to help find ______ (3) people.

BRADY: Just tell me ______ (4) you can remember about ______ (5) fire.

KEN: I ______ (6) I already told you ______ (7) whole story.

BRADY: Well, if you remember ______ (8) else, please call.

KEN: I sure will. I've asked my ______ (9), but he doesn't remember much ______ (10).

Answers: 1. Thanks 2. thing 3. those 4. everything 5. the 6. think 7. the 8. anything 9. brother 10. either

Now listen again and repeat the conversation.

Part 2. *Distinguishing* must *and* mustn't

Listen to these sentences and complete them with *must* or *mustn't*.

See Intro. p. xiii, Recognizing and distinguishing sounds 2 and 3

1. You ______ tell her about it.
2. You ______ do it again.
3. You ______ wash it in hot water.
4. You ______ send it to the cleaners.
5. You ______ stop there.
6. She ______ work today.
7. She ______ go there alone.
8. You ______ tell him.

Answers: 1. mustn't 2. must 3. mustn't 4. must 5. mustn't 6. must 7. mustn't 8. mustn't

Now listen again and repeat the sentences.

See p. 144 for the Pronunciation Tapescript.

(continued on next page)

Teaching Notes

Getting Started

1. Use Unit 8, Ex. A3 on Student's Book p. 67. Students work in pairs and tell their partners something they'd like to buy, using *when, as soon as, after* and *before.* You can bring in magazine pictures for cues.

2. Use Unit 8, Ex. C4 on Student's Book p. 71. Students make deductions about the person who lives in this room. Again, magazine pictures can be used instead of or in addition to the picture of Michael's room.

Introduction

 **1. Introductory Conversation.** See Intro. p. vii.

Preteaching

Words that are explained in Ex. 3 are not included below.
get involved Means *become part of.* The police will investigate alone.
easily Point out that the word comes from *easy.* The investigation will be easier if Ken doesn't get involved.
Begin at the beginning. Means start from the first thing that happened.
Go on. Means *Continue.*
smoky Means there was a lot of smoke in the air.
The next thing I knew, . . . Here, means *When I woke up, . . .*

Preparation

Elicit the storyline: Ken was hurt in the fire. He was released from the hospital, and now he's talking to Officer Brady. Ask focus questions: *What does Officer Brady want Ken to do?* (Tell him everything he can remember.) *Why didn't Ken see anything in Warehouse 5?* (It was too smoky.)

Exercise 2. See Intro. p. viii, Correct the information.
Answers: 1. Officer Brady doesn't want Ken to work with the police. Ken mustn't get involved. 2. Ken ran to Warehouse 5. 3. Ken heard a woman's voice, but he couldn't see anything. 4. Ken woke up in the hospital.

Exercise 3. See Intro. p. viii, Find a word or phrase . . .
Answers: 1. must 2. make out 3. positive 4. by ourselves

Exercise 4. See Intro. p. viii, Warm Up.
Develop Your Vocabulary: *Sure thing* and *Anytime* are idioms that mean *You're welcome.* Additional responses are *It was nothing./No problem.*

Optional: Describe situations for students and have them develop their own conversations, including thanking and responding to thanks, e.g.:
1. Your neighbor watered your plants for you while you were on vacation.
2. Your friend typed your term paper on his computer for you.
3. Your son did all the shopping and cleaning while you were sick.

 (continued on next page)

UNIT 9 Leave It to the Police

1 Officer Brady asked Ken Wilson to come to the police station. Listen to their conversation.

1
BRADY: Thanks for coming, Mr. Wilson.
KEN: Well, I wanted to talk to you. We *must* get the people who did this.
BRADY: But *you* mustn't get involved. We can investigate more easily by ourselves. Just tell me everything you can remember about the fire.

2
KEN: I don't know where to begin. It all happened so quickly.
BRADY: Well, just begin at the beginning.
KEN: OK. I smelled smoke and ran as fast as I could to Warehouse 5.
BRADY: Yes, go on. What did you do then?
KEN: I didn't know what to do. I just kept calling my brother's name.

3
BRADY: Did you see or hear anyone?
KEN: No, it was too smoky. I couldn't see anything. But I heard a woman's voice.
BRADY: A *woman's* voice? Are you positive?
KEN: Yes, but I couldn't make out what she was saying. Then someone hit me hard over the head. The next thing I knew, I was in the hospital.

2 Correct the information.

1. Officer Brady wants Ken to work with the police.
2. Ken was working in Warehouse 5.
3. Ken saw a woman in the warehouse.
4. Ken woke up in the warehouse.

3 Find a word or phrase in the conversation that means:

1. have to
2. understand
3. sure
4. without anyone else

4 Warm Up

Thank a classmate for doing something.

A: Thanks for *helping me with my homework.* I really appreciate it.
B: *You're welcome.* I was glad to do it.

DEVELOP YOUR VOCABULARY

(Student B)

That's OK.	My pleasure.
Sure thing.	Don't mention it.
Anytime.	. . .

Practice

A.

It all happened so **quickly.**

Spelling note: Regular adverbs

quick + ly ⟶ quickly
immediate + ly ⟶ immediately
capable + ly ⟶ capably
beautiful + ly ⟶ beautifully
happy (i) + ly ⟶ happily

Irregular adverbs

Adjective	*Adverb*
hard	hard
fast	fast
good	well

1 Talk about each picture by using the words in the box.

slow	incorrect	impolite
fast	sloppy	

1. The child spoke impolitely.

Could you please turn on the light?
Do it yourself!

1. speak

2. be dressed

What's the capital of the United States?
New York.

3. answer the question

4. drive

5. move

4. Your mother-in-law helped you do your income taxes.
5. Your friend took you out to dinner on your birthday.

A: Thanks for watering my plants. They really look great.
B: Sure thing. I was glad to do it. Did you have a good time on your vacation?

Practice A

Study Box. See Intro. p. viii.

quick Means *fast.*
immediate Means *right away, at once.*
capable Means able to do something efficiently or well.
responsible Means can be trusted to do the right thing or make the right decisions.

Adverbs of manner.
1. Use. Tell students that these adverbs tell how an action is done, e.g.: *quickly, slowly, easily, loudly, efficiently.*

2. Form. Regular adverbs are formed by adding *-ly* to the adjective. Regular spelling rules apply:

Keep the final *-e* in an adjective that ends with a vowel and a consonant, e.g., *immediately.*
Drop the final *-e* in an adjective that ends with two consonants, e.g., *capably, responsibly.*
Keep the final *-l* in an adjective, e.g., *beautifully.*
Change the final *-y* to *i*, e.g., *happily.*

Give practice in forming the adverbs of manner. Write some sentences on the board and ask students to redo them with adverbs and the verb in parentheses, e.g.:

Linda is an efficient reporter. (work) She works efficiently.
Johnny has a loud voice. (talk) He talks loudly.
This is an easy job for Tom. (do) He does the job easily.
Minh's motorcycle is slow. (move) It moves slowly.
Pete is a responsible parent. (act) He acts responsibly.
Frank and Angela had a quiet conversation. (talk) They talked quietly.

Exercise 1. See Intro. p. ix, Look at the pictures.
incorrect Means *not correct, wrong.*
sloppy Refer to picture 2, and teach the opposite—*neat.*
impolite Means *not polite.* Refer to picture 1 and the example.

Answers: 2. The boy is dressed sloppily. 3. The man answered the question incorrectly. 4. The driver is driving/drives the car fast. 5. The turtle moves/is moving slowly.

Exercise 2. See Intro. p. ix, Complete the sentences/paragraph.
courageous Means *brave.*
guilty Here, means feeling like you've done something wrong.
investigation Means the process of investigating—finding out the cause of something.

Remind students that adjectives, not adverbs, are used after some verbs, e.g.: *be, feel, seem, become.*

Answers: 2. Awful 3. courageously 4. guilty 5. responsibly 6. safe 7. careful 8. hard 9. quickly 10. complete

Exercise 3. See Intro. p. ix, Ask and answer questions.
fluently Means without hesitating.

Additional ideas are *play tennis well, use chopsticks correctly, sing beautifully, learn Russian quickly, live cheaply.*

Practice B

Study Box. See Intro. p. viii.

Comparison of adverbs. Teach the formation of the comparative:

Adverbs with *-ly* form their comparative with the phrase *more . . . than,* e.g., *more neatly than.*

One-syllable adverbs form their comparative with *-er,* e.g.: *sooner than, faster than, harder than.*

There are also some irregular forms: *well–better than, badly–worse than, far–farther than.*

Point out that in informal speech and writing, we would say, *Michael writes more neatly than her.* In formal speech and writing, we would say, *He writes more neatly than she does.*

Exercise 1. See Intro. p. ix, Look at the pictures.
grammatically Means without making grammar mistakes.
accurately Means without making mistakes, almost perfectly.
creatively Means with new and interesting ideas.
**playground* An area for children to play in, usually on special equipment, e.g., slides, swings, sand box, seesaw.
**outer space* Means the region beyond the earth's atmosphere. Remind students about the Johnson Space Center.
**dreamt* Past tense of *dream.*
**planet* One of the nine major bodies circling the sun: *Mercury, Venus, Earth, Mars, Jupiter, Saturn, Uranus, Neptune* and *Pluto.*
**woods* Means *forest,* an area with trees.
**bush* A low tree.

Answers: Comparative forms: writes more grammatically than, works harder than, spells more accurately than, writes better than, writes more creatively than.

2 Review and Build

Read Frank and Angela's conversation and complete it. The adjective form is given. Change it to the adverb form when necessary.

FRANK: I feel *terrible* (1. terrible) about the fire, Angela.

ANGELA: How bad was the damage, Frank?

FRANK: ______ (2. awful). The fire department fought ______ (3. courageous) to save the building, but they couldn't. I don't know what to tell the museum board.

ANGELA: You shouldn't feel ______ (4. guilty). You acted ______ (5. responsible). You put the paintings in a ______ (6. safe) place.

FRANK: I know. But why wasn't I more ______ (7. careful)?

ANGELA: What did the insurance company say?

FRANK: They said they'll try ______ (8. hard) to send the money ______ (9. quick), but before they do, they have to make a ______ (10. complete) investigation.

3 Tell a classmate about something you wish you could do.

A: I wish I could *speak English fluently.* What about you?
B: I wish I could *type fast.*

B.

Michael writes **more neatly than** Cindy. He works **harder than** her.

1 Michael's teacher is comparing two homework papers. Look at the papers and use the words in the box to compare them like this:

A: Who writes more neatly?
B: Michael writes more neatly than Cindy.

write neatly	spell accurately
write grammatically	write better
work hard	write creatively

Rewrite this, Cindy!

My Sumer vacation
by Cindy Lewis
I done meny things on my vacation. I had a very good time. I am sorry that skool has started agin. I went to the playgraun. I went to the pull Pool.

1

My Visit to Outer Space — Excellent!
by Michael Gómez
Last night I had a fantastic dream. I dreamt I visited the planet of Saturn. The dream started when I was walking in the woods and I saw a spaceship. While I watched through the bushes, I saw some little people come out of the spaceship.

2

2 **Review and Build**

An editor from the Houston *Sun* wants to hire a reporter. Two of Angela's students from her night class have applied for the job. The editor is calling Angela to get references about them. Listen to their conversation and make notes about each student.

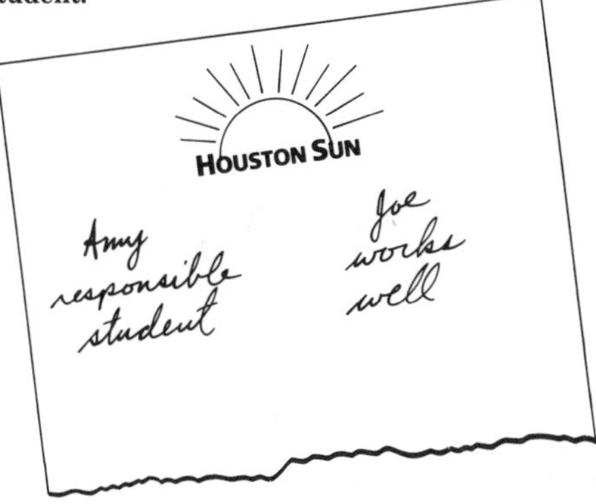

Now talk to a classmate and decide if the editor should hire Amy or Joe.

A: I think the editor should hire *Amy. She's more responsible* than *Joe.*
B: I agree. *Amy's a hard worker.*
OR Yes, but *Joe writes better.*
A: But . . .

C.

Ken didn't know **where to begin** his story. He didn't know **what to do.**

1 **Talk about each person's problem.**

1. A: What's the matter with Johnny?
   B: He doesn't know what to do now.

1

2

3

4

Exercise 2. See Intro. p. ix, Listening.
**regularly* Here, means that Amy doesn't miss classes.
unreliable Here, means that people can't depend on Joe.

Remind students that Angela teaches a journalism class at night.

Answers:

Amy	Joe
attends class regularly	unreliable
hard worker	hands in work late
hands in assignments on time	excellent writer
doesn't write creatively	interviews people well

Optional: Discuss as a whole class which set of characteristics are more important to an employer.

Practice C

Study Box. See Intro. p. viii.

Infinitive after question words. Point out that the infinitive after a question word has the meaning of *should, can* or *could.* The sentences in the Study Box mean *Ken didn't know where he should begin his story* and *He didn't know what he could/should do.*

Pronunciation point: Point out the intonation and the stress and reduction patterns:

Ken didn't know where to begin his story.

where to begin /wɛərṭəbɪgɪn/ what to do /wətədu/

Exercise 1. See Intro., p. ix, Look at the pictures.
Answers: 2. A: What's the matter with Angela? B: She doesn't know where to go. 3. A: What's the matter with Michael? B: He doesn't know who to ask. 4. A: What's the matter with Alice? B: She doesn't know how much to buy.

Optional: For additional practice, pairs of students read conversations like the following. Then, call on volunteers to make sentences with question words + infinitives.

A: Do you know when we should arrive at Sandra's party tonight?
B: No, I don't. Why don't we call her?
(They didn't know when to arrive at the party.)

A: What did you say when your boss told you about your promotion?
B: I was so surprised that at first I couldn't say anything.
(He/She didn't know what to say.)

A: I'd like to buy Jim a shirt for his birthday, but I don't know his size.
B: I think he wears a size 38.
(He didn't know what size to buy.)

Exercise 2. See Intro. p. ix, Listening.
**I've got that.* Means *I understand that.*
**righthand* Means *on the right side.*

Answers: 1. right 2. right 3. wrong 4. right
They're talking about (2) the washing machine.

Exercise 3. See Intro. p. ix, Ask and answer questions.
sister-in-law Means *brother's wife* or *husband's sister.*
ingredients Foods and spices used in a recipe.
complain Here, means tell what's wrong.
sink (n) Where you wash your hands and face in the bathroom or do the dishes in the kitchen. Use a magazine picture or make a simple drawing.

Additional ideas are *What/say to my boss when I quit. How/write a thank you note. Where/go on vacation. How much detergent/put in this washing machine. What/do next weekend. How many kids/ask to my daughter's birthday party.*

Encourage students to extend their conversations by talking about the suggestions.

Practice D

Study Box. See Intro. p. viii.

Review the meanings of *must, mustn't* and *don't have to* and give additional examples. Ask students to list regulations on their jobs, e.g.: *We must come to work on time, and we mustn't smoke in the office. But we don't have to work overtime if it's not convenient.*

Pronunciation point: Point out the reduction in:
must find /məsfaɪnd/ mustn't get /məsəngɛt/
doesn't have to see /dəzənhæftəsi/
Also note the /f/ in /hæftə/.

Point out the stress and intonation in:

Ken mustn't get involved.

Ken doesn't have to see Officer Brady again.

Exercise 1. See Intro. p. ix, Listening.
Answers: 2. A: What did she say about staying in bed? B: She said he doesn't have to stay in bed. 3. A: What did the doctor say about going back to work? B: She said he mustn't go back to work yet. 4. A: What did she say about going back for a checkup? B: She said he must come back in a week for a checkup. 5. A: What did the doctor say about making another appointment? B: She said he doesn't have to make one.

Optional: On the board, write a number of situations that might apply in your school. Ask volunteers to make sentences with *must, mustn't* and *don't have to.*

2 Michael Gómez is having a problem. He's asking a woman for advice. Listen to their conversation. Then read the sentences below and decide if they are right or wrong.

1. The woman knows how to use the machine.
2. Michael knows how much money to put in the machine.
3. Michael knows where to put the money.
4. Michael knows what to do after he puts the money in the machine.

Now listen to the conversation again and choose the machine that Michael and the woman are talking about.

1

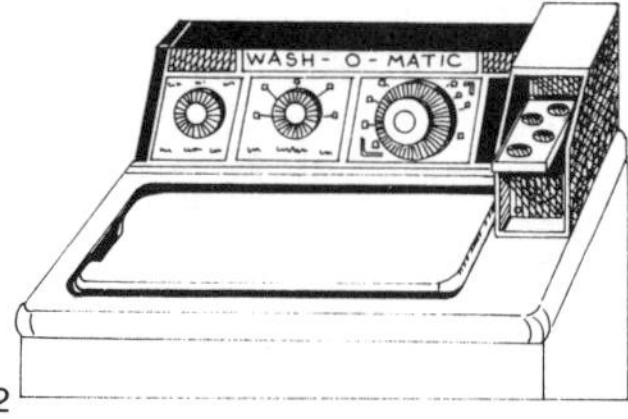

2

3

3 Ask a classmate for advice about a problem.

A: I have a problem. I don't know *what to buy my sister-in-law for her birthday.*
B: How about *a record? Everyone likes music.*

You can use these ideas:

where / buy *Mexican ingredients*
how / find *a good doctor*
who / complain to about *my broken sink*

D.

The police **must find** the arsonist.		
Ken	**must not** **mustn't**	**get** involved.
	doesn't have to	**see** Officer Brady again.

Note: *You mustn't do that* means *You can't do that* (because it's wrong or bad). *You don't have to do that* means *You can do it if you want* (but it isn't necessary).

1 Review and Build

After speaking to Officer Brady, Ken went to see his doctor. Listen to their conversation and check the things that Ken *must* do, *mustn't* do and *doesn't have to* do.

	must	mustn't	doesn't have to
1. get a lot of rest	✓		
2. stay in bed			
3. go back to work			
4. go back for a checkup			
5. make another appointment			

Now talk about what the doctor told Ken.

1. A: What did the doctor tell Ken about getting rest?
B: She said he must get a lot of rest.

2 Michael is still at the laundromat. He's reading the washing instructions on the clothing labels. Look at each label. Say what you *must* or *don't have to* do.

1. You don't have to iron it.
   OR You must dry it on low.

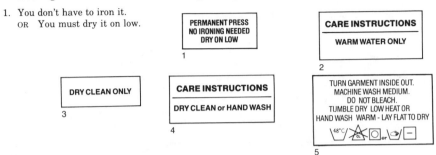

1
PERMANENT PRESS
NO IRONING NEEDED
DRY ON LOW

2
CARE INSTRUCTIONS
WARM WATER ONLY

3
DRY CLEAN ONLY

4
CARE INSTRUCTIONS
DRY CLEAN or HAND WASH

5
TURN GARMENT INSIDE OUT.
MACHINE WASH MEDIUM.
DO NOT BLEACH.
TUMBLE DRY LOW HEAT OR
HAND WASH WARM - LAY FLAT TO DRY

PUT IT ALL TOGETHER

Bill asked Linda to have coffee with him. Listen to the conversation and complete the statements.

1. Bill thanked Linda for coming
   a. alone.
   b. so fast.
   c. to interview him.
2. Bill told Linda he doesn't know
   a. what to do.
   b. who to talk to.
   c. when to leave.
3. Bill told Linda where to find
   a. another reporter.
   b. the man who spoke to him.
   c. a good restaurant.
4. Bill told Linda to go to the diner
   a. alone.
   b. with another reporter.
   c. with the police.
5. Bill says the diner isn't
   a. crowded.
   b. safe.
   c. famous.

Now look at these advertisements. Which one do you think is an ad for Rosie's Diner?

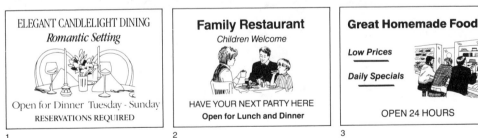

1
ELEGANT CANDLELIGHT DINING
Romantic Setting

Open for Dinner Tuesday - Sunday
RESERVATIONS REQUIRED

2
Family Restaurant
Children Welcome
HAVE YOUR NEXT PARTY HERE
Open for Lunch and Dinner

3
Great Homemade Food
Low Prices
Daily Specials

OPEN 24 HOURS

ON YOUR OWN

Think about some of the problems people had in this unit and discuss the following questions with your classmates.

1 When you first came to this country (or started this class), what were some things you didn't know how to do? How did you solve these problems?

2 What are some problems that a foreigner might have in your country? What advice would you give him or her?

Exercise 2. See Intro. p. x, Look at the document.
Elicit or tell students that these are labels found on the inside of clothing that tell you how you must wash and dry the clothing. If possible, show one on the inside of a sweater or jacket.

**permanent press* and **no ironing needed* Mime ironing. Materials made so that you don't have to iron them are called *permanent press.*
dry clean, hand wash and *machine wash* Methods of cleaning clothing. *Dry cleaning* is cleaning with chemicals rather than water. *Hand wash* means to wash the clothing yourself, e.g., in a sink, rather than in a washing machine. Refer to the picture on Student's Book p. 80 for *machine wash.*
medium (adj) Here refers to a water temperature that is not hot and not cold.
dry on low, tumble dry and *lay flat to dry* These are instructions for drying washed clothing. *Low* refers to the temperature. *Tumble dry* means to dry in a dryer (it lifts and drops the clothes). *Lay flat* means to spread on a flat surface. Teach the separable two-word verb *hang up* in this context.
**garment* Means a piece of clothing.
inside out Demonstrate with a sweater or jacket.

Answers: 2. You must wash it in warm water/mustn't wash it in cold or hot water. 3. You must dry clean it/mustn't wash it. 4. You don't have to dry clean/hand wash it. 5. You must turn it inside out. You don't have to hand wash it. You mustn't use bleach. You must dry it with low heat. You mustn't dry it with high heat. You don't have to lay it flat to dry. You mustn't hang it up to dry.

Put It All Together. See Intro. p. ix, Listening.

spoke Past tense of *speak.*
**candlelight dining* Means eating dinner by candlelight. Refer to the picture.
**reservations required* Means you must call the restaurant and tell when you are coming and with how many people.
homemade Means that the food is freshly made at the restaurant.

Answers: 1. b 2. a 3. b 4. b 5. b
The ad for Rosie's Diner is number 3.

On Your Own. See Intro. p. xi.

1. Use the Life Skills sections of the Student's Book for suggestions, e.g.: *talk about medical history or problems, take a telephone message, ask for directory assistance, shop in a supermarket, use food coupons.* Students can roleplay asking for and giving advice about these.

Reading

See Intro. p. xi.

Exercise 1.
Explain that *skimming* is a useful reading technique for getting specific information quickly. Point out the system of rating the quality and cost of a restaurant. Then ask students to complete the exercise. Ask volunteers for the answers and their reasons.

Answers: The reviewer likes Hamburger Haven better; she gave it four stars. The Szechuan Palace is more expensive; it has the $$ symbol, which means "moderate."

Exercise 2.
Students should try to guess new vocabulary from context. Words found in Ex. 4, which gives practice in this, are not defined here.
American Express, Visa, MasterCard and *Diner's Club* All refer to credit cards that are accepted by the restaurant.
self-service Means cafeteria-style; no waiters.

Exercise 3. See Intro. p. xi, Answer the questions.
Answers: 1. The decor leaves much to be desired. (She doesn't like it.) 2. The food is generally good. 3. Yes, they do. 4. Cash, American Express, Visa or MasterCard. 5. The customers serve themselves. 6. For lunch, Monday through Saturday. 7. Only with cash. 8. Szechuan Palace.

Optional: Bring in samples of other restaurant reviews for students to skim for information about credit cards, reservations and hours.

Reading

1 **Skimming. Look quickly at these two restaurant reviews. Which restaurant does the reviewer like better? How do you know? Which restaurant is more expensive?**

2 **Now read the reviews.**

The Houston Herald

Eating Out *by Cathy Wilson*

*	fair	$	inexpensive
**	good	$$	moderate
***	very good	$$$	expensive
****	excellent	$$$$	very expensive

Credit Cards: **Amex** American Express, **V** Visa, **MC** MasterCard, **DC** Diner's Club

♿ Accessible to the handicapped

SZECHUAN PALACE **

The Szechuan Palace is a new restaurant in downtown Houston which serves spicy Chinese cuisine. The food is generally good, but the decor leaves much to be desired. The room is very dark, and the tables are much too close together.

In spite of the lack of comfort, the Szechuan Palace is still worth a visit. I heartily recommend the chili-pepper chicken, the Szechuan green beans and the peas with crabmeat sauce.

Open for lunch and dinner Tuesday through Sunday. 3205 Montrose. Reservations necessary Friday and Saturday nights.
555–4892/$$/Amex·V·MC/♿

HAMBURGER HAVEN ****

Since it opened just six months ago, Hamburger Haven has become one of the most popular lunch spots in downtown Houston. Although it is self-service, it looks much more like a café than a typical fast-food eatery. The large number of plants creates a cheery atmosphere.

The food at Hamburger Haven is as good as the decor. They serve ten different types of hamburgers including Taco Burgers with jalapeño cheese, Pizza Burgers with mozzarella cheese and tomato sauce, and Alpine Burgers with swiss cheese and mushrooms. For those who are dieting, there is a well-stocked salad bar.

Open for lunch Monday through Saturday. 4309 Broad.
555–9216/$/No CC

3 **Comprehension. Answer these questions. If you don't understand a word in the reviews, try to guess its meaning without looking in the dictionary.**

1. What does the reviewer think of the decor at the Szechuan Palace?
2. How is the food at the Szechuan Palace?
3. Do they accept reservations at the Szechuan Palace?
4. How can you pay for your meal at the Szechuan Palace?
5. Who serves the meals at Hamburger Haven?
6. When is Hamburger Haven open?
7. How can you pay for your meal at Hamburger Haven?
8. Which restaurant has facilities for the handicapped?

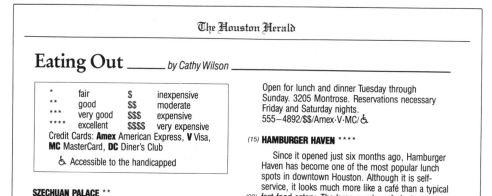

4 **Guessing the meaning from context. Match the words in column A with their definitions in column B.**

A	B
1. cuisine	a. usual
2. spicy	b. type of food
3. decor	c. restaurant
4. lack	d. to have a lot of
5. typical	e. the way a room looks
6. eatery	f. hot in flavor
7. to be well stocked	g. absence

5 **Discussion. What do you think? Discuss these questions with your classmates.**

1. The decor of a restaurant is very important to this reviewer. Is it important to you? Why?
2. Which of these restaurants would you rather eat in? Why?

Writing

Skill: Describing
Task: Writing a review

1 **You are going to write a review of a place you have eaten in recently. It can be a restaurant, a diner, the school cafeteria or someone's home.**

Think about the place and make notes about it as you answer these questions.

1. Is it big or small? Crowded or empty?
2. How is it decorated?
   a. Are there pictures on the walls?
   b. Are there flowers on the tables?
   c. What does the furniture look like?
3. What's the atmosphere like?
   a. Does it make you feel happy? Depressed?
   b. Is it warm and comfortable or cold and sterile?
   c. Is it noisy or quiet?
4. What kind of food do they serve there?
5. How is the food?
   a. What is the best dish?
   b. The worst?
6. Is it expensive?
7. What's the best thing about the place? The worst?

2 **Read the two restaurant reviews again. Then use your notes to write your review about the place you ate in.**

For pronunciation exercises for Unit 9, see page 115.

Exercise 4. See Intro. p. xii, Matching.
flavor (n) Here, means the way food tastes.
usual Means happening or seen most often, not unusual.

Answers: 1. b 2. f 3. e 4. g 5. a 6. c 7. d

Exercise 5. See Intro. p. xi, On Your Own.
1. Ask students to talk about restaurants they have eaten in that had a terrible decor but good food, or terrible food but a lovely decor. Which is preferable? How does the decor affect your enjoyment of the meal? They can also discuss what aspects of decor are important: Is it necessary to have a lot of room? Is the lighting important? The colors?

2. On what occasions might one restaurant be more appropriate than the other? With what friends would you enjoy one and not the other?

Writing

See Intro. p. xii.

Exercise 1.
Ask students to choose a restaurant or a home they would like to write about. They can think about the restaurants they talked about in Reading Ex. 5 to help them choose. Then, tell the class that writers often ask themselves questions as a way of deciding what to write. Writers take informal notes as they answer the questions and then organize those notes into their final piece of writing. Have students work individually to take notes in answer to the questions. As they do this, you can quickly check around the room to make sure students have chosen appropriate topics.

Exercise 2.
After students reread the two reviews, point out that each one starts out with a general statement about the restaurant and then describes the decor. The second paragraph of each describes the food and mentions specific dishes the reviewer noticed or liked. Suggest that their answers to question 7 might provide the overall impression students need to start their reviews. They can talk about food first and decor second or the other way around, but each paragraph should concentrate on one aspect of the review.

Optional: Students can write their reviews as letters to classmates recommending a local place to eat or describing an experience in someone's home.

For **Pronunciation** exercises for Unit 9, see p. 93.

UNIT 10

Language Summary

Functions

Asking for and giving information
Do you know what Thailand's most important export is? Sure. It's rice.
Expressing anger
I'm really upset that I didn't get a raise.
Expressing curiosity
I wonder where I'll be in ten years.
Giving advice
Take it easy. Maybe you should talk to your boss again.

Introduction

Vocabulary

eavesdrop	follow	snoop *v*

For recognition only
permission

Expression

Calm down.

Practice A

Structures

Should have **(advice)**
Linda should have called the police.
She shouldn't have gone to the diner alone.

Vocabulary

regret *n*

For recognition only

attention	confident	real *adj*
canvas	frame *n*	warning *adj*
carefully	original *n*	worthless

For recognition only—on cassette

hung *past part*	suddenly

Practice B

Structures

Embedded clauses
statements
I wonder where she is.
questions
Do you know what it means?

Vocabulary

almanac	population	turkey
atlas	rainfall	wonder *v*
average *adj*	repair shop	yearly
encyclopedia	residential *v*	yellow pages
export *v*	schedule *n*	
industry	thesaurus	

Expressions

For recognition only

Don't try anything funny.	out of town

Life Skills

Transportation
Making an airplane reservation
Asking and giving information about flights
Asking and giving directions
Understanding airport symbols
Understanding announcements

Vocabulary

baggage claim	escalator	newsstand
cancel	first-aid station	non-smoking (section)
cane	ground transportation	waiting area
currency exchange	information booth	
delay		

For recognition only

carrier (= airline)	gate	status
depart	round-trip	unassigned *adj*
flight monitor	smoking (section)	

For recognition only—on cassette

adjacent to	party (group of people)	seat belt
announcement	preboard	securely
assistance	proceed	take-off
extinguish	report *v*	
fasten		
page *v*		

Expressions

lost and found (department)

For recognition only—on cassette
smoking materials

On Your Own

Vocabulary

For recognition only
long-distance

Pronunciation

Pronunciation points

1. Distinguishing /y/ and /dʒ/
2. Understanding reduced *should've* and *shouldn't have*

Pronunciation exercises. *The pronunciation exercises for Unit 10 also appear in the Student's Book on p. 116.*

Part 1. *Distinguishing /y/ and /dʒ/*

Pete and Tom are talking about Linda again. Listen to their conversation and complete it.

See Intro. p. xiii, Recognizing and distinguishing sounds 2 and 3

PETE: Have ______(1) heard from Linda ______(2)?

TOM: ______(3). She called ______(4) a few minutes ago.

PETE: Where was she?

TOM: At some diner. I think that her ______(5) friend Bill was there too.

PETE: I don't like this. When's ______(6) coming back?

TOM: Not until ______(7) 18th. I hope Linda can stay out of trouble until then.

PETE: Yes. And I hope Bill can stay out of ______(8).

Answers: 1. you 2. yet 3. Yes 4. just 5. young 6. Angela 7. July 8. jail

Now listen again and repeat the conversation.

Part 2. *Understanding reduced* should've *and* shouldn't have

Listen and complete each conversation with *should've* or *shouldn't have.*

See Intro. p. xiii, Stress and intonation 3 and 4

1. A: What's the matter?
   B: I ______ watched that program.
2. A: What's wrong?
   B: I ______ bought that sweater.
3. A: What's the matter?
   B: We ______ gone on vacation.
4. A: Is something wrong?
   B: Yes. We ______ invited your sister to dinner.
5. A: Are you upset about something?
   B: Yes. You ______ told him about it.
6. A: What do *you* think?
   B: They ______ gotten married.

Answers: 1. should've 2. shouldn't have 3. should've 4. should've 5. shouldn't have 6. shouldn't have

Now listen again and repeat each conversation.

See p. 145 for the Pronunciation Tapescript.

Teaching Notes

Getting Started

1. Play a game to practice clauses with *when, before, after* and *as soon as.* Write sentence stems on the board and ask students to complete them individually with their own information. Then put students in groups of three. Students B and C try to guess what A does as soon as he or she, e.g., hears the telephone ring. They can guess several times to try to get an answer close to the truth. A reads his or her sentence, and the group goes on to the next player's sentence.

As soon as I hear the telephone ring, I . . .
After I get home in the evening, I . . .
Before I leave the house every morning, I . . .
When I want to remember something, I . . .

2. In pairs, students practice adverbs of manner. Distribute magazine pictures for cues and write adjectives on the board for students to transform into adverbs. Ask students to talk about the pictures, using adverbs, e.g.:

You can eat cheaply in that restaurant.
They play tennis very well.

Introduction

1. Introductory Conversation. See Intro. p. vii.

Preteaching

follow Linda plans to walk behind him and see where he goes.
Other new vocabulary is practiced in Ex. 3.

Preparation

Discuss the pictures. Ask: *Why's Linda wearing dark glasses and a scarf? Who do you think is coming up the stairs in picture 2?* Ask focus questions: *Where's Linda in picture 1?* (Rosie's Diner.) *Who sent Linda a threatening letter?* (Carol did.)

Exercise 2. See Intro. p. viii, Say *That's right . . .*
Answers: 1. That's wrong. 2. I don't know. 3. That's wrong. 4. That's right. 5. That's right.

Exercise 3. See Intro. p. viii, Find a word or phrase . . .
Answers: 1. snooping 2. wonder 3. What's up? 4. eavesdropping

Exercise 4. See Intro. p. viii, Warm Up.
Tell students they can also reassure someone who is upset before making a suggestion, e.g.: *Calm down. Things will work out./It'll be OK. Maybe you should . . .*

Develop Your Vocabulary. For calming someone down, add *Don't get so excited/worked up. Don't let it get you upset.* For making a suggestion, remind students of various expressions: *Why don't you . . ./You could always . . ./You might . . .*

Before starting the exercise, put some situations on the board. Elicit suggestions and other problems students want to talk about, e.g.:

My daughter failed her math test.
My friend didn't show up yesterday.
I couldn't find a birthday present for my boss.

UNIT 10 Snooping

1 Linda went to Rosie's Diner to find the man Bill told her about. Listen to the conversation.

1

LINDA: Tom, this is Linda. Is Angela there?
TOM: No, she isn't. She just left for the airport. What's up?
LINDA: Well, I'm at Rosie's Diner on Fulton. The guy Bill described is here. I'm going to follow him when he leaves. I just wanted someone to know.
TOM: You should let the police do . . .
LINDA: I've got to go—he's leaving. Bye!

2

CAROL: Do you know when Phil's coming?
LUKE: He said 4:00.
CAROL: Well, it's 4:15 now. I wonder where he is.
LUKE: Take it easy. He'll show up.

3

PHIL: Look who I found eavesdropping.
LINDA: Carol!
CAROL: Is she alone?
PHIL: Yeah, I think so.
CAROL: I sent you that letter to make you stop snooping. You should've listened, Linda.
LINDA: You . . . you started those fires. Why?
CAROL: I guess I can tell you now. You won't have a chance to tell anyone else.

2 Say *That's right, That's wrong* or *I don't know.*

1. Linda spoke to Angela.
2. Angela went to Dallas.
3. Linda told Tom where she was going.
4. Linda found the arsonists.
5. Carol isn't afraid of Linda.

3 Find a word or phrase in the conversation that means:

1. looking into someone's life without permission
2. want to know
3. What's happening?
4. listening secretly to a conversation

4 Warm Up

Pretend you are upset about something. A classmate will try to calm you down and make a suggestion.

A: I'm really upset *that I didn't get a raise.*
B: *Take it easy.* Maybe you should *talk to your boss again.*

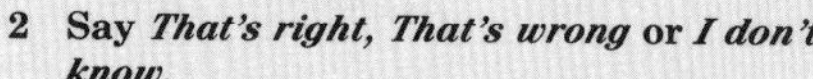

DEVELOP YOUR VOCABULARY

Calm down. Relax.
Don't be upset. . . .

Practice

A.

Linda	should have should've	called the police.
	shouldn't have gone to the diner alone.	

Note: *Should've* is pronounced "should of." *Shouldn't have* is pronounced "shouldn't of."

1 **Talk about what the people *should have* or *shouldn't have* done.**

1. Linda should've called the police.

1

2

3

4

5

6

7

8

Practice A

Study Box. See Intro. p. viii.

***Should have* (advice).** *Should have done* and *shouldn't have done* express the speaker's idea that an action in the past was a mistake, e.g.:

I feel sick. I should've eaten breakfast this morning. (I didn't eat breakfast.)
Ray spent a lot of money on clothes, and now he doesn't have enough to last the week. (Ray shouldn't have spent that money.)

Pronunciation point: Part 1 of the **Pronunciation** exercises can be used here to practice distinguishing between *should've* and *shouldn't have.*

Optional: Give additional practice. Call on volunteers to say what they should have or shouldn't have done, e.g.:

T: You didn't set your alarm clock, and you were late for work this morning.
S: I should've set my alarm clock.

Loni forgot to shop for food last weekend, and tonight there's nothing in the house for dinner.
We forgot to buy gas in the last town, and the tank is very low.
The student cheated on a test, and now he's in trouble.
We watched a terrible movie on TV last night and wasted three hours.
I didn't read the washing instructions before I washed that shirt, and now it's too small.
Martha loved Sal, but she didn't marry him. Now she's lonely.

Exercise 1. See Intro. p. ix, Look at the pictures.
If students don't recognize the characters, they can simply answer with *he* or *she.*

Answers may vary. 2. Cindy should've studied for her math test. 3. He shouldn't have parked there. 4. Michael should've read the instructions. 5. Tom should've come earlier. OR He should've called the theater first. 6. Johnny shouldn't have eaten that much cake. 7. Cathy should've brought her umbrella/raincoat. OR She shouldn't have forgotten her umbrella/raincoat. 8. Lan should've used a ladder. OR She should've been more careful.

Exercise 2. See Intro. p. ix, Listening.
Answer: Picture 2

Discuss the other pictures. The first shows what Tom thinks he should've done. The second shows what Pete thinks Tom should've done. The third shows what the two decide to do now.

Optional: Ask students what they think Tom should have done.

Exercise 3. See Intro. p. ix, Complete the sentences/paragraph.
Answers: 2. shouldn't have destroyed 3. should know 4. should examine OR should've examined 5. shouldn't have started 6. shouldn't be 7. shouldn't tell 8. should've listened 9. shouldn't have continued

Exercise 4. See Intro. p. ix, Ask and answer questions.
Additional ideas are *start school earlier/later, move to another city, buy a used car, learn English/to use a computer, gone to . . . on vacation last year.*

Encourage students to extend the conversation by asking questions, e.g.: *Why do you regret starting college now? Should you have worked a few years first? Why is that a good idea?*

Optional: Give situations like the following to pairs of students and ask them to discuss what the person should have and shouldn't have done:

1. Your friend borrowed a sweater that you really liked. He decided to wash it before he returned it because he got it quite dirty. The care instructions said to hand wash the sweater in cold water and then lay it flat to dry. But he decided to machine wash it in hot water because he wanted to get it really clean for you. He didn't read the instructions on the bottle of detergent and added too much detergent. The machine stopped, so he took the sweater out, rinsed it and hung it up to dry. He didn't bring it back himself or explain what happened. He mailed it to you, and his roommate told you the story. Your sweater is much too small, and the arms are very long. You are very angry.

2. Laura forgot to set her alarm yesterday. When she woke up, she saw she was quite late, so she just left the house and didn't call her boss. She decided to take her car instead of the train. However, there was a lot of traffic, and she became even later. When she got to the city, the parking lots were already full. She parked in front of a "No Parking" sign just to go in and tell her boss she was there. When she got back, there was a parking ticket on her car.

2 Tom is telling Pete about Linda's phone call. Listen to their conversation. Then choose the picture that shows what Pete thinks Tom should have done.

1

2

3

3 Review and Build

Carol is explaining her plan to Linda. Read their conversation and complete it with *should/shouldn't* or *should have/shouldn't have* and the correct form of the verb.

CAROL: You shouldn't have come (1. come) here, Linda.

LINDA: *You* ________ (2. destroy) those paintings. Why did you do it?

CAROL: Money. You're not rich. You ________ (3. know) how it feels to need money all the time.

LINDA: But how can you make money from paintings you burned?

CAROL: The paintings *weren't* burned.

LINDA: But the police found pieces of canvas and picture frames in the fire.

CAROL: They ________ (4. examine) them more carefully. The paintings that were burned were not the originals. They were worthless. We took the real ones out of the warehouse before we started the fire.

LINDA: And all those other fires?

CAROL: We didn't want this fire to get special attention. Maybe we ________ (5. start) so many, but it's too late now.

LINDA: Well, you sound very confident, but maybe you ________ (6. be). What are you going to do with me?

CAROL: Well, I ________ (7. tell) you this, but there's going to be another fire. This time in Warehouse 6. Unfortunately, someone's going to die this time. You ________ (8. listen) to my warning note. You ________ (9. continue) your investigation.

4 Ask a classmate to tell you about something he or she regrets.

A: What do you regret about your life?
B: I think I *should* have *become a police officer.* What about you?
A: Oh, I *shouldn't* have *gotten married so young.*
OR I don't really have any regrets.

B.

Where is she? When's he coming? What does it mean? How many people know? Is it true?	I wonder	where **she is.** when **he's coming.** what **it means.** how many **people know.** if **it's** true.

1 What is Carol Fullerton thinking? Begin with these words:

1. She wonders . . .

She wonders when Phil's coming.

2. She wants to know . . .
3. She doesn't understand . . .
4. She wants to know . . .
5. She wonders . . .

When's Phil coming? Where is he? Why is he late?
Is he in trouble? What does Linda really know?

Now say what Tom is thinking. Begin with these words:

6. He wonders . . .
7. He doesn't know . . .
8. He wants to know . . .
9. He doesn't understand . . .

Where's Linda now?
Is she still at Rosie's?
Is she in trouble?
Why does Linda always do things alone?

2 It's later. Look at Linda. What do you think she wonders? Complete her thoughts.

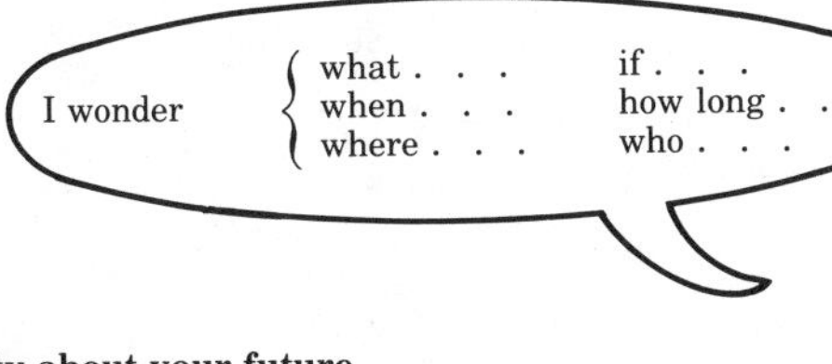

I wonder
what . . .
when . . .
where . . .
if . . .
how long . . .
who . . .

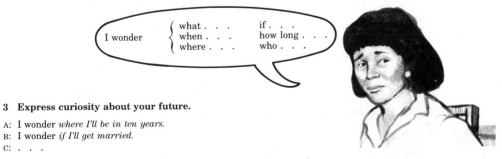

3 Express curiosity about your future.

A: I wonder *where I'll be in ten years.*
B: I wonder *if I'll get married.*
C: . . .

Practice B

Study Box. See Intro. p. viii.

Embedded clauses—statements.

1. Point out the change in word order when the question is embedded in a sentence:

Aux S V — S V

Where does he work? I don't know where he works.

2. Point out that for a *yes/no* question, the statement begins with *if* or *whether:*

Is Sandra absent today? I wonder if Sandra is absent today.

3. Point out that the question mark is not used when the question becomes part of a statement.

Optional: Give additional practice. Read questions like the following and ask students to make sentences with *I wonder* and *I don't know.*

T: Who is that man?
S: I wonder who that man is.
T: What time is it?
S: I don't know what time it is.

Where is your dictionary? How does this calculator work?
When does class begin? Why is your friend absent today?

Exercise 1. See Intro. p. ix, Make sentences.
Answers: 2. She wants to know where he is. 3. She doesn't undersand why he's late. 4. She wants to know if he's in trouble. 5. She wonders what Linda really knows.

Now say what Tom is thinking. . . .
Answers: 6. He wonders where Linda is now. 7. He doesn't know if she's still at Rosie's. 8. He wants to know whether she's in trouble. 9. He doesn't understand why Linda always does things alone.

Exercise 2. See Intro. p. ix, Make sentences.
If students still need help embedding, first elicit the questions themselves and write some on the board, e.g.:

What is Carol planning to do?
When are they going to start the fire?
Where is the fire going to be?
Is Tom looking for me?

Then call on volunteers to make sentences. Students can continue the exercise in pairs.

Exercise 3. See Intro. p. ix, Ask and answer questions.
Make suggestions and elicit others. Write them on the board, e.g.:

get my driver's license — stop smoking
find a bigger apartment — build my own computer
open my own business — cook Thanksgiving dinner

Study Box. See Intro. p. viii.

Embedded clauses—questions.

1. Point out the subject-verb word order for the questions embedded in another question:

Aux S V
What does it mean?

S V
Do you know what it means?

2. Tell students for questions with a modal and no question word, the embedded clause begins with *if* or *whether*, e.g.:

Will it rain tomorrow?	Do you know if it will rain tomorrow?
Should I take the bus or the train?	Do you know whether I should take the bus or the train?

Exercise 4. See Intro. p. ix, Ask and answer questions.

Bring in copies of these reference books:

thesaurus Lists words of the same, similar and opposite meaning.

encyclopedia A book or books containing articles on all branches of knowledge, usually arranged alphabetically by subject.

almanac A book published yearly that contains general information and statistics (e.g., population, rainfall, major exports).

atlas A book of maps.

yellow pages A telephone directory of business and services arranged alphabetically by type of business.

Answers: 2. Do you know what residential means? 3. . . . if turkeys can fly? 4. . . . what bus I can take to the library? 5. . . . if there are any good movies in town? 6. . . . what's on TV tonight? 7. . . . where Sri Lanka is? 8. . . . what another word for *agree* is? 9. . . . if there's a bicycle repair shop in town? 10. . . . what the weather is going to be like tomorrow?

Optional: Bring in copies of pages from various reference works and have students work in groups to make questions. The class plays a game: one group presents one of their questions; the other groups must decide which reference work to use and find the answer.

Exercise 5. See Intro. p. ix, Ask and answer questions.

population Means the number of people living in a certain place.

industry A type of business or manufacturing, e.g., the banking industry or the steel industry.

average (adj) Means a normal or typical amount. Show students how to calculate an average grade.

Exercise 6. See Intro. p. ix, Listening.

**try anything funny* Here, means try to trick them.

**out of town* Means went on a trip.

Answers: 2. I 3. should 4. say 5. you 6. are 7. you 8. haven't 9. called 10. Angela's 11. there 12. I 13. didn't 14. call 15. her 16. back 17. I'll 18. be 19. able 20. to

Do you know	what **it means?** why **they did** it? who **she is?** if **it's** here?

4 Ask a classmate one of the questions below. Begin with *Do you know* . . . ? If your classmate doesn't know the answer, he or she will tell you where to get the information.

Some places to find information:

dictionary	yellow pages
thesaurus	train schedule
encyclopedia	bus map
almanac	TV schedule
atlas	newspaper

1. What country exports the most rice?

A: Do you know *what country exports the most rice?*
B: I'm sorry, I don't know. Why don't you look *in an almanac?* OR *I think it's China.*

2. What does *residential* mean?
3. Can turkeys fly?
4. What bus can I take to the library?
5. Are there any good movies in town?
6. What's on TV tonight?
7. Where's Sri Lanka?
8. What's another word for *agree?*
9. Is there a bicycle repair shop in town?
10. What's the weather going to be like tomorrow?

5 Ask a classmate something about his or her country.

A: Do you know *what Thailand's most important export is?*
B: Sure. *It's rice.*
OR Sorry. I don't know.

Student A can use these ideas:

population	average income
major industries	yearly rainfall
major exports	

6 Linda has told the criminals that her friends at the *Herald* are going to be worried. Carol wants her to call and tell them she's fine. Listen to the conversation and complete it.

CAROL: Now you're going to call the *Herald.*

LINDA: But I have no idea what (1) ______ (2) ______ (3) ______ (4).

CAROL: I'm sure you'll think of something. They must wonder where ______ (5) ______ (6) and why ______ (7) ______ (8) ______ (9) them again. But you'd better not try to do anything funny.

LINDA: OK. *(She dials)* Hello. Mr. Tran? This is Linda Smith. Can you tell me if ______ (10) ______ (11)?

MINH: Angela's out of town for a week. Didn't you know that?

LINDA: Yes, I did. She must want to know why ______ (12) ______ (13) ______ (14) ______ (15) ______ (16) today. Please tell her that I'm not sure if ______ (17) ______ (18) ______ (19) ______ (20) meet her at 6:00 at El Fuego. My sister's sick, and I have to see her right away.

MINH: What's going on, Linda? Are you in . . .

LINDA: Thank you, Mr. Tran.

Life Skills

Transportation

1 **Angela flew to Chicago. A few weeks before, she called Northeastern Airlines to make a reservation. Listen to part of her conversation and complete it.**

AGENT: Northeastern.

ANGELA: Hello. I'd like to make (1) a round-trip _____ (2) on one of your flights from Houston to Chicago.

AGENT: OK. When would you like to _____ (3)?

ANGELA: On July _____ (4).

AGENT: And the _____ (5) flight?

ANGELA: July _____ (6).

AGENT: What _____ (7) of day would you like to leave?

ANGELA: In the _____ (8).

AGENT: Well, we have a _____ (9) flight and an _____ (10).

ANGELA: I'd prefer the _____ (11) one. And coming back on the 18th, I'd like a morning _____ (12) too.

AGENT: How about one leaving Chicago at _____ (13) A.M., arriving in Houston at _____ (14)?

ANGELA: That sounds fine. Can you tell me _____ (15) the fare _____ (16)?

AGENT: It's _____ (17) round trip.

ANGELA: I _____ (18) if I can make my seat reservation now too.

AGENT: Certainly. Do you _____ (19) smoking or non-smoking?

ANGELA: _____ (20).

AGENT: _____ (21) or aisle?

ANGELA: _____ (22), please.

AGENT: Please hold on while I check the computer.

Now look at these boarding passes and choose which one is Angela's.

	1	2	3	4
	Northeastern Airlines	Northeastern Airlines	Northeastern Airlines	Northeastern Airlines
NAME OF PASSENGER	Lentini/AMS	Lentini/AMS	Lentini/AMS	Lentini/AMS
FROM	Houston Tx	Houston Tx	Houston Tx	Houston Tx
TO	Chicago Il	Chicago Il	Chicago Il	Chicago Il
CARRIER	Northeastern	Northeastern	Northeastern	Northeastern
FLIGHT	400	400	400	400
DATE	11 July	11 July	11 July	11 July
TIME	930 A	1115 P	930 A	930 A
SEAT	Unassigned	5F	5F	5F

Life Skills

In this unit students will learn about making airline reservations and will practice asking and giving information about flights. They will also be introduced to symbols used in airport and other terminals and practice reading them to ask and give directions. In addition, they will practice listening to and understanding announcements.

Exercise 1. See Intro. p. ix, Listening.
**round-trip* A round-trip ticket is both for going to and coming from a place.
**smoking* The area of a plane or other place where people are permitted to smoke.
non-smoking The area where people may not smoke.
**carrier* Here, means *airline.*
**unassigned (adj)* Here, means no particular seat was reserved.

Go over the information on the *boarding pass,* the document that shows that the passenger has a ticket and is ready to *board* (get on) the plane. Point out the smoking and non-smoking symbols.

Answers: 2. reservation 3. leave 4. 11th 5. return 6. 18th 7. time 8. morning 9. 9:30 10. 11:15 11. earlier 12. flight 13. 10:00 14. 12:25 15. what 16. is 17. $229 18. wonder 19. want 20. Non-smoking 21. Window 22. Aisle

Now look at these boarding passes . . .
Answer: Boarding pass number 3 (9:30 departure, non-smoking, seat 5F)

Point out or elicit that (1) had an unassigned seat, (2) was for the wrong time and (4) was for the smoking section.

Optional: Students can roleplay a similar situation. You can suggest or pairs of students can decide on some travel plans. Students take turns as the agent and passenger.

Exercise 2. See Intro. p. x, Look at the document.
**flight monitor* Means a large screen that gives information about flights.
**status* Point out the information in this category.
**gate* Means the place to board the plane.
delayed (adj) Means the flight is not on time.
**cancelled (adj)* Means that because of bad weather or other reasons, that flight will not arrive.

Additional conversations:

PASSENGER: Can you tell me where to board the flight to Dallas?
AGENT: Yes. Flight 321 to Dallas is boarding at gate 5A.

PASSENGER: What time is the flight to Washington leaving?
AGENT: I'm sorry. That flight is delayed. Please watch the monitor for the new departure time.

Exercise 3. See Intro. p. xii, Matching.
Students should first try to infer the meaning from the symbols.

baggage claim Means the place to pick up suitcases after a flight.
first-aid station Means the place to receive medical care.
ground transportation Means buses, taxis and limos.
currency exchange Means the place to exchange foreign money.

Answers: 2. a 3. g 4. f 5. b 6. e 7. d 8. i 9. h

After students complete matching, ask them to find these places on the map on Student's Book p. 91.

2 When Angela got to the airport she looked at the flight monitor.

Northeastern Airlines

FLT	DEPARTING FOR	SCHED	STATUS	GATE
321	Dallas	7:30 a	On time	5A
604	San Francisco	8:15 a	On time	13B
110	New York	9:00 a	Now boarding	12A
400	Chicago	9:30 a	On time	11A
211	Washington	9:45 a	Delayed	21B
421	Detroit	10:21 a	Cancelled	7B
618	Miami	10:45 a	On time	18A
342	Toronto	11:30 a	On time	9B
701	Pittsburgh	12:00 p	Delayed	6B

Look at the monitor. Find out about the flights, like this:

YOU: Can you tell me what time the flight to Detroit leaves?
AGENT: I'm sorry, but it's been canceled.

Just for Fun

3 At the airport there are many symbols. Match the symbols in column A with the words in column B.

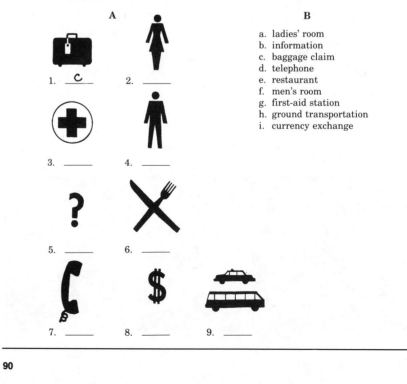

A

B

a. ladies' room
b. information
c. baggage claim
d. telephone
e. restaurant
f. men's room
g. first-aid station
h. ground transportation
i. currency exchange

4 Angela just asked someone for directions. Read the directions she was given. Then look at the map and decide where Angela wanted to go.

ANGELA: Excuse me. Can you tell me where __________ is?

CLERK: Yes. Go down this hall to the information booth. Turn left and walk to the telephones. The __________ is to the right of the phones.

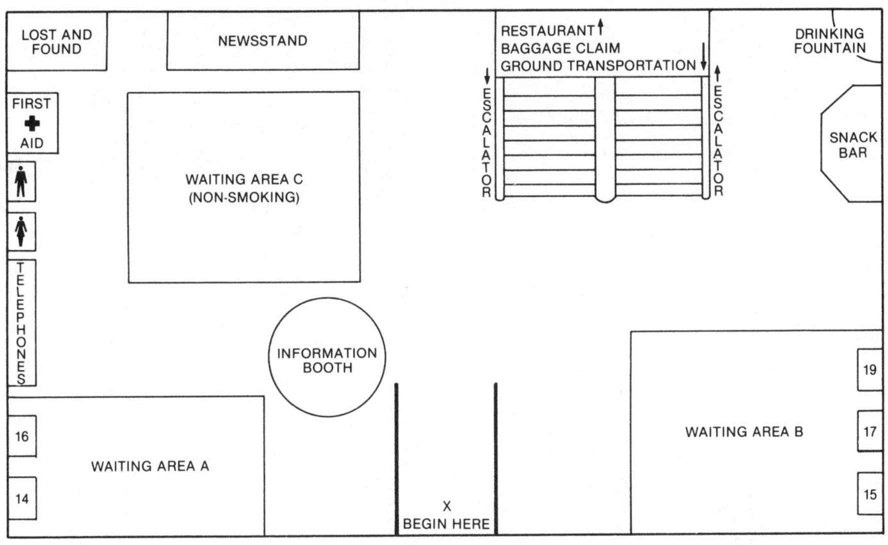

Now use the airport map and practice asking for and giving directions.

5 Listen to the announcements and choose the correct answers.

1. The passenger should
   a. call José López on the phone.
   b. board flight 24.
   c. go to the information booth near gate 24.
2. Angela can board now because
   a. her seat number is 5F.
   b. she uses a cane to walk.
   c. she is flying to Chicago.
3. James Walski
   a. is meeting someone at the airport.
   b. must go to the information booth.
   c. is going to a party.
4. A passenger with seat 35F should
   a. go to the information booth.
   b. board now.
   c. wait for another announcement.
5. This announcement was made
   a. in the airport terminal.
   b. in the airplane.
   c. in the airport restaurant.

ON YOUR OWN

Discuss these questions with your classmates.

1 How do you prefer to travel from one city to another (car, bus, train, boat, plane)?

2 What are some advantages and disadvantages of different types of long-distance transportation?

For pronunciation exercises for Unit 10, see page 116.

Exercise 4. See Intro. p. ix, Ask and answer questions.

escalator Means a moving staircase.

newsstand Means a place where newspapers, magazines and other small items are sold.

waiting area Means the area where passengers or friends wait for a flight.

Optional: Have students write directions as in the example and then work with a partner to practice giving directions.

Answer: Angela wanted to go to the ladies' room.

Exercise 5. See Intro. p. ix, Listening.

You may want to introduce vocabulary before each announcement.

1. **paging* Means *calling.*
   **report to* Here, means *go to.*
   **adjacent to* Means *next to.*
2. **preboard* Means board first, before the other passengers.
   **assistance* Means *help.*
   cane Draw one on the board. Remind students that Angela is slightly disabled.
3. **party* Here, means a group of people.
5. **take-off* Means at the time the plan lifts into the air.
   **seat belt* Mime fastening a seat belt.
   **securely* Here, means fasten it so it can't open.
   **extinguished* Means *put out.*
   **smoking materials* Cigarettes, cigars, pipes, matches.

Answers: 1. c 2. b 3. a 4. b 5. b

On Your Own. See Intro. p. xi.

1. Some factors to consider are the time available, the expense, how much you are carrying, how interested you are in the scenery. Ask students if they have ever taken a long trip by boat or train and if they enjoyed it. How was it different from traveling by plane?

2. Again, ask students about their own experiences. By car, travelers can choose their own routes and schedules. Buses are cheaper. All ground transportation gives the traveler more of a chance to see the countryside. Airplane travel enables you to visit a far-off place even on a short vacation or business trip, but jet lag can be a problem.

For **Pronunciation** exercises for Unit 10, see p. 103.

REVIEW 5

Exercise 1.
2. impolite 3. well 4. hard 5. fast 6. sloppy 7. terribly 8. careful 9. quickly 10. grammatically

Exercise 2.
2. grammatical 3. slowly 4. terrible 5. quickly 6. impolite 7. carefully 8. hard 9. well 10. fast

Exercise 3.
Answers will vary.

Exercise 4.
2. Cindy types faster than Michael. 3. Michael types more accurately than Cindy. 4. Michael types better than Cindy.

Exercise 5.
2. A ten-year-old speaks more grammatically than a two-year-old. 3. A bicycle moves more slowly than a motorcycle. 4. Adults act more responsibly than children. 5. Cats climb trees better than dogs.

Exercise 6.
2. I don't know how much I have to pay. 3. I don't know when I should leave. 4. I don't know who I should ask for information. 5. I don't know where I should wait.

REVIEW 5

1 Complete this chart with the correct adjectives or adverbs.

	Adjective	Adverb		Adjective	Adverb
1.	slow	*slowly*	6.	________	sloppily
2.	________	impolitely	7.	terrible	________
3.	good	________	8.	________	carefully
4.	hard	________	9.	quick	________
5.	________	fast	10.	grammatical	________

2 Complete these sentences with words from Exercise 1. Use a word only once.

1. I can't read this letter. Brad writes very *sloppily*.
2. *John walk* is not a ________ sentence.
3. Angela walks a little ________ because she hurt her leg.
4. There was a ________ storm last night, and one of the trees in our yard fell down.
6. You shouldn't be ________ to anyone.
5. Don't worry. I'll be done soon. I work very ____.
7. If you work ________, you won't make mistakes.
8. Linda works very ________. She even works on weekends.
9. Tom plays the piano ________. He's very talented.
10. The Bullet train is very ________. It travels about 130 miles per hour.

3 Write sentences about yourself using these adjectives and adverbs.

1. slow
2. fast
3. well
4. carefully
5. sloppy
6. hard

4 Michael is learning how to type in school. Look at the results of his typing test and of Cindy's typing test. Then compare Michael's and Cindy's typing. Use the words to the right and *than*.

Michael	Cindy
40 words per minute 2 mistakes	50 words per minute 10 mistakes

1. more slowly
Michael types more slowly than Cindy.
2. faster
3. more accurately
4. better

5 For each item, compare the two things or people. Use the verbs and adverbs in parentheses.

1. an airplane / a car (go fast)
An airplane goes faster than a car.
2. a two-year old / a ten-year old (speak grammatically)
3. a bicycle / a motorcycle (move slowly)
4. adults / children (act responsibly)
5. cats / dogs (climb trees well)

6 Lan Tran wants to take the train to Dallas. She has a lot of questions. Change her questions to statements using *I don't know* and an infinitive.

1. Which train should I take?
I don't know which train to take.
2. How much do I have to pay?
3. When should I leave?
4. Who should I ask for information?
5. Where should I wait?

7 Pete is talking to Michael. Complete their conversation with *must, mustn't* or *don't have to*.

MICHAEL: I don't have to (1) take this medicine, Dad, do I?

PETE: Yes. You ____ (2) take your medicine, or you won't get better.

MICHAEL: Well, can I go out?

PETE: No, the doctor said that you ____ (3) go out until tomorrow.

MICHAEL: Do I have to stay in bed?

PETE: No, you ____ (4) stay in bed, but you ____ (5) stay home and rest.

8 Read these situations. Then write two sentences about each one. Tell what the person *should have* and *shouldn't have* done.

1. Michael failed his English test.

He should've studied more.
He shouldn't have watched so much TV.

2. Brad bought an expensive car, and now he can't pay for it.
3. Pete's brother, Sam, married Paula because she was rich. Now Sam's very unhappy.
4. Cathy's sister, Miriam, left school when she was 16. Now she can't find a job.
5. Tom's wallet was stolen last night, and he had to walk home five miles because he didn't have bus fare.

9 Make sentences by combining the phrase and the question.

1. I wonder . . .
   How can I get to Chicago?

I wonder how I can get to Chicago.

2. Can you tell me . . .
   Where is the post office?
3. She doesn't know . . .
   Who is the prime minister of England?
4. Do you know . . .
   What time will he be back?
5. We would like to know . . .
   What are your plans?
6. Please tell her . . .
   When are you leaving?
7. I wonder . . .
   Is he American?
8. Would you let me know . . .
   How much does the gift cost?
9. I'm not sure . . .
   When is the class?
10. He needs to find out . . .
   Where does she live?

Just for Fun

10 Unscramble the letters to make words. Then match the words in column A with their opposites in column B.

	A			B	
1. d	woylls	slowly	a.	daylb	
2. ____	ipolte		b.	yopillsp	
3. ____	lewl		c.	sweor	
4. ____	ralyucfel		d.	saft	fast
5. ____	teebrt		e.	teimilop	

Exercise 7.

2. must 3. mustn't 4. don't have to 5. must

Exercise 8.

Answers will vary.

Exercise 9.

2. Can you tell me where the post office is? 3. She doesn't know who the Prime Minister of England is. 4. Do you know what time he'll be back? 5. We would like to know what your plans are. 6. Please tell her when you are leaving. 7. I wonder if he's an American. 8. Would you let me know how much the gift costs? 9. I'm not sure when the class is. 10. He needs to find out where she lives.

Exercise 10.

2. e, polite, impolite 3. a, well, badly 4. b, carefully, sloppily 5. c, better, worse

UNIT 11

Language Summary

Functions

Expressing disbelief
You're pulling my leg!
Reporting what someone said
Carol said her mother was sick.
Talking about likes and dislikes
What do you like about Toronto? I like the excitement.

Introduction

Vocabulary

joke *v*
secret
serious

For recognition only
unbelievable

Expressions

be in danger
first of all,
only child
out of town
Something's up.
You're joking!
You're pulling my leg!

Practice A

Structures

Reported speech—statements
She said her sister was sick.
He said he would buy a new car.

Vocabulary

especially
excitement
had *aux*
humid
hurry *v*
pick out

Expressions

all year round

For recognition only—on cassette
get away with it

Practice B

Structures

Reported speech
questions
He asked where she was.
He asked if I had met her.
commands
Carol told Phil to get the truck.
She told him not to use the front door.

Vocabulary

carry
crate
embarrassing *adj*
figure out
front door
religion
tie *v*
tight

Expression

I'd rather not say.

Reading

Skills

Predicting
Separating fact from opinion

Vocabulary

air
association
cancer
citizen
environment
government
group *n*
illegal
inhale
legislator
lobby *v*
lung
nonsmoker
numerous
prove
proven *past part*
representative *n*
right *n*
secondhand
smoke *v*
smoke-free
smoker
supporter

For recognition only
anti-smoking
bill (plan for a law)
fact
force *v*
grateful
hazard *n*
legislature
measure *n* (bill)
opposed *adj*
pass *v* (a bill)
proof
propose
reason *n*
scientific
support *n*
support *v*

Expressions

such as

For recognition only
be made law
there is no reason why . . .
take a risk

Writing

Skill

Stating an opinion

Task

Writing a letter

Vocabulary

For recognition only
statement

Pronunciation

Pronunciation points

1. Distinguishing /l/ and /r/
2. Distinguishing statements, questions and exclamations by intonation

Pronunciation exercises. *The pronunciation exercises for Unit 11 also appear in the Student's Book on p. 116.*

Part 1. *Distinguishing /l/ and /r/*

Listen and complete these sentences.

See Intro. p. xiii, Recognizing and distinguishing sounds 3 and 4

1. I got a _______ strange _______ from _______ .
2. _______ ? I don't _______ it.
3. _______ the _______ _______ away.
4. What _______ did she say?
5. She was going to go to a _______ .
6. She's _______ with _______ .

Answers: 1. very, call, Linda 2. Really, like 3. Call, police, right 4. else 5. restaurant 6. living, Angela

Now listen again and repeat the sentences.

Part 2. *Distinguishing statements, questions and exclamations by intonation*

Minh and Cathy are talking about Linda. Listen to their conversation and complete it by choosing the correct punctuation—an exclamation point (!) after the exclamations, a period (.) after the statements and a question mark (?) after the questions.

MINH: I got a really strange phone call (.) ? [1]

CATHY: Really . (?) [2] What was strange about it (?) ! [3]

MINH: Linda wanted to talk to Angela . (!) [4]

CATHY: You're kidding . (!) [5] What else did she say . (?) [6]

MINH: She said she had to take care of her sister (.) ? [7]

CATHY: Her sister . (!) [8] Linda's an only child (.) ? [9]

Answers: The answers are circled in the sentences above.

Now listen again and repeat the conversation.

See p. 146 for the Pronunciation Tapescript.

Teaching Notes

Getting Started

Students practice embedded questions, first individually, then in pairs or groups. Write sentence stems on the board:

I wonder/I want to know/I'd like to know/I don't understand

Students work individually to write out five or more things they would really like to know, e.g.:

I'd like to know how a laser works.

I wonder if there are people on Mars.

They then work with a partner or a group and share their questions. Groups can share the most interesting questions with the whole class.

Introduction

1. **Introductory Conversation.** See Intro. p. vii.

Preteaching

secret (adj) Means something other people don't know about.

Preparation

Elicit the storyline: *Linda was following the man who hit Bill. She was caught and now the arsonists are forcing her to call her office and tell her co-workers she is all right.* Ask focus questions: *Who did Linda ask to speak to?* (Angela.) *What reason did Linda give for not meeting Angela?* (Her sister was sick.)

Exercise 2. See Intro. p. viii, Give a reason.
Students' inferences may differ from those below. Accept any reasonable answer. 1. She asked if Angela was there. 2. She's been staying with her. 3. Something's wrong. OR She was trying to give Minh a secret message. 4. Linda's an only child, but she said her sister was sick.

Exercise 3. See Intro. p. viii, Find a word or phrase . . .
Answers: 1. You're kidding! 2. only child 3. out of town 4. Something's up.

Exercise 4. See Intro. p. viii, Warm Up.
**unbelievable* Means the listener can't believe it.
You're joking! and *You're pulling my leg!* Both mean *You're not serious.*

Ask students about some surprising events they've experienced and how their friends and family reacted when they heard the news. After discussing the new expressions, ask them for expressions of disbelief in their own language.

Pronunciation point: Parts 1 and 2 of the **Pronunciation** exercises are appropriate for this section of the Unit.

UNIT 11 Something's Up

1 Minh is talking to Cathy at the *Herald.* Listen to their conversation.

1

MINH: I got a very strange phone call from Linda just now.
CATHY: Really? What was strange about it?
MINH: Well, first of all, she asked me if Angela was here.
CATHY: You're kidding! She must know that Angela's out of town. After all, she's been staying with her!

2

MINH: I know. And then she kept calling me "Mr. Tran." Something's up, and I don't like how it sounds.
CATHY: I think you're right. She must be in danger.
MINH: I wonder if she was trying to give me a secret message.

3

CATHY: What else did she say?
MINH: She said she couldn't meet Angela at some restaurant . . . because her sister was sick.
CATHY: Her sister? Linda's an only child!
MINH: We've got to do something!
CATHY: You're right. We'd better call Officer Brady right away.

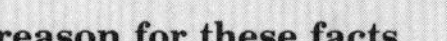

2 Give a reason for these facts.

1. Minh thinks Linda's phone call was strange.
2. Linda should know that Angela's out of town.
3. Linda called Minh "Mr. Tran."
4. Cathy wants to call Officer Brady.

3 Find a word or phrase in the conversation that means:

1. You're not serious.
2. without brothers or sisters
3. away from home
4. Something's wrong.

4 Warm Up

Tell a classmate something that sounds unbelievable. He or she will express disbelief.

A: *I just won $1,000,000 in the lottery.*
B: *You're kidding!*
A: *Yeah,* I'm just kidding.
OR *No,* I'm serious. *I really did.*

DEVELOP YOUR VOCABULARY

(Student B)
I don't believe it!
You're joking!
You're pulling my leg!
Oh, come on.
Are you serious?
. . .

Practice

A.

"My sister**'s** sick," she said.	She said her* sister **was** sick.
"We**'re** leaving soon," he said.	He said they* **were** leaving soon.
"I**'ve** left a note," she said.	She said she* **had** left a note.
"I**'ll** buy a new car," he said.	He said he* **would** buy a new car.
"I **can't** meet Angela," she said.	She said she* **couldn't** meet Angela.

*Note the pronoun changes.

she had = she'd
she would = she'd

1 Carol, Phil, Luke and Linda are talking. Listen to their conversations and complete them. Then report what each person said.

1. Carol said it was late. Phil said . . .

1

2

3

4

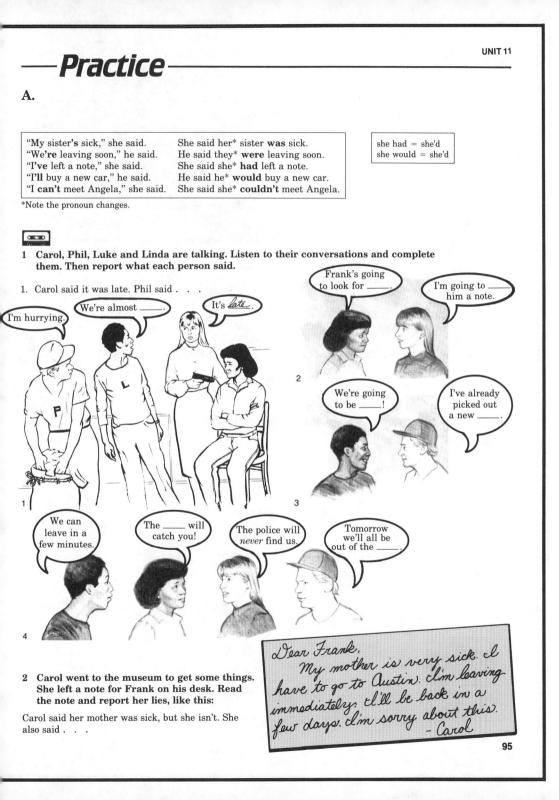

2 Carol went to the museum to get some things. She left a note for Frank on his desk. Read the note and report her lies, like this:

Carol said her mother was sick, but she isn't. She also said . . .

Dear Frank,
My mother is very sick. I have to go to Austin. I'm leaving immediately. I'll be back in a few days. I'm sorry about this.
- Carol

Practice A

Study Box. See Intro. p. viii.

Reported speech—statements.

1. Point out that the exact words of the speaker are put between quotation marks. Point out that *that* can be used before the embedded clause, e.g.:

She said that her sister was sick.
He said that they were leaving.

2. Explain that when the main verb of the sentence is in the past tense, the verb in the embedded clause will be in the past tense also. This is true in both spoken and written English even though the situation still exists in the present, e.g.:

"I **enjoy** working at the *Herald*," she said.
She said she **enjoyed** working at the *Herald*.

An exception is when you report something that was just said, e.g.:

A: What did Mom just say? I couldn't hear her.
B: She said she wants you to turn the TV down.

3. Remind students that the past tense of *will* is *would* and the past tense of *can* is *could*.

Exercise 1. See Intro. p. ix, Listening.
hurry (v) Means *rush;* move or work fast.
**get away with it* Means not be caught or punished.

Point out that when reporting, *tomorrow* becomes *the next day*.

Answers: 1. ready/Carol said it was late. Phil said he was hurrying. Luke said they were almost ready. 2. you, leave/Linda said Frank was going to look for Carol. Carol said she was going to leave him a note. 3. rich, car/Luke said they were going to be rich. Phil said he had already picked out a new car. 4. police, country/Luke said they could leave in a few minutes. Linda said the police would catch them. Carol said the police would never find them. Phil said the next day they would all be out of the country.

Exercise 2. See Intro. p. ix, Look at the pictures.
Tell students that they should report both the lie that Carol told and the truth. Note in the example, the truth—*but she isn't*—is outside the reported speech clause and remains in the present tense.

Answers: She said she had to go to Austin, but she doesn't OR but she's really leaving the country. She said she would be back in a few days, but she won't. She said she was sorry, but she's not.

Exercise 3. See Intro. p. ix, Listening.
Ex. 3 and 4 should be done in the same class session.

Answer: . . . he was interested in the job and he would call you in a few days.

Exercise 4. See Intro. p. ix, Listening.
Answers: I've just been speaking to she sounds just like the woman at the warehouse fire I'm positive that it's the same voice I'm sure she's involved with the fires

What important information did Ken . . .
Tell students to use their dictation to write the next part of the exercise.

Answers: 1. Ken said he has just been speaking to Frank Jordan's assistant, Carol Fullerton. 2. Ken told Brady she sounded just like the woman at the warehouse fire. 3. Ken said he was positive that it was the same voice. 4. Ken told Brady he was sure she was involved with the fires.

Optional: Put the sentences on the board and have students check their own work for correct pronouns and verb tenses.

Exercise 5. See Intro. p. x, Look at the document.
Give students some alternative for reporting statements:

informed Brad that . . . told interviewer that . . .
remarked that . . . complained that . . .
noted that . . .

Answers: 1. . . . that she really loved it. She told the interviewer that she especially liked the nightlife. Cindy said the only thing that she didn't like was the weather. She complained that it was too hot and humid. 2. Carlos Ramírez said he was from Baytown, a small town near Houston. He said he liked it because the people were friendly, but he complained that it was not very exciting, so he said he was thinking of moving to Houston. 3. Betsy Carson said she had lived in Houston all her life and she was going to live in Houston forever. She said she loved the weather because she could swim almost all year round. She noted that the people were the best she had ever met.

Optional: Have students write this exercise first and then read their reports.

3 While Carol was in Frank's office, she answered the telephone. Listen to the conversation and complete the message Carol left for Frank.

WHILE YOU WERE OUT

M ______

TELEPHONED		PLEASE CALL	
CALLED TO SEE YOU		WILL CALL AGAIN	

Message *He called to thank you for the flowers, and he said*

4 Dictation

Ken called Officer Brady to give him some important information. Listen to their conversation. Then listen again and complete it.

KEN: Officer Brady? This is Ken Wilson.
BRADY: Yes, Mr. Wilson. How can I help you?
KEN: Well, this may sound crazy, but . . .
BRADY: Yes?
KEN: Well, ______ Frank Jordan's assistant, Carol Fullerton, and . . .
BRADY: Yes, go on.
KEN: Well, ______.
BRADY: Are you sure?
KEN: Yes, ______.
BRADY: Do you know her?
KEN: No, but ______.

What important information did Ken give Officer Brady? Complete these statements.

1. Ken said ______.
2. Ken told Brady ______.
3. Ken said ______.
4. Ken told Brady ______.

5 While everyone else is busy, Brad is interviewing people on the street for the *Herald's* "What's Your Opinion?" column. Read the column and report what the people said, like this:

Cindy Baker said she had been living in Houston for the past ten years. She also said . . .

The Houston Herald

What's Your Opinion?

What do you like or dislike about Houston?

Carlos Ramírez
Well, I'm from Baytown, a small town near Houston. I like it because the people are friendly, but it's not very exciting, so I'm thinking of moving to Houston.

Cindy Baker
I've been living in Houston for the past ten years, and I really love it. I especially like the nightlife. The only thing I don't like is the weather. It's too hot and humid.

Betsy Carson
I've lived in Houston all my life, and I'm going to live in Houston forever. I love the weather because I can swim almost all year round. And the people are the best I've ever met.

6 Now ask some classmates how they feel about where they live. Take notes and then report their answers to the class.

A: What do you like about *Toronto?*
B: I like *the excitement.*
A: What do you dislike about *Toronto?*
B: . . .

A: *Maria* said *she* liked *the excitement in Toronto. She said* . . .

B.

He asked,	"Where is she?" "When is she leaving?" "Are you sure?" "Have you met her?" "Will you tell me her address?"	He asked	where **she was.** when **she was leaving.** if **I* was** sure. if **I* had met** her. if **I* would tell** him* her address.

*Note the pronoun changes.

1 Report the questions.

1. CATHY: Where's Linda?
   MINH: I don't know. Can you figure out her message?

Cathy asked where Linda was. Minh asked . . .

2. CATHY: Have you heard from Linda?
   BRAD: No. What's wrong?
3. TOM: What are we going to do?
   PETE: I don't know. Will the police be able to find her?

2 Officer Brady called Frank at home to ask him questions about Carol. Read their conversation.

BRADY: How long has Carol Fullerton worked for you?
FRANK: About six months.
BRADY: Is she from Houston?
FRANK: No, she isn't. She's from Austin.
BRADY: Have you seen her today?
FRANK: No, I haven't. Why do you ask?
BRADY: I called her home, and she wasn't there. Where is she?
FRANK: She's in Austin. Her mother's sick.
BRADY: Can I have her phone number there?
FRANK: I'm sorry. I don't have it.
BRADY: When will she be back?
FRANK: She said she'd be back in a few days.

Now Frank is talking on the phone to Angela. Continue their conversation by reporting the five other questions that Officer Brady asked.

FRANK: Officer Brady called and asked me a lot of questions about Carol.
ANGELA: Like what?
FRANK: He asked me how long she had worked for me.
ANGELA: What else did he ask?
FRANK: He asked . . .

Exercise 6. See Intro. p. ix, Ask and answer questions.
Students can work with these ideas: education/schools, transportation, shopping, job opportunities, climate, people, housing, cost of living.

Practice B

Study Box. See Intro. p. viii.

Reported speech—questions. Point out the word order in the reported question is the normal subject—verb sentence order. Point out that the tenses shift as they do for reported statements.

Give some additional ways to report questions:
wanted to know . . . wondered . . .

Optional: Write some simple conversations on the board. Two volunteers read them, and a third reports what was said, e.g.:

A: What time is it?
B: I don't know. I'm not wearing my watch.
C: A asked what time it was. B said she didn't know because she wasn't wearing her watch.

Exercise 1. See Intro. p. ix, Make sentences.
Have pairs of students read the conversation, as in the optional exercise above. Extend the exercise by asking students to write other short questions and answers that storyline characters might have said.

Answers: 1. . . . if she could figure out her message. 2. Cathy asked if Brad had heard from Linda. Brad asked what was wrong. 3. Tom asked what they were going to do. Pete asked if the police would be able to find her.

Exercise 2. See Intro. p. ix, Ask and answer questions.
Practice the first conversation with the whole class, and then have pairs of students read it together. Repeat this procedure for the second conversation, where Frank is reporting Brady's questions.

Answers: He asked if she was from Houston. He wanted to know if I had seen her today. He asked where she was. He asked if he could have her phone number in Austin. He asked when she would be back.

Exercise 3. See Intro. p. ix, Ask and answer questions.
embarrassing (adj) Means something that makes you feel uncomfortable. Here, a question that is too personal.
I'd rather not say. Means *I'd prefer not to tell you.*
religion Give some examples: *Catholic, Moslem, Hindu.*

Elicit and discuss any cultural differences about what questions are too personal. An American, for example, would probably not object to a question about religion but wouldn't want to answer one about money or age. Chinese often need to know the age of a new acquaintance in order to know whether to treat that person as an elder sibling or a younger sibling. Since barriers dissolve as friendships develop, point out some ways of broaching these subjects, e.g.: *Do you mind if I ask how old you are? Would it be all right to ask why you aren't married yet? You'd be such a good parent, I was wondering why you don't have children. Would you mind telling me how much you paid for your house?*

Study Box. See Intro. p. viii.

Reported speech—commands. Point out that the infinitive is used to report commands. Also note that *not* precedes the infinitive in negative commands.

Optional: Do a round robin drill. One student gives a simple command. The next student reports what was said and gives another, e.g.:

A: Open the door.
B: She said to open the door.
Don't turn on the TV.
C: He said not to turn on the TV.

Exercise 4. See Intro. p. ix. Make sentences.
tie . . . tight Refer to the picture.

Answers: Carol told Phil to get the truck. She also told him not to use the front door. Phil told Luke to carry the crate to the truck. He told Linda not to make any noise. Luke told Carol to help him get Linda into the crate. He told Phil to hurry and leave.

Optional: Ask students to talk about advice they gave or received in various circumstances, e.g.:

just starting school — starting to drive a car
moving to a new country or city — buying a house

Write situations on the board and elicit others. Students work in pairs or small groups and decide which topics to discuss.

Put It All Together. See Intro. p. ix, Listening.

Answers: 3. was 4. going 5. to 6. 6:00 7. strange 8. Spanish 9. look 10. up 11. means 12. f-u-e-g-o

3 Find out if your classmate has ever been asked an embarrassing question.

A: Has anyone ever asked you an embarrassing question?
B: Yes. One time *someone* asked me *how much money I made.*
A: What did you say?
B: I said *I'd rather not say.*

Student B can use these ideas:

What's your religion?	Why don't you have children?
How much do you weigh?	Why aren't you married?
How old are you?	. . .

Carol **told** Phil	**to get** the truck. **not to use** the front door.

4 Review and Build

Carol, Luke and Phil are almost ready to leave. Read the conversation and report the commands, like this:

Linda told Luke not to tie her hands too tight.

LINDA: Don't tie my hands too tight.
CAROL: Phil, go get the truck. Don't use the front door.
PHIL: Luke, carry the crate to the truck. Linda, don't make any noise.
LUKE: Carol, help me get her into the crate. Hurry and leave, Phil.

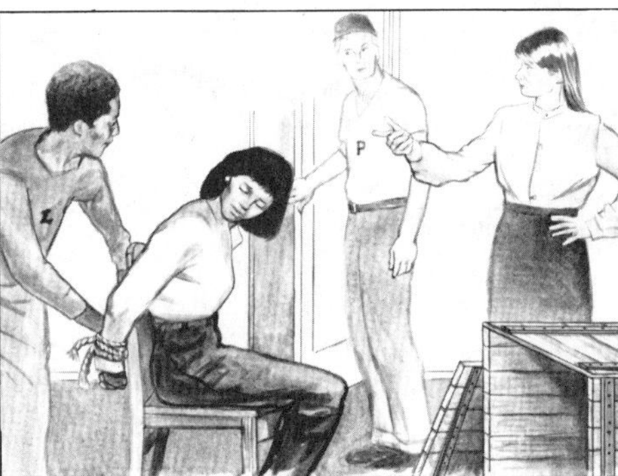

PUT IT ALL TOGETHER
Cathy and Minh are telling Officer Brady about Linda's strange telephone call. Listen and complete their conversation.

BRADY: This does sound strange. Go on. Tell me everything you can remember.
MINH: Well, Linda said she couldn't meet Angela at some restaurant because she had (1) to (2) see her sister.
CATHY: Didn't she also say what time she ____ (3) ____ (4) ____ (5) meet Angela and the name of the restaurant?
MINH: Yes. She said she was going to meet Angela at ____ (6). But I didn't really understand the name of the restaurant.
CATHY: Try to remember. This is important.
MINH: It was a ____ (7) name. Something like "fwaygo."
BRADY: That sounds like ____ (8).
CATHY: Yes, and I think Linda studied Spanish. Let's ____ (9) it ____ (10) in the dictionary.
BRADY: I don't know what it ____ (11), but I think it's spelled ____–____–____–____–____ (12). Here, I found it! Aha! I think I know what Linda meant. We'd better get going!
CATHY: OK. Let me leave a message for Pete and Tom.

Now look at the dictionary page and think about what Linda said. Why did Linda:

1. mention 6:00?
2. name the restaurant El Fuego?

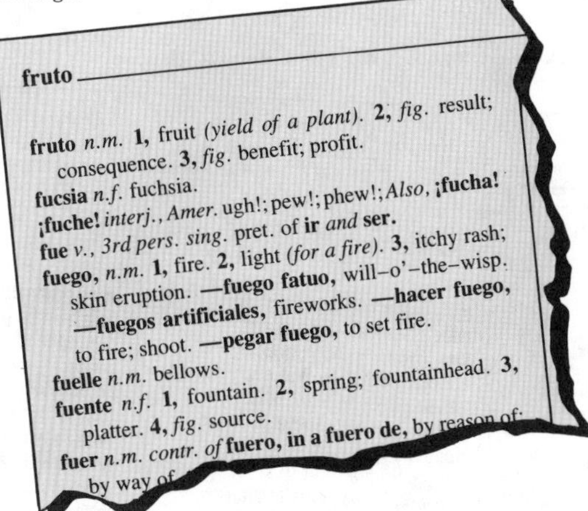

fruto

fruto *n.m.* **1,** fruit *(yield of a plant).* **2,** *fig.* result; consequence. **3,** *fig.* benefit; profit.
fucsia *n.f.* fuchsia.
¡fuche! *interj., Amer.* ugh!; pew!; phew!; *Also,* **¡fucha!**
fue *v., 3rd pers. sing.* pret. of **ir** *and* **ser.**
fuego, *n.m.* **1,** fire. **2,** light *(for a fire).* **3,** itchy rash; skin eruption. **—fuego fatuo,** will-o'-the-wisp. **—fuegos artificiales,** fireworks. **—hacer fuego,** to fire; shoot. **—pegar fuego,** to set fire.
fuelle *n.m.* bellows.
fuente *n.f.* **1,** fountain. **2,** spring; fountainhead. **3,** platter. **4,** *fig.* source.
fuer *n.m. contr. of* **fuero, in a fuero de,** by reason of; by way of

Complete Cathy's message for Pete and Tom. (The message is printed upside down below.)

Dear Pete and Tom,
We've gone to find Linda. Meet us at ________.
Cathy

Meet us at Warehouse 6.

ON YOUR OWN
Think of Brad's interview for the *Herald's* "What's Your Opinion?" column on page 96. Then discuss these questions with your classmates.

1 What do you like or dislike about the city or town you are now living in?

2 What did you like or dislike about the city or town you grew up in?

Now look at the dictionary page . . .
Have students work in pairs to discuss the questions and complete the message. Call on volunteers to answer questions 1 and 2.

Optional exercises for practicing reported speech:
1. Have students write letters to each other about things they are doing and thinking. Ask them to use statements, questions and commands in their letters. Students then get together in groups and report what was said, e.g.:

> I just got a letter from Felipe. He said he got an A in math last semester and was thinking about majoring in computer programming. He wanted to know how I was getting along with my boss. He told me to try to get to work on time more often.

2. Elicit some topics for impromptu speeches and put them on the board. Call on one volunteer to give the first one-minute speech on a topic of his or her choice. The class takes notes and then reports what the speaker said. Each speaker chooses the next student to speak.

On Your Own. See Intro. p. xi.

Remind students of their discussion for exercise A6 on Student's Book p. 97.

Reading

See Intro. p. xi.
Vocabulary for recognition only:
anti-smoking Tell students *anti-* means *against,* e.g., *anti-war.*
legislature The government body that makes new laws.
support (n and *v)* Here, means to agree with a new law; also, the actions people take to try to get a new law passed.
measure (n) Means a *bill* (see below).
oppose Means disagree with a new law.
hazard (n) Means *danger.*
scientific proof Means formal experiments or evidence.
There is no reason why . . . That is, nonsmokers should not have to . . .
forced Means have to do something one doesn't want to do.
pass Here, means make a bill into law by voting on it.
grateful Means *thankful.*

Vocabulary for active use:
bill Here, means a plan for a new law.
illegal Means against the law.
legislator A *law-maker.*
representative A *legislator.* This person is elected by citizens and represents (acts for) their interests.
numerous Means *many.*
lobbying groups Groups with special interests. Point out the examples in the text.
such as Means *for example.*
secondhand smoke Point out the definition that follows in the text.
inhale Means *breathe in.*
right (n) Something a person should be able to do, e.g., *the right to vote.*
environment Means the conditions around a person.
proven Past participle of *prove* (to show something is true).

Elicit what the class knows about proposing and passing a new law. Supply the new vocabulary as it is needed for the discussion:

> A representative proposes a new bill. The bill is discussed by the legislature. Lobbying groups try to influence legislators to vote a certain way, and some bills are also discussed in editorials. Finally, a vote is taken. If the bill passes, it becomes a new law.

Exercise 1.
Call on volunteers. Ask students what they saw in the text to help them predict.

Exercise 2. See Intro. p. xi, Answer the questions.
Answers: 1. It should be illegal to smoke in government offices. 2. Representatives and lobbying groups. 3. Secondhand smoke may cause cancer. People should have the right to a smoke-free environment. 4. People should have the right to smoke. No one has proven that secondhand smoke causes cancer. 5. The supporters of the anti-smoking bill. 6. Quit smoking or quit their jobs.

(continued on next page)

Reading

An editorial is a newspaper article in which the editor of the newspaper gives his or her opinion about important issues.

1 Predicting. Look quickly at this editorial. What issue does it discuss?

The Houston Herald

AN ANTI-SMOKING BILL

The state legislature is considering a bill that would make it illegal to smoke in government offices. The bill was proposed by state legislator Tom Ortega and has the support of the many other representatives, as well as of numerous lobbying groups such as the Citizens for Clean Air and the Lung Association. Those who support the measure say that secondhand smoke—smoke that you inhale while you are near a smoker—may cause lung cancer in nonsmokers. In addition, they say that everyone has the right to work in a smoke-free environment. Those opposed to the bill say that people have a right to smoke and no one has ever proven that secondhand smoke can cause cancer.

We agree with the bill's supporters. Smoking has been shown to be a health hazard. In our opinion, even if there is no scientific proof yet that secondhand smoke causes cancer, there is no reason why nonsmokers should be forced to take this risk. If the bill is passed, workers in government offices will have to either quit smoking at work or quit their jobs. We think that those who choose to quit smoking will be grateful for this bill. It may save their lives.

2 Comprehension. Now read the article and answer the questions.

1. What does the anti-smoking bill say?
2. Who supports the anti-smoking bill?
3. Why do the bill's supporters think the bill should be made law?
4. Why do some people believe that the bill should not be passed?
5. Who does the editor agree with?
6. If the bill passes, what will the government workers have to do?

3 Separating facts from opinion. Read these statements. According to the editorial, which ones are facts and which ones are opinions?

1. Tom Ortega supports the anti-smoking bill.
2. The anti-smoking bill would make smoking in government offices illegal.
3. The Citizens for Clean Air support the bill.
4. Secondhand smoke is dangerous.
5. People have a right to smoke.
6. If the bill is passed, smokers will not be able to smoke while they work in government offices.
7. The anti-smoking bill may save people's lives.

4 Discussion. What do you think? Discuss this question with your classmates.

Do you think smoking in public places should be illegal? Why or why not?

Writing

Skill: Stating an opinion
Task: Writing a letter

1 A newspaper editorial is usually written in this way:

1. statement of the problem
2. arguments on both sides of the problem
3. statement of the editor's opinion
4. reasons for the editor's opinion

Reread the editorial on page 100. Find sentences that are examples of each of the four parts above.

2 Look at the editorial again. Find the three phrases that introduce the editor's opinion.

1. We agree 2. 3.

3 Write a letter to the editor of a newspaper, either agreeing or disagreeing with the editorial on smoking. Before you write, list the reasons for your opinion. Try to use the phrases that you listed in Exercise 2, but remember to change the pronouns from *we* to *I* and from *our* to *my*.

Reasons:

For pronunciation exercises for Unit 11, see page 116.

Exercise 3. See Intro. p. xi, Answer the questions.
Point out that *facts* are clearly true or false. *Opinions* must be argued and evidence must be shown to convince the reader.

Answers: 1. fact 2. fact 3. fact 4. opinion 5. opinion 6. fact 7. opinion

Exercise 4. See Intro. p. xi, On Your Own.
After discussion, put reasons for students' opinions on the board.

Writing

See Intro. p. xii.
Have students bring editorial pages from local newspapers. Point out the Letters to the Editor sections. Mention this is a good way to share your opinions.

Exercise 1.
1. The state legislature is considering a bill . . . 2. *See Ex. 3 on Student's Book p. 100.* 3. We agree with the bill's supporters. 4. In our opinion, even if there is no proof . . ./We think that those who choose . . . *Also, see Ex. 3.*

Exercise 2.
Write these on the board as volunteers call out the answers.

Answers: 2. In our opinion 3. We think

Exercise 3.
Refer students to the reasons they developed in the discussion in Ex. 4 on Student's Book p. 100. Help them model their letters on those from the Letters to the Editor page. Students can work in pairs to develop their reasons and then draft their letters individually.

Optional: Choose an issue in your school, e.g.: *smoking in the cafeteria, a daycare center for students, student parking.* Have students write letters to the school newspaper on the issue.

For **Pronunciation** exercises for Unit 11, see p. 115.

UNIT 12

Language Summary

Functions

Agreeing and disagreeing
I don't think he ought to invite Johnny and Ellen Wilson. I agree./Oh, I think he ought to invite them.
Expressing opinions
I think think they ought to give Linda a medal.
Talking about past expectations
I thought this class was going to be very difficult.

Introduction

Vocabulary

ammunition
motive
press *n* (newspapers, magazines)
shoot
shootout
surrender
trio

For recognition only
bravery
charge *n* (for breaking the law)
collector
deadly
discover
drama
gun battle
gunfight
gunman
hideout
kidnap
let (= allow)
medal
ought to
priceless
question *v*
replace
rescue *v*
robber
store *v*
which *rel pron*

Expressions

run out of *trans*

For recognition only
attempted murder
group of
know nothing of
pay attention
take *her* prisoner
told of

Practice A

Structure

Future in the past—*was/were going to*
Carol was going to be a scientist.

Vocabulary
difficult

Practice B

Structures

Let* and *make
Did your parents let you stay up late when you were a child?
No, they made me go to bed before 8:00.

Expressions

stay up (= not go to sleep)
wear make-up

Practice C

Structure

Ought to
I think they ought to give Linda a medal.

Vocabulary

chief
medal
trophy

For recognition only—on cassette
award *n*

Expression

close to *adj*

Life Skills

Employment
Getting information about employee benefits
Getting information about company rules
Understanding paycheck deductions
Understanding a paycheck stub

Vocabulary

Blue Cross
Blue Shield
dental coverage
disability (insurance)
life insurance
major medical (health insurance)
punch in
uniform *n*

For recognition only

dues
earnings
federal
gross *adj* (= total)
net *adj*
pay period
percentage
union
regular
retain
take-home pay
though (= however)
times (= multiplied by)
total *adj*
unemployment compensation

On Your Own

Vocabulary

For recognition only
ability

Expression

For recognition only
length of time

Pronunciation

Pronunciation points

1. Distinguishing blends with /l/ and /r/
2. Practicing reduced *going to*
3. Understanding reduced *going to, want to* and *ought to*

Pronunciation exercises. *The pronunciation exercises for Unit 12 also appear in the Student's Book on p. 116.*

Part 1. *Distinguishing blends with /l/ and /r/*

Listen and complete these sentences.

See Intro. p. xiii, Recognizing and distinguishing sounds 2 and 3

1. They ________ the ________ on the ________ .
2. The ________ was very ________ .
3. The ________ had a ________ ________ .
4. They were going to ________ to ________ .
5. Now Linda can take a ________ .

Answers: 1. placed, crate, truck 2. prisoner, frightened 3. trio, dramatic, plan 4. fly, Brazil 5. break

Now listen again and repeat the sentences.

Part 2. *Practicing reduced* going to

Listen and repeat these sentences.

See Intro. p. xiii, Stress and intonation 2 and 4

1. Carol was going to be a scientist.
2. She was going to be rich and famous.
3. She was going to travel a lot.
4. She was going to sell the stolen paintings.

Part 3. *Understanding reduced* going to, want to *and* ought to

Frank and Angela are talking about Carol. Listen to their conversation and complete it.

See Intro. p. xiii, Stress and intonation 3 and 4

FRANK: I can't believe Carol ________ (1) kill Linda.

ANGELA: Well, it's true. The police ________ (2) put her in jail for a long time.

FRANK: I'm ________ (3) go see her. I ________ (4) know why she did this.

ANGELA: She really ________ (5) give you a full explanation.

Answers: 1. was going to 2. are going to 3. going to 4. want to 5. ought to

Now listen again and repeat the conversation.

See p. 147 for the Pronunciation Tapescript.

Teaching Notes

Getting Started

Use Unit 11, Ex. A6 on Student's Book p. 97. Students work with a new partner and talk about how they feel about where they live. They can then form small groups and report what their partners said.

Introduction

1. Newspaper Article. See Intro. p. xi, Reading.

Preteaching

New vocabulary not dealt with in Ex. 3:
shoot Means fire a gun. Refer to the context—a gun battle began.
ammunition Means bullets for the gun.

Vocabulary for recognition only:
**drama* Here, means an exciting situation.
**take someone prisoner* Means keep someone against his or her will.
**charges (n)* Means the crimes the police said they committed.
**kidnap* Means take someone prisoner.
**attempted murder* Point out that *attempt* means *try.*
**priceless* Here, means the pictures are so valuable that they cannot be bought.
**store (v)* Means keep some place.
**replace* Refer to the context—they put worthless paintings in place of the priceless paintings.
**pay special attention to* Means *notice.*
**collector* Someone who collects valuable objects such as coins or paintings.
**knew nothing* Means *didn't know anything.*
**deadly plans* Means plans to do something that would cause a death.
**ought to* Means *should.*
**medal* Mime pinning a medal on someone.
**bravery* Means *courage.*

Preparation

Ask students where in the newspaper this article appears. (On the front page.) Ask a focus question: *Why did the arsonists set the fires?* (Their motive was robbery. They didn't want the police to pay special attention to the Warehouse 5 fire.)

Exercise 2. See Intro. p. xii , Put these steps in the right order.
Answers: a. 7 b. 4 c. 2 d. 6 e. 1 f. 8 g. 3 h. 5

Exercise 3. See Intro. p. viii, Find a word or phrase . . .
Answers: 1. surrender 2. shootout OR gun battle 3. trio 4. press 5. motive

UNIT 12 Caught!

1 Listen to this article from the *Herald*.

The Houston Herald

Arsonists Arrested, Reporter Rescued

HOUSTON—After a dramatic shootout last night, Houston police arrested two men and a woman who they believe are responsible for five warehouse fires in the Houston area.

The drama began when the police received information that the three were planning to burn down Warehouse 6 on Palmer Road. When the police arrived at the scene, they found the trio removing a large crate from a truck. When the police tried to question them, the two men started shooting and a ten-minute gun battle began. It ended when the gunmen ran out of ammunition and the police made them surrender. No one was hurt, but when the police opened the crate, they found *Herald* reporter Linda Smith inside. The arsonists took Ms. Smith prisoner after she discovered their apartment hideout. Arrested on charges of arson, robbery, kidnapping and attempted murder were Carol Fullerton, 28, Luke Davis, 35, and Phil Watts, 32, all of Houston.

According to police detective George Brady, the arsonists' motive was robbery. Before they set fire to Warehouse 5 last week, they stole a group of priceless paintings which the Houston Art Museum was storing there. The robbers then replaced the valuable art with worthless paintings and burned down the warehouse so that no one would discover the robbery. All the other fires were started so that the police would not pay special attention to the fire in Warehouse 5 where the art was originally.

The arsonists say that they were hired by wealthy art collector Evans Collier, who was going to buy the paintings from them. Mr. Collier's lawyer would not let him speak to the press. His lawyer said, however, that Mr. Collier knew nothing of the arsonists or their plans.

Herald reporter, Tom Kirby, who was present at the scene, said that Ms. Smith had called the newspaper with a secret message that told of the arsonists' deadly plans. Part of that message was in Spanish. "Linda always thought her Spanish was bad. She didn't know that one day it was going to help save her life."

Officer Brady also said, "Ms. Smith was very helpful to the police. She ought to get a medal for bravery."

2 Put these events in order.

a. ___ The police found Linda.
b. ___ Luke and Phil started to shoot.
c. ___ The police arrived at Warehouse 6.
d. ___ The police arrested Luke, Phil and Carol.
e. _1_ The arsonists arrived at Warehouse 6.
f. ___ The arsonists told the police about Evans Collier.
g. ___ The police tried to talk to the arsonists.
h. ___ Luke and Phil ran out of ammunition.

3 Find a word or phrase in the article that means:

1. give up
2. a gunfight
3. three people
4. newspaper reporters
5. a reason for doing something

Practice

A.

Carol **was going to be** a scientist, but that never happened.

1 Carol is thinking about her life. Look at the pictures and say what she thought her life was going to be like.

1. Carol was going to be a scientist.

1

2

3

4

5

2 Talk about what you thought your English class was going to be like before it began.

A: I thought the class was going to be *very difficult.*
B: I thought I was going to *have a lot of problems understanding the teacher.*

3 Review and Build

Can you remember the story? Did these people do these things? Make statements using *was/were going to* or the past tense. Do not use any negatives.

1. Carol / sell the paintings
Carol was going to sell the paintings, but she didn't.
2. Carol / steal the paintings
Carol stole the paintings.
3. Luke, Phil and Carol / kill Linda
4. Linda / find the arsonists
5. Phil / buy a new car
6. Luke / put Linda in a crate
7. Carol, Phil and Luke / leave the U.S.
8. An art collector / buy the paintings
9. Officer Brady and Cathy / rescue Linda
10. Luke, Phil and Carol / burn down Warehouse 5

Practice A

Study Box. See Intro. p. viii.

Future in the past—*was/were going to.*
1. Use. *Was going to be* expresses that plans the speaker had did not work out. It is also used with expressions like *I thought . . .* or *I had no idea . . .* to express what the speaker thought would happen but didn't.

2. Form. Remind students that the base form of the verb is used after *going to.* Give examples of the expression with plural subjects: *They were going to study medicine, but the tuition was too high.* Give examples of questions: *Who was going to go with them? What were you going to do after the movies? Were they going to drive?*

Pronunciation point: Note the reduction: /wəzgənə/. Part 2 of the **Pronunciation** exercises can be used here.

Optional: Give additional practice:
1. Write some professions on the board, e.g., *firefighter, pilot, astronaut.* Students talk about what they were going to be:

A: What did you want to be when you were little?
B: When I was five, I thought I was going to be an astronaut.

2. Read some situations like the following to the class. Ask volunteers to make statements with *was going to.*
a. Sula planned to get up early to study for her French test. She didn't hear her alarm clock, however, so she didn't get a chance to review. (Sula was going to get up early and study, but she didn't hear her alarm clock.)

b. Luis and Felipe wanted to play baseball Saturday afternoon. However, it rained, and they went to the movies instead.

Exercise 1. See Intro. p. ix, Look at the pictures.
Answers: 2. She was going to live in the country/in a big house. 3. She was going to discover a new vaccine. 4. She was going to get married and have two children. 5. She was going to travel.

Exercise 2. See Intro. p. ix, Ask and answer questions.
difficult Means *hard, not easy.*

Exercise 3. See Intro. p. ix, Make sentences.
Answers: Accept any reasonable statement for the clause after *was going to.* 3. Luke, Phil and Carol were going to kill Linda. 4. Linda found the arsonists 5. Phil was going to buy a new car, but he couldn't. 6. Luke put Linda in a crate. 7. Carol, Phil and Luke were going to leave the U.S., but the police found them first. 8. An art collector was going to buy the paintings, (but they were returned to the museum). 9. Officer Brady and Cathy rescued Linda. 10. Luke, Phil and Carol burned down Warehouse 5.

Practice B

Study Box. See Intro. p. viii.

***Let* and *make*.**

1. Meaning. *Let* means *permit. Make* suggests that there is no choice. To illustrate the difference, write statements on the board:

> Mr. Acoste said, "You must learn these verbs tonight. There will be a test tomorrow." Mrs. Yuan told her class, "You may use your books for the test."

Tell the class that Mr. Acoste made his students memorize the verbs. Mrs. Yuan let her students use their books.

2. Form. Point out the word order:

	Let/Make	Object	Action
Angela	let	Linda	stay with her.

Note that the base form of the verb is used after *let* or *make.* Give examples of different tenses and subjects: *This school lets students park in the school parking lot, but it makes them pay a fee for parking every semester. Last year they only let the faculty use the parking lot, but registration went down.*

Pronunciation point: Note the reduction with pronouns: /lɛmi/ /lɛṭɪm/ /lɛṭər//lɛṭəm/

Optional: Give additional practice. Write sentences on the board and have students make statements with *let* or *make.*

> Maira told her friend Victor he could use her camera. (She let him use her camera.)
>
> "You have to clean your room before you go out today," Mr. Wing told his son. (He made him clean his room.)

Exercise 1. See Intro. p. ix, Look at the pictures.
Answers: 2. They let her drink a glass of water. 3. They made her call her office. 4. They let her eat some bread. 5. They made her get into a crate.

Exercise 2. See Intro. p. ix, Listening.
Answers: 2. made 3. didn't let 4. let 5. didn't let 6. let 7. made 8. didn't let

B.

> Angela **let** Linda **stay** with her.
> Linda **didn't let** the anonymous letter **frighten** her.
> Carol **made** Linda **sit** in a chair.

1 Tell what the criminals *let* and *made* Linda do.

1. They made her sit in a chair.

1

2

3

4

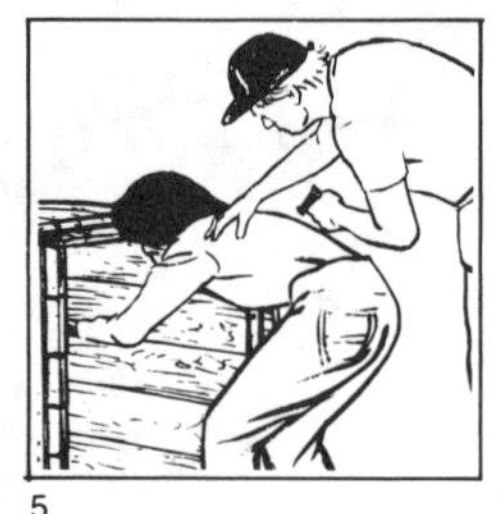
5

2 Listen to the conversation Pete and Michael had yesterday. Then look at the list and decide if Pete *let, didn't let* or *made* Michael do the following things.

	Let	Didn't let	Made
1. go out and play	✓		
2. call his grandmother			
3. drink a glass of soda			
4. drink a glass of chocolate milk			
5. have cookies			
6. invite a friend to dinner			
7. do his homework before dinner			
8. do his homework with a friend			

Now ask and answer questions like this about Pete and Michael.

A: Did Michael want to go out and play?
B: Yes, and Pete let him.

A: Did Michael want to call his grandmother?
B: No, but Pete made him.

3 Talk about your childhood.

A: Did your *parents let* you *stay up late* when you were a child?
B: Yes, *they* did.
OR No, *they made* me *go to bed before 8:00.*

Student A can use these ideas:

study a lot	wear make-up
clean the house	eat food you didn't like
stay home alone	go on dates
go to the movies with your friends	take care of your brothers and sisters

C.

They **ought to give** Linda a medal.

Note: *Ought to* means *should.* It is not usually used in questions or negative statements.

1 Some of the *Herald* staff is talking about Linda. Listen to the conversation and choose the things they say they ought to do for her.

1. buy her a present
2. take her out to dinner
3. have a party for her
4. give her a trophy
5. give her a raise

2 Pete is planning a surprise party for Linda. He can only invite ten people in addition to Linda, Michael and himself.

Look at this list of possible guests. Who do you think he ought to invite? Who don't you think he ought to invite? Why?

A: I don't think he ought to invite *Johnny and Ellen Wilson. They're too young.*
B: I agree.
OR Oh, I think he ought to invite *them. Linda seems close to Cathy and her kids.*

Angela Lentini	Cathy Wilson
Frank Jordan	Ken Wilson
Suzanne	Steve Wilson
Alice Thomas	Ellen Wilson
Bill Thomas	Johnny Wilson
Officer Brady	Tom Kirby
Brad Kimball	Chief of the Fire Department
Minh Tran	
Lan Tran	

3 What do you think ought to happen to these people in the story?

1. A: I think they ought to give Linda a medal.
 B: I think she ought to . . .

1

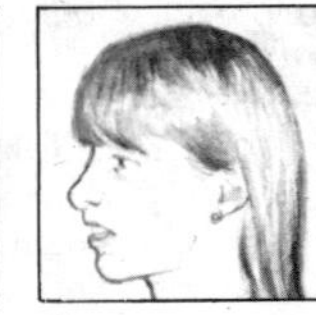
2

3

4

5

6

7

Exercise 3. See Intro. p. ix, Ask and answer questions.
stay up Means not go to bed.
make-up Give examples: *lipstick, eye shadow.*

Additional ideas are *choose your own clothes, talk on the telephone, spend time with your grandparents.*

Practice C

Study Box. See Intro. p. viii.

Ought to. *Ought to* can also express probability, e.g., *The bus ought to be here in five minutes.* Point out that the base form of the verb follows *ought to.*

Pronunciation point: Point out the reduction: /ɔṭə/

Optional: Give additional practice. Read the following sentence and ask volunteers what the subject out to do.

Maria's mother is arriving by plane tonight. Maria knows the flight number but isn't sure what time the plane arrives. (She ought to call the airport.)
You and your friend have rented a car for the weekend. It's a beautiful day. (We ought to . . .)
Eric and Yolanda just arrived in downtown Houston. They're lost. They see a police officer. (They ought to . . .)
I lost my credit card. (You ought to . . .)

Exercise 1. See Intro. p. ix, Listening.
**award (n)* Here, means a formal way, e.g., a letter or money, to recognize what Linda did.

Answers: 3, 4 and 5

Exercise 2. See Intro. p. ix, Ask and answer questions.
close to (adj) Means be good friends with someone.
chief Means head of, e.g., a Fire Department or Police Department.

Exercise 3. See Intro. p. ix, Ask and answer questions.
Have the class discuss their answers in groups. Ask the groups for their opinions. Encourage the class to discuss disagreements.

A: I think Officer Brady ought to get a promotion.
B: I don't. He's too good at his job. I think he should get a raise, but he ought to stay in the Arson Divison.

Exercise 4.

Have students work in pairs or teams and compete to finish the puzzle first. Alternatively, the puzzle can be assigned as homework and checked in class.

Answers:

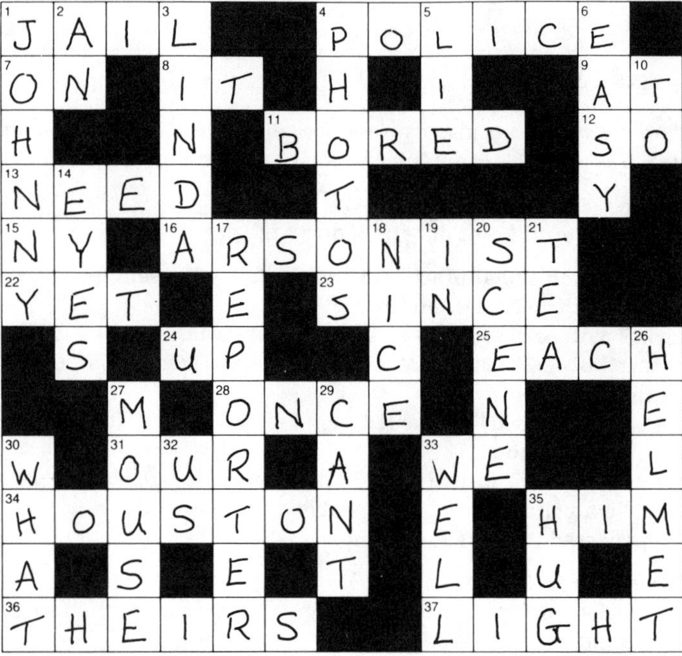

Pronunciation point: Parts 2 and 3 of the **Pronunciation** exercises can be used here.

Just for Fun

4 Complete this crossword puzzle.

The *Herald* Crossword Puzzle

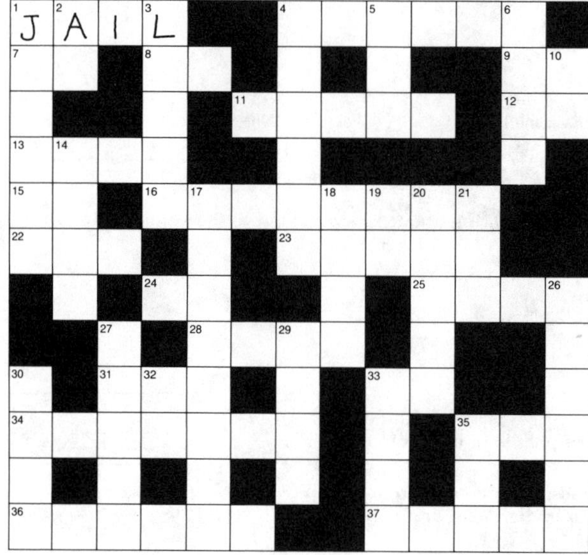

Across

1. Where the arsonists will probably go
4. Officer Brady works for them
7. Opposite of *off*
8. Can you tell me what time ___ is?
9. Be good ___ doing something
11. Opposite of *interested*
12. I think ___.
13. Find necessary
15. Biggest city in the U.S. (abbreviation)
16. Person who starts fires
22. Have you done it ___?
23. She's lived here ___ 1986.
24. Look it ___ in the dictionary.
25. They take care of ___ other.
28. One time
31. Your and my
33. You and I
34. Home of the *Herald*
35. He hurt ___self.
36. His and hers
37. Opposite of *dark*

Down

1. Boy's name
2. ___ informant gives information.
3. She found the arsonists
4. What Minh Tran takes
5. Not tell the truth
6. Opposite of *hard*
10. Ought ___
14. We see with them
17. Linda Smith's profession
18. ___ to meet you.
19. Be interested ___ something
20. Location
21. Kind of drink
26. Motorcyclist's hat
27. As quiet as a ___
29. Isn't able to
30. I don't know ___ to do.
32. You and me
33. Good (adverb)
35. Embrace

Life Skills

Employment

1 Ken Wilson is going to start working as a welder at one of Frank Jordan's businesses—Jordan Ironworks. Ken is asking his supervisor, Allan, some questions about company benefits. Listen and complete their conversation.

KEN: I've got some questions about company benefits (1).

ALLAN: Sure. What would you like to know?

KEN: Well, first of all, I'd like to know about ____ (2) ____ (3).

ALLAN: You get major medical health insurance, which helps cover your ____ (4) visits and your ____ (5) bills. You don't get dental coverage, though.

KEN: Does the major medical ____ (6) immediately?

ALLAN: No. It starts after you've been here for ____ (7) ____ (8).

KEN: And what about life ____ (9)? I've got a wife and two kids.

ALLAN: You also get that after three months on the ____ (10). And you get disability.

KEN: And how much ____ (11) time do I get?

ALLAN: ____ (12) ____ (13) after a ____ (14), ____ (15) weeks after ____ (16) years, and ____ (17) weeks after ____ (18) years.

KEN: That doesn't sound bad.

ALLAN: Yeah, we've got a pretty good union here.

Now ask and answer questions about someone's job benefits, like this:

A: Does your wife get health insurance?
B: Yes, she does. She gets Blue Cross/Blue Shield. OR No, she doesn't.

2 Ken is talking to another worker at Jordan's Ironworks. He's asking him some questions about company rules. Look at the pictures and ask and answer questions with *let* or *make*.

1. A: Do they make you punch in and out?
   B: Yes, they do.

1. punch in and out

2. take breaks

3. listen to music

4. wear a uniform

5. smoke on the job

6. work overtime

Now ask and answer questions about someone's job. Use the ideas in the pictures above.

Life Skills

In Unit 12 students will learn how to ask questions about employee benefits and company rules. In addition, they will learn about the standard deductions from a paycheck, as well as other information given on a paycheck stub.

Exercise 1. See Intro. p. ix, Listening.
Tell students that when someone starts a new job, he or she needs to ask questions about company benefits. One important fringe benefit is insurance. Here are some of the kinds of insurance that a company might provide:
major medical Health insurance that pays for a large percentage of medical expenses, both in and out of the hospital. This includes doctor visits, medicines, X-rays and other procedures.
dental coverage Insurance for dentist bills.
life insurance Money paid to other family members (or anyone else the insured person had specified) when the insured person dies. For example, if Ken died, Cathy and the children would collect his life insurance.
disability insurance Money to replace a worker's salary if the worker gets sick or injured and can't work.
**though* Means *however.*
**union* An organization of workers which arranges the workers' contract with the company. The union usually pressures the company for better benefits for its workers, e.g., insurance, vacation and pension.

Answers: 2. health 3. insurance 4. doctors' 5. hospital 6. begin 7. three 8. months 9. insurance 10. job 11. vacation 12. One 13. week 14. year 15. two 16. two 17. three 18. three

Now ask and answer . . . See Intro. p. ix, Ask and answer questions.
Blue Cross and *Blue Shield* Popular kinds of insurance. *Blue Cross* pays for hospital expenses; *Blue Shield* for doctors.

Add:
tuition assistance Money to pay for school tuition.
pregnancy leave Vacation, paid or unpaid, when a worker has a baby. The job is held open until the worker returns.
credit union An employee's organization that offers banking services to its members. They usually lend at a lower rate of interest than a bank.

Exercise 2. See Intro. p. ix, Look at the pictures.
Answers: 2. A: Do they let you take breaks? B: Yes, they do. 3. A: Do they let you listen to music? B: No, they don't. 4. A: Do they make you wear a uniform? B: Yes, they do. 5. A: Do they let you smoke on the job? B: No, they don't. 6. A: Do they make you work overtime? B: Yes, they do.

For Your Information. See Intro. p. x.
unemployment compensation Money that replaces income if a worker is laid off.
gross earnings Means salary before all deductions.
union dues Money paid every month to support the union.
percentage Give the symbol (%).
federal Refers to the national government of the U.S., rather than to a state or city government.
take-home pay Means salary after deductions. These benefits are discussed in the On Your Own section on Student's Book p. 109.

Exercise 3. See Intro. p. x, Look at the document.
REG Means *regular rate of pay.* Note that the next category is *OT* for *overtime.*
retain Means *keep.*
pay period Means the period the employee is being paid for with this check.

Point out the deductions explained in the For Your Information box: *UC*, *DC* and *Union* under *Deductions and Adjustments; Federal Income Tax* and *FICA* under *Description.*

Answers: 2. 44 3. one and a half times 4. $736.00 5. the same as 6. more than 7. federal tax only

For Your Information

Paycheck deductions

When you receive a paycheck, there will usually be several deductions. Money for health insurance (MED), unemployment compensation (UC) and disability compensation (DC) is taken out of your total (gross) earnings. Union dues may also be deducted. A percentage of your earnings is deducted for federal income taxes and for social security (FICA). Some states and cities also have taxes. The money that is left after deductions is your take-home pay (net pay).

3 Ken has received his first paycheck. Look at his paycheck stub and then complete the sentences.

EMPLOYEE NAME: Ken Wilson
PERIOD: Week
EMPLOYEE NUMBER: 080111-0670
SOCIAL SECURITY NO.: 555-01-9011
PERIOD ENDING: 8-7-90

THIS PAY PERIOD EARNINGS			DEDUCTIONS AND ADJUSTMENTS				OTHER PAY INFORMATION
TYPE	HOURS/UNITS	AMOUNT	TYPE	AMOUNT	TYPE	AMOUNT	
REG @ $16	40	640 00	UC	5 66			
OT @ $24	4	96 00	DC	9 00			
			UNION	8 00			

DESCRIPTION	THIS PAY	YEAR TO DATE
EARNINGS	736 00	736 00
FED. INCOME TAX	144 80	144 80
FICA	50 68	50 68
STATE TAX		
LOCAL TAX		
OTHER TAX		
DED/ADJ	22 66	
NET PAY	517 86	

DEPOSITED TEXAS SAVINGS BANK

STATEMENT OF EARNINGS & DEDUCTIONS
DETACH AND RETAIN FOR YOUR RECORDS

1. Ken gets paid once a week. (once a month / once a week / every two weeks)
2. Ken worked ______ hours this week. (40 / 44 / 16)
3. Ken's overtime pay is ______ his regular pay. (two times / the same as / one and a half times)
4. Ken's gross earnings are ______. ($736.00 / $16.00 / $517.86)
5. Ken's year-to-date earnings are ______ his earnings for this pay period. (the same as / more than / less than)
6. In Ken's next check, his year-to-date earnings will be ______ his earnings for the pay period. (the same as / more than / less than)
7. If you work in Houston, you have to pay ______. (local, state and federal taxes / state and federal taxes / federal tax only)

ON YOUR OWN

Discuss these questions with your classmates.

1 What kinds of job benefits do you think are important?
2 Do you think everyone should have the same job benefits? If not, what should they depend on (length of time at the job, age, ability, need)?
3 How much vacation time do you think people should get?
4 What job benefits do people get in your country? How much vacation time do they get?

For pronunciation exercises for Unit 12, see page 116.

On Your Own. See Intro. p. xi.

1. Review the benefits discussed in Life Skills. Ask students when they would use each one. Ask if they have ever needed these benefits or have known anyone who did. In what specific ways did they help or would they have helped?

2. Does the importance vary with age, whether one is married, whether one has children, for example? Ask students to give reasons for their answers.

REVIEW 6

Exercise 1.
2. Carol said they had to hurry. 3. Pete said Linda was in trouble. 4. Minh said he couldn't understand her message. 5. Angela said she wouldn't be back until Tuesday.

Exercise 2.
2. Linda asked if they (he/she) could untie her hands. 3. Pete asked if Michael had done his homework. 4. Minh asked if the police would find Linda. 5. Cathy asked when Officer Brady was coming.

Exercise 3.
2. couldn't understand 3. was 4. called OR had called 5. was coming

Exercise 4.
3. Pete told Michael to do his homework. 4. Angela told Brad to get her the Lewis file. 5. Suzanne told Pete not to forget to write her a letter. 6. Lan told Minh to call her before 6:00. 7. Carol told Luke to hurry up. 8. Luke told Phil not to make so much noise. 9. Officer Brady told Mr. Jordan to tell him everything.

REVIEW 6

1 Change these statements to reported speech.

1. Linda said, "I want some water."

Linda said she wanted some water.

2. Carol said, "We have to hurry."
3. Pete said, "Linda's in trouble."
4. Minh said, "I can't understand her message."
5. Angela said, "I won't be back until Tuesday."

2 Change these questions to reported speech.

1. Angela asked, "Where's the Lewis file?"

Angela asked where the Lewis file was.

2. Linda asked, "Can you untie my hands?"
3. Pete asked, "Have you done your homework, Michael?"
4. Minh asked, "Will the police find Linda?"
5. Cathy asked, "When's Officer Brady coming?"

3 Angela is in Dallas. She called the *Herald*. Read the conversation she had with Minh.

ANGELA: Hello, Minh. Is Linda there?
MINH: No, she isn't.
ANGELA: Where is she?
MINH: No one knows. She's missing. She called earlier and gave me a message, but I can't understand it. Actually, I'm sure she's in trouble.
ANGELA: Have you called the police?
MINH: Yes.
ANGELA: Well, I'm coming back right now.

Next Angela called her husband, Frank. Complete the message she left on his answering machine.

I have to come back to Houston immediately. I just called and spoke to Minh. He said that Linda was (1. be) missing. She called the *Herald* and left a message, but he said he ________ (2. can understand–*neg.*) it. He said she ________ (3. be) in trouble. He told me that they ________ (4. call) the police, but I think I should be there. I told him that I ________ (5. come) back right away. I'll see you tonight.

4 Change these commands to reported speech.

1. Cathy said, "Be quiet, kids."

Cathy told the kids to be quiet.

2. Ken said, "Don't stay up late, children."

Ken told the children not to stay up late.

3. Pete said, "Do your homework, Michael."
4. Angela said, "Get me the Lewis file, Brad."
5. Suzanne said, "Don't forget to write me a letter, Pete."
6. Lan said, "Call me before 6:00, Minh."
7. Carol said, "Hurry up, Luke."
8. Luke said, "Don't make so much noise, Phil."
9. Officer Brady said, "Tell me everything, Mr. Jordan."

5 Read Pete's letter to Suzanne. Change the underlined words to direct speech.

1. Angela said, "Take a vacation, Linda."

Dear Suzanne,

I'm sure you've heard about all the excitement we've had here. Luckily everything's OK now. Linda had a rough time, and (1) Angela told her to take a vacation. But (2) Linda said that she was fine. (3) She told us she just wanted to get back to work. That woman is amazing!

Guess what! Frank Jordan is looking for a new assistant. (4) Angela asked me if I knew anyone who had a background in art. (5) I told her that I knew someone who might be interested. It's really the perfect job for you, Suzanne. (6) Angela said to tell you to send Frank a résumé as soon as possible.

6 When you were a child, what did you decide you were going to do when you grew up? Write five sentences.

EXAMPLE: When I was a child, I decided I was going to be an engineer.

7 Write sentences about what parents *should let, shouldn't let* and *should make* their children do.

1. eat good meals

Parents should make their children eat good meals.

2. stay up late
3. go out with their friends sometimes
4. drink a lot of soda
5. be polite to adults
6. watch too much TV
7. make some of their own decisions
8. do their homework
9. have fun

8 Your friends want to improve their English. Tell them five things that they *ought to* do. You can choose from the list below or make your own suggestions.

take English classes
read the dictionary
listen to the radio
be quiet in class
make friends with some Americans
read English newspapers
speak correctly all the time
buy lots of grammar review books
go to English movies
ask questions when they don't understand
speak English as much as possible
memorize the alphabet
ask their friends to translate for them

Exercise 5.

2. Linda said, "I'm fine." 3. Linda said, "I just want to get back to work." 4. Angela asked, "Do you know anyone who has a background in art?" 5. I said, "I know someone who might be interested." 6. Angela said, "Tell her to send Frank a résumé as soon as possible."

Exercise 6.

Answers will vary.

Exercise 7.

Possible answers: 2. They shouldn't let their children stay up late. 3. They should let them go with their friends sometimes. 4. They shouldn't let them drink a lot of soda. 5. They should make them be polite to adults. 6. They shouldn't let them watch too much TV. 7. They should let them make some of their own decisions. 8. They should make them do their homework. 9. They should let them have fun.

Exercise 8.

Answers will vary.

Tapescripts

(The page numbers refer to pages in the Student's Book.)

UNIT 1

Page 3, Ex. 2

Angela Lentini is introducing Pete Gómez to some other members of the news staff. Listen and write what she says about each person.

1. ANGELA: Pete, this is Cathy Wilson. She writes articles on health and food. Now she's writing a story on new restaurants.
   CATHY: Glad to meet you, Pete.
   PETE: Glad to meet you too.
2. ANGELA: And meet my assistant, Brad Kimball. He does a lot of different things. He's helping Linda with the arson story right now.
   BRAD: Hi, Pete.
   PETE: Nice to meet you, Brad.
3. ANGELA: And this is Minh Tran. He takes great pictures. He's also working on the arson story.
   MINH: How do you do, Pete?
   PETE: How do you do?

Page 5, Ex. 2

Linda Smith and Tom Kirby are having lunch. Read the sentences below. Then listen to their conversation and choose the correct answers.

TOM: What are you going to do after work, Linda?
LINDA: I'm not sure, Tom. Maybe see a movie.
TOM: Why don't you see *Una Vida Peligrosa?* I saw it, and it's great.
LINDA: But *you* speak Spanish. *I* won't understand anything.
TOM: You studied Spanish, Linda! You'll probably understand a lot.
LINDA: Oh, I really can't go to a movie, Tom. I have too much work. I need to work on this arson story.
TOM: You work too hard, Linda. You really need to have some fun too.

Page 7, Put It All Together

Linda called Pete to tell him about another fire. Listen to their conversation and decide which story will be in tomorrow's newspaper.

OPERATOR: Houston *Herald.*
LINDA: Pete Gómez, please.
(Telephone rings)
PETE: Pete Gómez.
LINDA: Pete, this is Linda. Remember those fires I told you about? Another one's just started. I'm standing on the corner of Franklin and Lamar, and there's a big fire across the street. It's in a clothing factory.
PETE: Is there anyone working there now?
LINDA: No, I don't think so. Usually about 200 people work there, but no one's working today.
PETE: Should I call the fire department?
LINDA: They're already here, but I don't think they can put the fire out before it destroys the whole building. Tell Minh to jump on his motorcycle and come down here. I want some pictures of this factory burning down.
PETE: OK, I'll do that right now.

TAPESCRIPT FOR PRONUNCIATION EXERCISES

Page 112

Part 1

Listen and complete these sentences.

1. Tom writes sports news.
2. He doesn't like computers.
3. He prefers to use a typewriter.
4. Linda usually writes stories about politics.
5. Now she's doing a story about all those warehouse fires.

Now listen again and repeat the sentences.

Part 2

Listen to these sentences and complete each one with the correct object pronoun.

1. Look it up in the dictionary.
2. Why don't you call her up?
3. Drop him off at the library.
4. Pete's handing them in.
5. Yes, do it over.
6. Please point her out to me.

Now listen again and repeat the sentences.

Part 3

Listen to these sentences and mark the word that has the most stress in each sentence.

Example: I think it's right. (The word "think" has the most stress in that sentence.)

1. Well, I think so.
2. But you speak Spanish.
3. It's very difficult.
4. I won't understand anything.

Now listen again and repeat the sentences.

UNIT 2

Page 12, Ex. 3

Linda is telling Pete about Bill Thomas's life. Listen to their conversation and write Bill's age for each event and his age now.

PETE: How's Bill Thomas?
LINDA: No one knows. He's still unconscious. That poor kid.
PETE: How do you know him?
LINDA: I've known his family for a long time. They moved into the apartment next door to me when Bill was only four, and they've lived there ever since. When Bill was six, his father died. There were a lot of kids in the family and not much money.
PETE: That's too bad.
LINDA: Bill got into trouble a lot. The police arrested him for the first time when he was twelve. When he was sixteen, he quit school. A year later, he was sent to prison for arson. He spent two years there. When he got out, he realized he was only nineteen and still had time to change. So, he got a job working as a mechanic, and last year at the age of twenty, he went back to school and got his high school diploma.
PETE: Sounds like he's changed a lot.
LINDA: He has. He's twenty-one now and has his future all planned. He started studying to be a computer programmer at Houston Business Institute just two months ago. I *know* he didn't start those fires!

Page 13, Ex. 1

Pete is asking Linda about Angela Lentini. Listen to their conversation and decide if Angela completed the action or is still doing it.

PETE: What can you tell me about Angela Lentini? I really don't know anything about her.
LINDA: Well, she was born in Toronto and went to school there. Then she got a job teaching journalism at the University of Houston, and she's taught there for the past ten years.
PETE: Sounds like she doesn't have much free time. Is she married?
LINDA: She's been married for about three years, I think. Her husband is Frank Jordan, the Director of the Houston Art Museum.
PETE: Where does she live?
LINDA: She lived in the suburbs for a long time, but she's had an apartment in town since she got married.
PETE: And what about her interests? What does she like to do when she's not working?
LINDA: Well, she skied until her accident, and she's played the piano since she was a child.

Page 16, Ex. 2

Linda Smith is calling the hospital to get some information about Bill. Listen and complete the conversation.

OPERATOR: City Hospital.
LINDA: Hello, I'd like some information about Bill Thomas. He's a new patient at your hospital.
OPERATOR: One minute. I'll connect you to the nurses' station on his floor.
NURSE: Fifth floor, Nurse Spencer.
LINDA: Hello. This is Linda Smith. Can you please tell me the condition of Bill Thomas?
NURSE: Are you related to the patient?
LINDA: I'm a close friend of the family.
NURSE: I see. Well, his condition is listed as critical.
LINDA: Oh. Can you tell me what the visiting hours are?
NURSE: They're from 1:30 to 3:30 in the afternoon and 6:00 to 8:30 at night.
LINDA: And what room is he in?
NURSE: 501. It's on the fifth floor, East Wing. But only family can see him now.
LINDA: Thank you.

TAPESCRIPT FOR PRONUNCIATION EXERCISES

Page 112

Part 1

Linda is talking to her new neighbor Vicky. Listen to their conversation and complete it.

VICKY: How long have you lived in Houston, Linda?
LINDA: Oh, I've been here all my life. I was born in Houston. What about you?
VICKY: We moved to Texas in November because I got a better job here.
LINDA: By the way, have you met Bill and Alice? They live in apartment 2B.
VICKY: Yes. They seem very nice.

Now listen again and repeat the conversation.

Part 2

Listen to these sentences and complete them with *has, hasn't, have* or *haven't.*

1. Alice hasn't seen Bill.
2. The doctors have examined him.
3. Hasn't he woken up?
4. The police haven't found the driver.
5. Alice has called her sister.

Now listen again and repeat the sentences.

Part 3

Listen to these questions and mark the word that has the most stress in each question.

1. Why didn't you call the police?
2. Why didn't you call the police?

Now listen again and match the questions with the answers in your book.

1. Why didn't you call the police?
2. Why didn't you call the police?

UNIT 3

Page 21, Ex. 2

Pete is talking on the phone to his girlfriend, Suzanne. He's telling her about the blackout. Listen and complete their conversation.

SUZANNE: I heard about the blackout on the news. Are you and Michael OK?
PETE: Oh, we're both fine.
SUZANNE: What were you doing when the lights went out?
PETE: I was interviewing someone about the next election.
SUZANNE: Oh? What did you do then?
PETE: I was using a cassette recorder with batteries, so we just continued the interview.
SUZANNE: And what about Michael? Where was he when the lights went out?
PETE: He was doing his homework at home. When the lights went out, he just turned on a flashlight and continued.

Page 24, Ex. 1

Before Angela left for Dallas, she told Brad what she wanted people at the *Herald* to do. Brad made a list. Listen to the conversation and write the name of the person next to each job.

ANGELA: These are the things I want people to do while I'm in Dallas. Could you make a list, Brad?
BRAD: Sure, Ms. Lentini.
ANGELA: First of all, I'd like you to get the information about the warehouses for Linda as soon as possible.
BRAD: No problem. Would you like me to interview the fire commissioner?
ANGELA: No. I want Linda to do that. You can help Pete Gómez.
BRAD: OK.
ANGELA: Ask Tom to interview the manager of the Houston Comets.
BRAD: What about Cathy?
ANGELA: Cathy should talk to the owner of Shop and Save supermarket. And I'd like Minh to take pictures of the store. Oh, and remind Minh also to take pictures of the museum renovation.
BRAD: Is that all?
ANGELA: Uh . . . no. I want Tom to call George Davidson, and Linda should rewrite that story about the mayor. That's it.

Page 25, Put It All Together

Bill Thomas has come out of his coma. Officer Brady is asking him some questions. Read the notes below. Then listen to the conversation and choose the notes that Officer Brady made.

BRADY: Why did you tell Linda Smith to meet you on Sunday, Bill?
BILL: I . . . uh . . .
BRADY: You're in trouble, Bill. When we searched your car we found gasoline and a map showing the location of the last warehouse fire.
BILL: What? That stuff's not mine. *He* put it there to make me look guilty.
BRADY: He? Who's he?
BILL: OK, I'll tell you. I was working at the garage one day when a man came up and asked me to do a little job for him.
BRADY: Job? What kind of job?
BILL: He knew I used to start fires. That's what he wanted me to do. But I told him no.
BRADY: Who is this man?
BILL: I don't know him. I never saw him before, but I could describe him.
BRADY: OK. I'll send a police artist to see you this afternoon. Now, what do you remember about the accident?
BILL: Not much. I was walking along, and suddenly this car came right at me and hit me.
BRADY: Do you think it had something to do with this arson business?
BILL: I'm not sure. Maybe someone found out I was going to talk to Linda. The man told me not to go to the police. Now I'm worried about my mom too.

TAPESCRIPT FOR PRONUNCIATION EXERCISES

Page 113

Part 1

A. Listen to these verbs in the present and past tenses. How many syllables do you hear—1, 2 or 3?

Example: **connect** (You hear two syllables.)
connected (You hear three syllables.)

1.	try	tried	7.	talk	talked
2.	use	used	8.	work	worked
3.	protect	protected	9.	hate	hated
4.	finish	finished	10.	happen	happened
5.	visit	visited	11.	start	started
6.	need	needed	12.	want	wanted

Now listen again and repeat each word.

B. 1. Which words in Exercise A have the same number of syllables in the present and in the past?
2. Which words in Exercise A have *more* syllables in the past than in the present?
Note that these words end in a *t* or *d* sound in the present tense.

C. Listen and repeat this conversation.

A: What did you do yesterday?
B: I visited my aunt. She wanted me to help her paint her bedroom.
A: What did you do after you painted the room?
B: Oh, we just talked about people we used to know.

Part 2

Listen and repeat these sentences. Notice that *used to* and *use to* are pronounced the same way.

1. Angela used to live in Toronto.
2. Pete used to be married.
3. Tom didn't use to speak Spanish.
4. Did Linda use to paint?
5. Minh didn't use to ride a motorcycle.

UNIT 4

Page 30, Ex. 4

Linda and Pete are talking. Read the statements below. Then listen to their conversation and say if the statements are right or wrong.

PETE: What's the matter, Linda?
LINDA: Oh, I've been waiting for Officer Brady to call me since this morning.
PETE: Has he spoken to Bill?
LINDA: Yes, but I don't know what he told him. I've been trying to write tomorrow's story, and I can't finish it until I talk to Brady.
PETE: Why don't you just talk to Bill?
LINDA: I'd like to, but the doctors have been examining him for hours. They want to make sure he's OK before they let him go home.
PETE: You know, Linda, if Bill's accident *wasn't* an accident, it could get dangerous. Maybe you should give the story to someone else.
LINDA: No, I've been working on this story for weeks, and I'm not going to give it up now.

Page 32, Ex. 4

Bill Thomas is trying to identify the man who asked him to start the fires. Officer Brady is showing him three police sketches. Listen to the conversation and choose the correct sketch. Then talk about it with a classmate.

BRADY: Well, take a look at these three sketches, Bill. Do any of these look like him?
BILL: Sort of. This one's nose is too small, and his hair isn't light enough.
BRADY: What about this one?
BILL: Well, it looks a little like him, but he's too old and his hair's too long. I think *this* is the man. The other two men's ears aren't big enough. And they're too old, and their hair's too dark. Yes, I'm almost sure this is the guy.

Page 36, Ex. 1

Cathy is at Peers Department Store. She is talking to a salesperson. Listen and complete their conversation.

CATHY: I'd like to return this dress.
SALESPERSON: What seems to be the problem with it?
CATHY: Well, I usually take a size 10, but this is too small on me.
SALESPERSON: Would you like to exchange it for a larger size?
CATHY: No, I'd prefer to get a refund. I bought it only five days ago.
SALESPERSON: Do you have your receipt?
CATHY: Yes, here it is.
SALESPERSON: OK. We'll be glad to give you your money back.

TAPESCRIPT FOR PRONUNCIATION EXERCISES

Page 113

Part 1

Steve Wilson is talking to his friend Bob. Listen to their conversation and complete it.

BOB: What's the matter?
STEVE: My brother can't find a job.
BOB: He's a good welder. Where's he been looking?
STEVE: He looks in the paper every day.
BOB: I remember when I was unemployed. It's hard, but I'm sure he'll find another job soon.

Now listen again and repeat the conversation.

Part 2

Listen to these sentences and complete them with *can* or *can't*.

1. We can't go to the movies.
2. Johnny can play outside.
3. You can find a job.
4. They can't stop at the store.
5. The Wilsons can't spend a lot of money.

Now listen again and repeat the sentences.

Part 3

Listen to these sentences. Notice the difference in pronunciation between stressed *too* and unstressed *to*.

1. It's too hot to drink.
2. They're too tired to work.
3. She's too young to vote.
4. It's too expensive to buy.
5. I'm too busy to talk.

Now listen again and repeat the sentences.

Page 41, Ex. 3

Listen to the conversations. Then describe these people with an adjective from the box.

1. JOHNNY: Oh, boy! Look at that spaceship!
   KEN: It's really big, isn't it?
2. ELLEN: Mommy, I had a bad dream. I don't want to sleep alone.
   CATHY: That's OK, Ellen. You can sleep with us tonight.
3. KEN: Do you have any openings for welders?
   WOMAN: I'm sorry. We aren't going to need any new welders for six months.
4. JOHNNY: Please buy me some candy. Please, please, please. I want some now!
   CATHY: I just told you you can't have candy before dinner.
5. KEN: Did you have a hard day?
   CATHY: Yes. All I want to do is go to sleep.

Page 42, Ex. 3

Linda is calling the Houston *Herald*. Listen to the conversation and choose the correct message form.

OPERATOR: Houston *Herald*.
LINDA: Pete Gómez, please.

OPERATOR: Just a moment.
(Telephone rings)
OPERATOR: I'm sorry. He's not at his desk. Would you like to leave a message?
LINDA: Yes. This is Linda Smith. Please tell him I won't be able to meet with him this morning because I've gone to speak to Officer Brady.
OPERATOR: Would you like him to call you back?
LINDA: No, that won't be necessary.

Page 45, Put It All Together

Cathy and Ken are talking about his problem. Listen and complete their conversation.

CATHY: You look so depressed, Ken. You're driving yourself crazy.
KEN: I know, but I can't stop myself from thinking about work.
CATHY: Don't be so discouraged. I'm sure you'll be able to find something soon.
KEN: I know. I tell myself that every day, but nothing happens. It's really very depressing. Two years ago I was able to get a job without any problem.
CATHY: But times are a lot harder now, Ken.
KEN: You're right, Cath. I should stop worrying.
CATHY: Let's go to a movie. We need to enjoy ourselves a little. We can ask your brother to take care of the kids. I think we need some time alone with each other.

TAPESCRIPT FOR PRONUNCIATION EXERCISES

Page 113

Part 1

Listen and complete these sentences.

1. I'm not getting anywhere.
2. Two heads are better than one.
3. Johnny's excited.
4. They're writing to each other.
5. She can't read the letter.

Now listen again and repeat the sentences.

Part 2

Listen and complete each sentence with the adjective you hear.

1. She's very interesting.
2. He's excited.
3. They're not frightened.
4. He's tiring.
5. Is she boring?

Now listen again and repeat the sentences.

Part 3

Sometimes an unstressed syllable is reduced so much it disappears. Listen to these sentences and cross out the vowel that you *don't* hear in each underlined word.

Example: The movie was frightening.
(You don't hear the "e.")

1. I thought the book was interesting.
2. Bill's studying business.
3. Let's do something different.
4. That's Minh's best camera.

Now listen again and repeat the sentences.

UNIT 6

Page 49, Ex. 2

Linda is talking to Cathy. Listen to their conversation and find out what Linda will do if she gets another threatening letter.

CATHY: You look really upset, Linda. What's the matter?
LINDA: I'm worried that I'll get another anonymous letter.
CATHY: What will you do if that happens? Will you stop working on the story then?
LINDA: No, I won't. If I get another letter, I'll work even harder on this story.
CATHY: Will you ask for police protection if you're threatened again?
LINDA: Well, of course I'll call Officer Brady. But I won't ask for protection.
CATHY: But you have to, Linda! You could really be in a lot of danger. You can't stay in your apartment alone. Why don't you come and stay with us?
LINDA: Thanks. But you and Ken have your own problems. If I get another letter, I'll speak to Angela about it. She'll be able to help me.

Page 51, Ex. 2

Officer Brady is returning Linda's phone call. Listen to their conversation. Then choose the letter Linda received.

BRADY: Ms. Smith? This is Officer Brady.
LINDA: Oh, Officer Brady. Thank you for returning my call.
BRADY: What's the matter? You sound upset.
LINDA: Yes. I received an anonymous letter in the mail today.
BRADY: What does it say?
LINDA: It tells me to stop working on the arson story.
BRADY: Does it say anything else?
LINDA: Yes . . . that if I *don't* stop, I'll be sorry.
BRADY: Hmm. I don't like how this sounds. Listen, I'll be right over.

Page 54, Ex. 1

Cathy Wilson received a phone call while she was away from her desk. Listen to the call and then complete the message. Use today's date and the correct time.

OPERATOR: Houston *Herald.*
MS. DUPONT: Hello. Can I speak to Cathy Wilson, please?
OPERATOR: I'm sorry, but she's not at her desk. Would you like to leave a message?
MS. DUPONT: Yes. Please tell her that Ms. Dupont from the French Café is returning her call.

OPERATOR: Ms. Dupont?
MS. DUPONT: Yes. D-U-P-O-N-T.
OPERATOR: OK. Anything else?
MS. DUPONT: Yes. Please tell her that I enjoyed meeting her last night at my restaurant and that I will call her again tonight if I finish work before 10:00.
OPERATOR: OK. You enjoyed meeting her last night, and you'll call her if you finish work before 10:00.
MS. DUPONT: That's right.
OPERATOR: Does she have your number?
MS. DUPONT: I think so. It's 525–9110.
OPERATOR: 525–9110?
MS. DUPONT: Yes. Thank you very much.
OPERATOR: You're welcome. Goodbye.
MS. DUPONT: Goodbye.

Page 54, Ex. 2

Pete Gómez is calling directory assistance to ask for someone's phone number. Listen to the conversation and complete it.

OPERATOR: Hello. Mrs. Ketcham.
PETE: Hello. Can I have the number of John Baretta?
OPERATOR: Can you spell the last name, please?
PETE: It's B-A-R-E-T-T-A.
OPERATOR: V as in Victor?
PETE: No, B as in Bob.
OPERATOR: And do you know the address?
PETE: Yes, 25 Grove Street.
OPERATOR: The number is 271–9830.
PETE: 271–9830?
OPERATOR: Yes, that's right.
PETE: Thank you.

Page 55, Ex. 4

Pete is calling John Baretta. He is not there. Listen to John's answering machine and choose the message Pete left for him.

JOHN: Hello. This is John Baretta. I'm sorry I can't answer your call now, but if you leave your name, number, time you called and a brief message, I'll get back to you as soon as possible. Please wait for the beep.

TAPESCRIPT FOR PRONUNCIATION EXERCISES

Page 114

Part 1

Pete and Tom are talking about Linda. Listen to their conversation and complete it.

PETE: I'm really concerned about Linda.
TOM: I know. She always works too hard.
PETE: No, it's not that. I'm worried about that letter she got when she returned to the office today.
TOM: Oh, I heard about that. What does Officer Brady think?
PETE: I don't know. But I'm nervous. I don't want Linda to get hurt.

Now listen again and repeat the conversation.

Part 2

Listen to these sentences. Notice how the voice rises and then falls in the *if*- clause.

1. If Pete finds an apartment, he'll move.
2. If Ken gets a job, he'll be happy.
3. If Michael doesn't study, he won't pass.
4. If Cathy calls, I'll tell you.
5. If Linda isn't careful, she'll get hurt.

Now listen again and repeat the sentences.

Part 3

A. Listen and repeat these *yes/no* questions. Remember that your voice goes up at the end.

1. Have you seen Linda?
2. Are you enjoying working in Houston?
3. Can I take a message?
4. Could I have the day off?

B. Now listen and repeat these *wh*-questions. Remember that your voice goes down at the end.

1. Who sent it?
2. What's it about?
3. What's the matter?
4. Where's Linda?

MIDTERM TEST

TAPESCRIPT FOR LISTENING COMPREHENSION TEST

See page 158 of the Teacher's Manual.

Tom is interviewing Derek Mahoney for a television program. You will hear Tom's part of the conversation. Circle the correct answers for Derek's part of the conversation.

51. TOM: Friends, meet Derek Mahoney. Derek is a player for the Houston Grinders.
52. TOM: Derek usually plays football, but right now he's doing something different.
53. TOM: That sounds great, Derek. Who are you working for?
54. TOM: How long have you done this kind of work?
55. TOM: Why did you decide to coach?
56. TOM: You used to play on a neighborhood team, didn't you?
57. TOM: What advice can you give young players when they get discouraged?
58. TOM: But most kids cannot become professionals. So, what should these good players do?
59. TOM: That reminds me. We hear you're planning to quit playing. Is it true?
60. TOM: Thanks for talking with me today, Derek.

UNIT 7

Page 59, Ex. 2

Linda's having dinner with Ken and Cathy. Listen and complete their conversation.

LINDA: Are you excited about starting your new job, Ken?
KEN: Well, I'm certainly looking forward to working again. I'm really tired of staying home.
CATHY: Ken's going to keep on looking for a job as a welder. Being a security guard is just temporary.
LINDA: I understand. It's better to have a job at something you're good at doing.
KEN: Yes, but I'm thankful to my brother for finding me this job. It's great to be able to read the paper without getting depressed.
CATHY: Talking about being depressed, Linda, how do you feel about staying at Angela's? You probably miss being at home.
LINDA: Oh, it's OK. Last night her husband's assistant, Carol Fullerton, came over for dinner.
CATHY: How was that? Is she nice?
LINDA: A little strange. She was *very* interested in hearing all about the arson story.

Page 63, Put It All Together

Two men are talking. Listen and complete their conversation.

LUKE: Well, is everything all set for Saturday night?
PHIL: Yes. We'll meet you at 1:00 A.M.
LUKE: Which warehouse is it?
PHIL: Number 5. It's on the west side of Palmer Road, south of Warehouse 6.
LUKE: What do you know about security?
PHIL: There are two doors. The main door is on the south side. The doors are locked when the workers go home at 6:00.
LUKE: What about the windows?
PHIL: There are two on the east side and three on the west side.
LUKE: Are they all protected by alarms?
PHIL: Yes, they are. The alarm box is located on the right side of the main door.
LUKE: What other security is there?
PHIL: Well, there's a guard. His desk is to the left of the main door.

TAPESCRIPT FOR PRONUNCIATION EXERCISES

Page 114

Part 1

Listen and complete these sentences.

1. Linda's writing a special story.
2. Reporting is routine.
3. Linda's work isn't always interesting.
4. She received a threatening letter.
5. Angela doesn't remember mentioning the report.

Now listen again and repeat the sentences.

Part 2

A. When we speak quickly, the word *and* is sometimes pronouncd *n* and the word *or* is sometimes pronounced *er*. Listen and repeat these phrases.

1. Linda and Carol
2. Cathy and Ken
3. writing about politics and investigating crimes
4. a couple of people at the paper and the police
5. an editor or a social worker
6. painting or reading
7. Wisconsin or Kansas
8. oranges or grapes

B. Now listen to these sentences and complete them with *and* or *or*.

1. She writes about politics or crime.
2. We can celebrate tomorrow and Saturday.
3. Let's invite Frank and Angela.
4. Cathy likes jogging or bicycling.
5. I think corn is grown in Kansas and Illinois.
6. I'd like apple pie or ice cream, please.

Now listen again and repeat the sentences.

Part 3

Listen to these sentences. Put a period after each statement and a question mark after each question.

1.a. She's here. b. She's here?
2.a Routine? b. Routine.
3.a They're eating? b. They're eating.
4.a It's 10 o'clock. b. It's 10 o'clock?
5.a He's not sure. b. He's not sure?

Now listen again and repeat the sentences.

UNIT 8

Page 67, Ex. 2

Minh is talking to his wife, Lan, about their plans for the future. Listen to their conversation and put the pictures in the right order.

LAN: I'd really like to move. We need a two-bedroom apartment.
MINH: I know. I promise you that we'll move as soon as I get a raise.
LAN: When will that be?
MINH: Oh, I forgot to tell you. I spoke to Angela about it today. She said she'll give me a raise next month.
LAN: Well, that's not too far away.
MINH: And we can start looking for a new place before I get my raise.
LAN: It'll be so wonderful to have another bedroom.
MINH: Speaking of another bedroom, when is my mother coming to visit?
LAN: She wants to come this month, but why don't we ask her to wait? After we move, she'll be a lot more comfortable.
MINH: That's a good idea. Oh, we're going to need another bed, aren't we?
LAN: Yes. But we can't get it before we move. We don't have any place to keep it.
MINH: That's OK. We can buy it after we move but before my mother comes.

Page 68, Ex. 2

Angela and her husband, Frank, are talking about what happened to Ken Wilson. Listen and choose the get-well note they sent Ken in the hospital.

FRANK: That's terrible about Ken and his brother. How are they feeling?
ANGELA: Well, Steve was released from the hospital last night.
FRANK: And what about Ken?
ANGELA: He's still in the hospital, but he was given a very good report by his doctors and should be getting out soon.
FRANK: That's good. You know, we should send him some flowers.
ANGELA: I already did. They were delivered this morning. I also told him to call you about that job you mentioned.
FRANK: Good. I'd really like to help him out.

Page 71, Ex. 3

Listen to these people. Then make a deduction about each one. Use *must be* and an adjective.

1. MAN: *(coughing)* May I speak to Dr. Homayun, please?
2. WOMAN: *(crying)*
3. MAN: I told you never to do that again!
4. WOMAN: Guess what! I got the job!
5. MAN: *(yawning)* I'd better stay home tonight.
6. WOMAN: *(hears footsteps)* John, is that you? *(more footsteps)* Who's there?
7. MAN: *(laughing)*

Page 72, Ex. 1

Rob, Ken Wilson's co-worker, is at Stop and Save. He is having trouble finding some of the things on his shopping list. Listen and complete his conversation with a clerk.

ROB: Excuse me. Where can I find paper towels?
CLERK: In aisle 2, left side, right across from the cleaning supplies.
ROB: OK. Thanks a lot.

TAPESCRIPT FOR PRONUNCIATION EXERCISES

Page 115

Part 1

A. Listen and complete these sentences.

1. Ken works the night shift.
2. Are you sure?
3. Don't mention this to anyone.
4. You shouldn't go alone.
5. Can you repeat the conversation?
6. Rob has to go to Stop and Save.

Now listen again and repeat the sentences.

B. Listen to this tongue twister and repeat it as fast as you can. How many times can you say it without making a mistake?

She sells seashells by the seashore.

Part 2

Listen and complete each sentence with the verb you hear.

1. Ken wasn't hired after Christmas.
2. Bill wasn't arrested last year.
3. The doors are locked at 6:00.
4. Rice is grown in Arkansas.
5. Paychecks aren't given out every week.

Now listen again and repeat the sentences.

Part 3

Listen to these sentences. Notice the rising and then the falling intonation in the clause with the time expression *(when, as soon as, after* or *before).*

1. When Rob leaves, he'll go home.
2. As soon as I know, I'll tell you.
3. After Pete's done, he'll call Suzanne.
4. Before Linda has dinner, she'll visit Bill.
5. When I get my license, I'll buy a car.

Now listen again and repeat the sentences.

UNIT 9

Page 79, Ex. 2

An editor from the Houston *Sun* wants to hire a reporter. Two of Angela's students from her night class have applied for the job. The editor is calling Angela to get references about them. Listen to their conversation and make notes about each student.

EDITOR: I'm just calling to find out about two of your students. What can you tell me about Amy Stark?
ANGELA: Well, she's a very responsible student and a hard worker. She attends class regularly and does all her assignments on time.
EDITOR: How's her writing?
ANGELA: That's the problem. She doesn't write very creatively.
EDITOR: How about Joe Taylor?
ANGELA: Well, he often hands his work in late. In fact, he's a little unreliable.
EDITOR: What about his writing?
ANGELA: He's an excellent writer, and he interviews people well too. I'd say he's a good reporter but not a great worker.

Page 80, Ex. 2

Michael Gómez is having a problem. He's asking a woman for advice. Listen to their conversation. Then read the sentences below and decide if they are right or wrong.

MICHAEL: Excuse me. Can you please show me how to use this machine?
WOMAN: Sure. First, you have to put your money in.
MICHAEL: I'm not sure how much to put in.
WOMAN: You need four quarters.
MICHAEL: OK. I've got that, but now I don't see where to put them.
WOMAN: Here, on the top righthand side of the machine.
MICHAEL: Oh, I see now.
WOMAN: Do you know what to do next?
MICHAEL: Sure. Thank you.

Page 80, Ex. 1

After speaking to Officer Brady, Ken went to see his doctor. Listen to their conversation and check the things that Ken *must* do, *mustn't* do and *doesn't have to* do.

DOCTOR: Well, how are you feeling today, Mr. Wilson?
KEN: Not bad, Dr. Feldbau. But I'm still getting these headaches.
DOCTOR: That's not unusual. You've had a concussion. You must be sure to rest a lot. I hope you're not being too active.
KEN: Do I have to stay in bed?
DOCTOR: No, but you can't go back to work yet. Just try and take it easy for a while.
KEN: OK. Is there anything else I should do?
DOCTOR: Just come back in a week for a check up, and I'll examine you again.
KEN: OK. I'll make an appointment with the receptionist.
DOCTOR: You don't really need one. Just come during my office hours.

Page 81, Put It All Together

Bill asked Linda to have coffee with him. Listen to the conversation and complete the statements.

BILL: Thanks for coming so quickly, Linda. I have to talk to you. I don't know what to do.
LINDA: About what?
BILL: I haven't told you everything I know about the fires.
LINDA: What haven't you told me?
BILL: I think I know where to find him.
LINDA: Find who?
BILL: The man who spoke to me.
LINDA: You do! Why didn't you tell me before?
BILL: Because I was afraid. Especially after you got that anonymous letter.
LINDA: I understand. Just tell me where to find this guy.
BILL: Well, he often goes to Rosie's Diner for lunch. That's where I met him. He works in the shoe factory across the street. Lots of those guys go there for lunch.
LINDA: All right. Thanks, Bill.
BILL: Linda, you mustn't go alone. Rosie's Diner is a dangerous place. Take another reporter with you.
LINDA: Don't worry. I'll be fine.

TAPESCRIPT FOR PRONUNCIATION EXERCISES

Page 115

Part 1

Officer Brady is talking to Ken again. Listen to their conversation and complete it.

BRADY: Thanks for coming again, Mr. Wilson.
KEN: Sure thing, Officer Brady. I want to help find those people.
BRADY: Just tell me everything you can remember about the fire.
KEN: I think I already told you the whole story.
BRADY: Well, if you remember anything else, please call.
KEN: I sure will. I've asked my brother, but he doesn't remember much either.

Now listen again and repeat the conversation.

Part 2

Listen to these sentences and complete them with *must* or *mustn't*.

1. You mustn't tell her about it.
2. You must do it again.
3. You mustn't wash it in hot water.
4. You must send it to the cleaners.
5. You mustn't stop there.
6. She must work today.
7. She mustn't go there alone.
8. You mustn't tell him.

Now listen again and repeat the sentences.

UNIT 10

Page 86, Ex. 2

Tom is telling Pete about Linda's phone call. Listen to their conversation. Then choose the picture that shows what Pete thinks Tom should have done.

TOM: Pete, I'm worried about Linda. She called a little while ago from some diner called Rosie's. She said she was following someone. Maybe I should've called Officer Brady.
PETE: Oh, I don't think you should worry too much. Linda can take care of herself.
TOM: Well, maybe. But she hung up so suddenly. I'm afraid she may be in trouble. She shouldn't have gone alone.
PETE: Hmm. I see what you mean. I guess you should've gone to Rosie's right away.
TOM: Yeah, maybe it's not too late. Why don't we go now?
PETE: OK. Let's get going.

Page 88, Ex. 6

Linda has told the criminals that her friends at the *Herald* are going to be worried. Carol wants her to call and tell them she's fine. Listen to the conversation and complete it.

CAROL: Now you're going to call the *Herald.*
LINDA: But I have no idea what I should say.
CAROL: I'm sure you'll think of something. They must wonder where you are and why you haven't called them again. But you'd better not try to do anything funny.
LINDA: OK. *(She dials)* Hello. Mr. Tran? This is Linda Smith. Can you tell me if Angela's there?
MINH: Angela's out of town for a week. Didn't you know that?
LINDA: Yes, I did. She must want to know why I didn't call her back today. Please tell her that I'm not sure if I'll be able to meet her at 6:00 at El Fuego. My sister's sick, and I have to see her right away.
MINH: What's going on Linda? Are you in . . .
LINDA: Thank you, Mr. Tran.

Page 89, Ex. 1

Angela flew to Chicago. A few weeks before, she called Northeastern Airlines to make a reservation. Listen to part of her conversation and complete it.

AGENT: Northeastern.
ANGELA: Hello. I'd like to make a round-trip reservation on one of your flights from Houston to Chicago.
AGENT: OK. When would you like to leave?
ANGELA: On July 11th.
AGENT: And the return flight?
ANGELA: July 18th.
AGENT: What time of day would you like to leave?
ANGELA: In the morning.
AGENT: Well, we have a 9:30 flight and an 11:15.
ANGELA: I'd prefer the earlier one. And coming back on the 18th, I'd like a morning flight too.
AGENT: How about one leaving Chicago at 10:00 A.M., arriving in Houston at 12:25?
ANGELA: That sounds fine. Can you tell me what the fare is?
AGENT: It's $229.00 round trip.
ANGELA: I wonder if I can make my seat reservation now too.
AGENT: Certainly. Do you want smoking or non-smoking?
ANGELA: Non-smoking.
AGENT: Window or aisle?
ANGELA: Aisle, please.
AGENT: Please hold on while I check the computer.

Page 91, Ex. 5

Listen to the announcements and choose the correct answers.

1. Western Airlines paging passenger José López. Please report to the information booth adjacent to gate 24. José López, please report to the information booth adjacent to gate 24.
2. In just a moment, we will begin boarding for flight 400 to Chicago. We will *pre*board passengers needing a little extra time or assistance. Please have your boarding pass available.
3. Can I have your attention please? James Walski, please meet your party at USA Airlines, gate 36. James Walski, please meet your party at USA Airlines, gate 36.
4. Attention passengers flying Northeastern Airlines flight 400 to Chicago. We will now begin boarding by seat number. Those passengers in rows 26 to 46, please proceed to gate 11A.
5. We are now ready for take-off. Please make sure that your seat belts are securely fastened and that you have extinguished all smoking materials.

TAPESCRIPT FOR PRONUNCIATION EXERCISES

Page 116

Part 1

Pete and Tom are talking about Linda again. Listen to their conversation and complete it.

PETE: Have you heard from Linda yet?
TOM: Yes. She called just a few minutes ago.
PETE: Where was she?
TOM: At some diner. I think that her young friend Bill was there too.
PETE: I don't like this. When's Angela coming back?
TOM: Not until July 18th. I hope Linda can stay out of trouble until then.
PETE: Yes. And I hope Bill can stay out of jail.

Now listen again and repeat the conversation.

Part 2

Listen and complete each conversation with *should've* or *shouldn't have.*

1. A: What's the matter?
   B: I should've watched that program.
2. A: What's wrong?
   B: I shouldn't have bought that sweater.
3. A: What's the matter?
   B: We should've gone on vacation.
4. A: Is something wrong?
   B: Yes. We should've invited your sister to dinner.
5. A: Are you upset about something?
   B: Yes. You shouldn't have told him about it.
6. A: What do *you* think?
   B: They shouldn't have gotten married.

Now listen again and repeat each conversation.

UNIT 11

Page 95, Ex. 1

Carol, Phil, Luke and Linda are talking. Listen to their conversations and complete them. Then report what each person said.

1. CAROL: It's late.
   PHIL: I'm hurrying.
   LUKE: We're almost ready.
2. LINDA: Frank's going to look for you.
   CAROL: I'm going to leave him a note.
3. LUKE: We're going to be rich!
   PHIL: I've already picked out a new car.
4. LUKE: We can leave in a few minutes.
   LINDA: The police will catch you!
   CAROL: The police will *never* find us.
   PHIL: Tomorrow we'll all be out of the country.

Page 96, Ex. 3

While Carol was in Frank's office, she answered the telephone. Listen to the conversation and complete the message Carol left for Frank.

CAROL: Mr. Jordan's office.
KEN: Is Mr. Jordan there?
CAROL: No, I'm sorry he isn't. Who's calling, please?
KEN: This is Ken Wilson. Is this his secretary?
CAROL: No, this is his assistant, Carol Fullerton. Can I take a message?
KEN: Yes. I just called to thank him for the flowers he and Angela sent me in the hospital. Please tell him that I *am* interested in the job and I'll call him in a few days.

Page 96, Ex. 4, Dictation

Ken called Officer Brady to give him some important information. Listen to their conversation. Then listen again and complete it.

KEN: Officer Brady? This is Ken Wilson.
BRADY: Yes, Mr. Wilson. How can I help you?
KEN: Well, this may sound crazy, but . . .
BRADY: Yes?
KEN: Well, I've just been speaking to Frank Jordan's assistant, Carol Fullerton, and . . .
BRADY: Yes, go on.
KEN: Well, she sounds just like the woman at the warehouse fire.
BRADY: Are you sure?
KEN: Yes, I'm positive that it's the same voice.
BRADY: Do you know her?
KEN: No, but I'm sure she's involved with the fires.

Page 98, Put It All Together

Cathy and Minh are telling Officer Brady about Linda's strange telephone call. Listen and complete their conversation.

BRADY: This does sound strange. Go on. Tell me everything you can remember.
MINH: Well, Linda said she couldn't meet Angela at some restaurant because she had to see her sister.
CATHY: Didn't she also say what time she was going to meet Angela and the name of the restaurant?
MINH: Yes. She said she was going to meet Angela at 6:00. But I didn't really understand the name of the restaurant.
CATHY: Try to remember. This is important.
MINH: It was a strange name. Something like "fwaygo."
BRADY: That sounds like Spanish.
CATHY: Yes, and I think Linda studied Spanish. Let's look it up in the dictionary.
BRADY: I don't know what it means, but I think it's spelled f-u-e-g-o. Here, I found it! Aha! I think I know what Linda meant. We'd better get going!
CATHY: OK. Let me leave a message for Pete and Tom.

TAPESCRIPT FOR PRONUNCIATION EXERCISES

Page 116

Part 1

Listen and complete these sentences.

1. I got a very strange call from Linda.
2. Really? I don't like it.
3. Call the police right away.
4. What else did she say?
5. She was going to go to a restaurant.
6. She's living with Angela.
7. Listen to the radio.

Now listen again and repeat the sentences.

Part 2

Minh and Cathy are talking about Linda. Listen to their conversation and complete it by choosing the correct punctuation—an exclamation point (!) after the exclamations, a period (.) after the statements and a question mark (?) after the questions.

MINH: I got a really strange phone call.
CATHY: Really? What was strange about it?
MINH: Linda wanted to talk to Angela!
CATHY: You're kidding! What else did she say?
MINH: She said she had to take care of her sister.
CATHY: Her sister! Linda's an only child.

Now listen again and repeat the conversation.

UNIT 12

Page 104, Ex. 2

Listen to the conversation Pete and Michael had yesterday. Then look at the list and decide if Pete *let, didn't let* or *made* Michael do the following things.

MICHAEL: Dad, can I go out and play now?
PETE: Sure, but first you have to call Grandma.
MICHAEL: Oh, Dad, do I really have to?
PETE: Yes, you do.
MICHAEL: OK. I'll do it now. And then is it OK if I have a soda?
PETE: No, you're drinking too much soda. It's not good for you.
MICHAEL: Can I have chocolate milk and cookies, then?
PETE: You can have some chocolate milk but not cookies. But first, call your grandmother!
MICHAEL: Oh, and I wanted to invite my friend Rosa for dinner. She's in my class.
PETE: That's a good idea. But what about your homework?
MICHAEL: I can do it in the morning before school.
PETE: *That's* not a good idea. If you want to have your friend over, you must do your homework *before* dinner.
MICHAEL: Can Rosa and I do our homework together?
PETE: No, I prefer you to do it alone.

Page 105, Ex. 1

Some of the *Herald* staff is talking about Linda. Listen to the conversation and choose the things they say they ought to do for her.

ANGELA: You know, Linda did such a great job on the arson story and she had such an awful experience at the end, we really ought to do something special for her.
PETE: I know. What can we do to cheer her up?
CATHY: I thought about giving her a present, but I couldn't think of anything good.
PETE: Yeah, I thought about going out to a restaurant, but that's not special enough.
CATHY: I know. We ought to give her a surprise party.
PETE: Yeah, we can have it at my apartment.
ANGELA: A party's a good idea, but we ought to do something more.
PETE: I think she ought to get some kind of award for bravery.
ANGELA: I agree. Let's get her a trophy. And I ought to give her a raise too.

Page 107, Ex. 1

Ken Wilson is going to start working as a welder at one of Frank Jordan's businesses—Jordan Ironworks. Ken is asking his supervisor, Allan, some questions about company benefits. Listen and complete their conversation.

KEN: I've got some questions about company benefits.
ALLAN: Sure. What would you like to know?
KEN: Well, first of all, I'd like to know about health insurance.
ALLAN: You get major medical health insurance, which helps cover your doctors' visits and your hospital bills. You don't get dental coverage, though.
KEN: Does the major medical begin immediately?
ALLAN: No. It starts after you've been here for three months.
KEN: And what about life insurance? I've got a wife and two kids.
ALLAN: You also get that after three months on the job. And you get disability.
KEN: And how much vacation time do I get?
ALLAN: One week after a year, two weeks after two years, and three weeks after three years.
KEN: That doesn't sound bad.
ALLAN: Yeah, we've got a pretty good union here.

TAPESCRIPT FOR PRONUNCIATION EXERCISES

Page 116

Part 1

Listen and complete these sentences.

1. They placed the crate on the truck.
2. The prisoner was very frightened.
3. The trio had a dramatic plan.
4. They were going to fly to Brazil.
5. Now Linda can take a break.

Now listen and repeat the sentences.

Part 2

Listen and repeat these sentences.

1. Carol was going to be a scientist.
2. She was going to be rich and famous.
3. She was going to travel a lot.
4. She was going to sell the stolen paintings.

Part 3

Frank and Angela are talking about Carol. Listen to their conversation and complete it.

FRANK: I can't believe Carol was going to kill Linda.
ANGELA: Well, it's true. The police are going to put her in jail for a long time.
FRANK: I'm going to go see her. I want to know why she did this.
ANGELA: She really ought to give you a full explanation.

Now listen again and repeat the conversation.

FINAL TEST

TAPESCRIPT FOR LISTENING COMPREHENSION TEST

See page 162 of the Teacher's Manual.

Brad is talking to a new reporter, Crystal Chase. You will hear Brad's part of the conversation. Circle the correct answers for Crystal's part of the conversation.

51. BRAD: I think you'll like working at the Houston *Herald*, Crystal.

52. BRAD: When will you get your first assignment?

53. BRAD: You're kidding! You must be a very experienced reporter.

54. BRAD: Did Angela tell you what you'll cover?

55. BRAD: Linda knows a lot about that. You ought to talk to her.

56. BRAD: But I think Angela's going to make her take a vacation for a while.

57. BRAD: Speaking of vacations, were you told about company benefits?

58. BRAD: Great. Oh, this is your computer terminal. Most reporters use the computer now.

59. BRAD: One more thing. You mustn't smoke in the office.

60. BRAD: Well, good luck, Crystal. Call me if you need help.

Workbook Answer Key

UNIT 1

1 1. e, c, a 2. b 3. d
2 2. prefer 3. cover 4. do over 5. cover 6. prefer 7. doing, over 8. power
3 2. I'm glad to see you're using video. 3. Yes, we just started using it last year. 4. The students are very happy with it.
4 *Answers will vary.*
5 3. 're working 4. have 5. seem 6. 'm covering 7. need 8. 'm eating
6 *Answers will vary.*
7 1. can 2. might 3. cannot 4. should 5. shouldn't
8 1. do *(is used in the present progressive)* 2. quickly *(not an adverb of frequency)* 3. work *(not a modal auxiliary)* 4. newsroom *(not a person)* 5. us *(not a subject pronoun)*
9 2. Tom still prefers to use a typewriter. 3. Linda can't finish an article in one day.
10 *Answers will vary.*
11 *Across:* 2. point out 3. look over 5. drop off 6. hand in 7. call up
Down: 1. look up 2. put out 4. bring back
12 2. drop it off 3. look it over 4. point out 5. bring back 6. look up 7. call you up
13 2. I have to pick her up after school. 3. Michael hands it in every day. 4. The chauffeur dropped him off at the airport.
14 2. he 3. We 4. they 5. They 6. we
15 2. However 3. but 4. and
16 *Answers will vary.*

UNIT 2

1 2. a 3. d 4. c
2 *Answers will vary.*
3 *Answers will vary.*
4 *Answers will vary slightly.* 2. A: How long has he been married? B: For a long time. 3. A: How long has he had a motorcycle? B: Since he came to this country. 4. A: How long has he worked at the *Herald?* B: Since 1984.
5 *Answers will vary.*
6 *Some possible answers:* in, it, no, nor, not, far, fat, fit, for, oar, of, on, or, ran, rat, rot, man, mat, a, an, ant, arm, art, tan, tar, tin, to, ton
7 2. have worked 3. have turned in 4. have done, over 5. have traveled 6. have met 7. have forgotten 8. has seemed 9. has been 10. have not been
8 In her twenty years in the newspaper business, she served many good editors, and many good writers worked for her. She turned in many articles, and then she did them over. She traveled all over the world. In her travels, she met hundreds of people, and she forgot several foreign languages! Her job seemed terrible sometimes, and it was wonderful often. But she was never bored.
9 2. experience 3. education 4. bilingual
10 2. A: How long has he lived in Houston? B: For two months. OR Since March 1. 3. A: When was he the editor of his college newspaper? B: From 1975 to 1976. 4. A: How long has he worked as a reporter? B: For thirteen years. OR Since 1977. 5. A: When did he graduate from college? B: In 1976.
11 *Answers may vary slightly.* 2. To buy (a) new (pair of) glasses. 3. To meet people. 4. To look for a new job.
12 2. What is your address? 3. 682–7734 4. No. 5. My mother, Juana Sánchez. Her phone number is 667–4117. 6. Are you allergic to any drugs?
13 1. condition 2. related 3. good 4. visiting 5. floor 6. Wing

UNIT 3

1 *Answers will vary.*
2 *Answer may vary slightly.*
I was working when I heard about the blackout. As soon as I heard the news, I tried to call you. But all the phone lines were busy after they reported the power failure. When you called the office, I was going home.
3 *Answers may vary.* 3. used to see 4. see skyscrapers 5. used to meet 6. meet crowds of people
4 *Answers will vary.*
5 *Answers will vary.*

6 2.–5. warned, reminded, encouraged, asked

W	A	R	N	E	D	X	A	V	R	A
A	M	E	T	Y	P	F	B	I	W	S
N	O	M	R	U	Z	J	C	R	D	K
T	L	I	J	N	E	A	O	Z	Q	E
E	E	N	C	O	U	R	A	G	E	D
D	E	D	U	U	L	C	K	E	E	D
P	O	E	P	U	L	A	T	E	D	V
A	R	D	I	S	T	O	F	R	A	T

7 2. Pete encouraged Tom to use a computer. 3. Michael asked Pete (his father) to take him to the game on Saturday. 4. Brad reminded Minh to take pictures of the museum renovation. 5. Angela warned Frank to be careful.

8 *Answers will vary.*

9 *Answers will vary. Possible answers:* 1. Because people were using their air conditioners full blast and the plant couldn't take it. OR Because a turbine blew up. 2. By noon. 3. No, it hasn't. This is the biggest power blackout ever.

10 2. hung up 3. huge 4. find out 5. receiver
Explanations will vary. Possible explanations:
(hung up) The conversation was over, so Peter put down the telephone.
(huge) Peter needed five steps to get across the office.
(find out) Peter gives the woman some information after she asks, "What did you find out?"
(receiver) Peter has just answered the telephone. Also, the receiver "receives" the voice.

11 1. blew up 2. damage 3. Repairpersons 4. blackout 5. massive

12 *Answer may vary slightly.* As soon as he got outside, he took out the keys to his tiny sports car. He usually laughed at himself as he got his long legs under the steering wheel. But today he drove off without a smile after he turned the radio on full blast to quiet his thoughts.

UNIT 4

1 2. a 3. e 4. d 5. b

2 *Answers may vary slightly.* 2. A: How long have Ann and Betty been swimming? B: For an hour and a half. 3. A: How long has Juanita been typing? B: For a long time. 4. A: How long have Roger and Lois been waiting for the bus? B: Since 1:00.

3 3. 's been happening 4. for 5. 's been looking 6. since 7. 's been sending out 8. 's been trying 9. since 10. 's, painted 11. 's taken

4 *Answers may vary slightly.* 2. Mike's too young to join the Army. 3. Greg's too clumsy to dance. 4. Jasu is efficient enough to be a secretary.

5 *Answers will vary. Some possible answers:* 1. He practiced enough to become very good. He practiced enough to play on the team. He was good enough to play on the team. He was not tall enough to be a professional. He was intelligent enough to be a coach. He loved the game enough to be a coach (to teach it).
2. Sara is talented enough to work for a famous designer. She used to be too disorganized to be a success. She was too disorganized to remember important meetings. Pete is efficient enough to help Sara. He is efficient enough to know where everything is. Sara is successful enough to plan her own show.

6 *Answers will vary.*

7 *Adjectives:* pretty, strong, easy, sick

H	A	P	P	Y	X	R
L	P	R	W	A	H	I
Q	U	E	Z	Z	I	C
A	S	T	R	O	N	G
W	I	T	U	E	I	O
B	C	Y	E	A	S	Y
I	K	O	E	C	D	U

8 *Answers will vary. Some possible answers:* 1. I thought it was too modern. 2. Then it won't be quiet enough. 3. The second one wasn't as big as the first one. 4. Yeah, you're right. It's probably too expensive for us.

9 *Across:* 1. refund 3. receipt 5. small 7. size 8. charge *Down:* 2. exchange 4. too 6. finance

10 1. 37 2. 38 3. 42 4. 38

11 1. peaceful *(not a negative adjective)* 2. size *(not an article of clothing)* 3. weather *(not an adjective)* 4. ugly *(not a positive adjective)*

UNIT 5

1 1. Two heads are better than one. 2. Why don't you take a break and get a bite to eat with me? 3. I'm not getting anywhere with this story.

2 *Across:* 4. describe 6. told 9. matter 10. two 12. one *Down:* 1. me 2. better 3. help 5. sketch 7. doing 8. getting 11. OK

3 1. frightening 2. annoying, annoyed 3. confused, confusing 4. embarrassing, embarrassed

4 1. bored 2. Discouraged 3. Tired 4. interesting 5. exciting 6. encouraging 7. confusing 8. pleased

5 1. haven't been able to 2. be able to 3. was able to 4. 'll be able to

6 1. TO: Linda
Minh wasn't able to get the finished pictures of the fire yet, but he'll be able to give them to you tomorrow morning.
2. TO: The Captain
Bill wasn't able to identify the driver. Our artist was able to get a good sketch from Bill's description, though.
3. TO: Angela Lentini
Your husband was able to get tickets for the next concert. He'll be in a meeting until 4:00, but he'll be able to call you again after that.

7 2. ourselves 3. yourself 4. himself 5. themselves

8 1. themselves 2. herself 3. each other 4. themselves OR each other 5. himself 6. herself

9 *Answers may vary slightly.* 1. She's talking to herself. 2. She can put them on herself. OR She's putting them on herself. 3. No, they're staring at each other.

10 How You Write Is How You Are

11 *Answers may vary slightly.* 1. Dallas is closer to my parents, so we can visit them often. 2. the children don't want to move because they like their school. 3. it will be difficult to sell our house now; therefore, we won't be able to buy a home in Dallas.

UNIT 6

1 1. e, a 2. c 3. b 4. d

2 *Answers will vary.*

3 1. anonymous 2. urgent 3. threatening 4. dangerous 5. dangerous 6. anonymous 7. urgent 8. threatening

4 *Answers will vary. Some possible answers:* 1. many more families drive to the museum 2. college students and older people won't want to go there 3. there are more people 4. if we have to hire more guards

5 *Answers will vary. Some possible answers:* 2. If you use Data computers, you'll do well in school. 3. If you wear Cougar running shoes, you'll run very fast.

6 *Answers will vary. Possible answers:* 2. You'd better not forget your umbrella. 3. We'd better move to a bigger apartment. 4. You'd better stop talking.

7 1. had better 2. Would 3. should 4. might 5. can

8 2.–9. started, have trouble, continue, suggest, consider, avoid, keep, remember

S	T	A	R	T	E	D	M	P	U	R
H	A	V	E	T	R	O	U	B	L	E
E	C	O	N	T	I	N	U	E	O	M
A	D	I	S	L	I	K	E	I	Z	E
R	O	D	M	O	R	E	A	W	S	M
S	I	K	R	O	P	E	C	Q	U	B
L	E	G	O	R	B	P	S	W	O	E
S	U	G	G	E	S	T	X	P	U	R
C	O	N	S	I	D	E	R	O	A	K

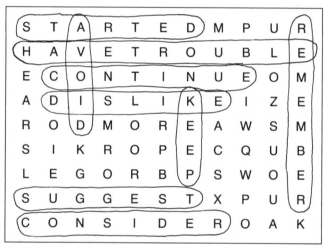

9 3. remember 4. enjoying 5. started 6. feeling 7. avoid 8. doing 9. suggest 10. quitting

10 *Answers will vary. Verbs to be used:* consider, continue, keep, have trouble

11 1. d 2. b 3. c 4. a

12 1. TO: Frank Jordan TIME: 3:00 P.M. M:S. Lentini OR Your wife (CHECK: TELEPHONED and PLEASE CALL) MESSAGE: She'll be out for an hour. Please call her back at around 4:00.
2. TO: Bill Thomas TIME: 1:30 M:S. Linda Smith (CHECK: TELEPHONED and WILL CALL AGAIN) MESSAGE: She'll call again at about 2:00.

UNIT 7

1 1. b. see c. By the way d. enjoying e. am
2. a. annoyed b. annoying c. two heads are better than one
3. a. I don't believe it b. telling c. 'd

2 2. f 3. e 4. a 5. c 6. b

3 2. seeing 3. doing 4. bringing 5. arriving OR coming
6. coming OR arriving 7. being 8. serving

4 1. Studying 2. keeping 3. Rewarding

5 2. Oil is found in Texas. 3. Oranges are grown in Florida.
4. They grow wheat in Idaho.

6 *Answers will vary.* 2. Oil is found in Texas, so my ship will pass Florida, Virginia and Maryland. 3. Oranges are grown in Florida. Therefore, orange juice will be very expensive.
4. Because they grow wheat in Idaho and Kansas, I will go there to find material for cereal and flour. OR Because I need wheat to make cereal and flour, I will go to Idaho and Kansas to find the material I need.

7 1. Classified Ads a. opened b. arranged c. mailed
d. answered e. delivered
2. Home a. watching b. telling c. feeling d. planning
e. enjoying
3. Local News a. avoiding b. Warning c. told

8 *Answers will vary.*

9 *Answers will vary.*

UNIT 8

1 *Across:* 2. good 4. shift 7. hard 8. believe 10. OK
Down: 1. mortgage 3. hired 4. salary 5. fine 6. meet
9. like

2 *Answers will vary.*

3 1. . . .as soon as he gets a raise 2. 'll start looking before he gets his raise 3. 'll be more comfortable after we move

4 *Answers may vary slightly.* 2. I'll go shopping before I come home. 3. I'll walk the dog as soon as I get home. 4. I'll put the food in the refrigerator after I walk the dog.

5 *Answers will vary.*

6 3. were not permitted 4. was kept 5. are told 6. were spoken to 7. are hurt 8. were noticed 9. was annoyed

7 *Answers will vary. Some possible answers:* 2. *(should include an adverb of frequency)* Linda usually writes her articles in the office. 3. *(should include a past tense marker or subordinate clause in the past tense)* The painting was destroyed yesterday. The painting was destroyed when the warehouse burned down. 4. *(should include a time expression showing action currently in progress)* This year he's learning how to use a computer. 5. *(should include an expression with* for *or* since*)* We have lived in this neighborhood since 1980/for ten years.

8 2. worked 3. left 4. was promoted 5. studied 6. has
7. to entertain 8. are educated 9. lives 10. saves
11. asked 12. get 13. 'll have 14. goes 15. 'll start

9 *Answers will vary. Some possible answers:* She must not have much free time because she has a family and a full-time job. She must be a good cook because she knows a lot about food. She must be in good shape because she likes to jog. Her daughter must be very young because she doesn't go to kindergarten yet.

10 *Answers will vary.*

11 1. False 2. True 3. False 4. True 5. True

12 1. b 2. d 3. e 4. a 5. c
Conversation: 2. 1 3. dishwashing liquid 4. paper products
5. fresh fruits and vegetables 6. 5

UNIT 9

1 2. c 3. b 4. a 5. f 6. h 7. d 8. i

2 2. slowly 3. carefully 4. courageously 5. completely
6. hard 7. honestly 8. well 9. sloppily 10. politely

3 *Answers will vary: Some possible answers:* 2. He wanted to learn Chinese correctly because he knew it was going to be useful in his career. 3. He tries to live cheaply, but that is difficult when you have children. 4. She investigates her stories courageously, and she writes well too.

4 2. faster 3. more courteously than 4. excellently
5. creatively

5 *Answers will vary. Some possible answers:* 1. he dresses more neatly 2. He also works harder 3. writes better

6 *Answers will vary.*

7 *Answers may vary.* 2. I don't know who to talk to. 3. I don't know how to fix this sink. 4. I don't know where to buy the ingredients for Chinese cooking.

8 *Answers may vary.* 2. No, you mustn't touch the paintings. 3. Ellen, you mustn't take the statue home. OR Ellen, you must leave the statue here. 4. Sorry, Ellen. You have to (must) leave your snack in the cafeteria. OR You mustn't bring food here. 5. Stop, Johnny. You mustn't run here. 6. you don't have to be quiet.

9 *Answers may vary.* 1. They serve French food (cuisine). 2. Yes, it is. OR Yes, it's very expensive. 3. No, I don't think so. 4. Yes, (I think) we should.

10 *Answers will vary.*

UNIT 10

1 *Across:* 3. send 5. What's up 7. Take 9. came 11. eavesdropping 13. did, do 16. Did, say 18. was showing 19. sounds
Down: 1. was talking 2. snoops 4. knew 6. to begin 8. read 10. Are 12. positive 14. ran 15. easy 17. couldn't

2 *Answers will vary.* 2. . . .shouldn't have written it sitting on the floor. OR . . .should've written it at my desk (at a table). 3. . . .shouldn't have talked in class. OR . . .should've paid attention (listened in class). 4. I shouldn't have read it while I was watching TV. OR I should've turned off the TV.

3 *Answers will vary. Some possible answers:* Carol's family should have told her they weren't rich. They shouldn't have sent her to such expensive schools. Carol should have found a job in high school. She shouldn't have traveled. She should have gotten a job that paid better.

4 *Answers will vary. Some possible answers:* 2. I'd like to know who painted it. 3. I wonder if it's real. 4. I'd like to know where the artist is now. OR I wonder where they found this painting. 5. I don't understand why that fork looks like that. 6. I'd like to know how much the museum paid for it.

5 *Answers will vary.*

6 *Answers will vary. Some possible answers:* I wonder why the man was carrying a briefcase. I wonder why he forgot his briefcase. I wonder what was in the briefcase. I wonder if it was something valuable. I'd like to know where the man was going. I wonder what he said to the boy. I wonder how much money he gave him.

7 *Answers will vary. Some possible questions:* Do you know what the weather will be like in Miami tomorrow? . . .how long it will rain in Dallas? . . .where there will be good weather? . . .if the weather will be clear in Houston tomorrow? . . .who stars in "Blue Balloon"? . . .what happened in "Randy's Hope" today? . . .how to spell the past tense of *forget?*

8 2. I'm not sure. We should have checked the review before we came. 3. I wonder if they take U.S. Express credit cards. 4. I think so. But I don't understand why it's so crowded. 5. Waiter, we'd like to know how long we'll have to wait. 6. About an hour. I'm afraid you should have made a reservation.

9 *Answers may vary slightly.* 1. No, it's not. It's delayed. 2. What gate do I go to (Where do I go for) flight 110 to New York? 3. At 11:30. It's on time. 4. I'm sorry. That flight has been cancelled.

10 *Answers may vary slightly.* 1. Where's the restaurant? 2. Where can I get a bus (a taxi/ground transportation)? 3. Where's the lost-and-found? 4. Is there a waiting room for non-smokers?

11 *Answers will vary.*

UNIT 11

1 1. b 2. c 3. f 4. g 5. e 6. d 7. a

2 2. was 3. did not think 4. would be 5. were 6. were 7. could

3 2. were 3. were married 4. was set 5. is 6. said 7. said 8. asked 9. felt 10 didn't 11. is 12. wore 13. carried 14. stood

4 *Answers to the questions will vary.* 2. I asked the Fire Chief if it was a good training exercise and why. He told me. . . 3. I asked the photographer what his best photograph was. He said. . .

5 *Answers may vary slightly.* 2. . . .she told me to stop feeding her. 3. She told me to turn on the TV. 4. About 45 minutes. Then she told me to read her a story. 5. About 7:30, she told me to kiss her goodnight. 6. Well, no. At 8:30 she told me to give her a glass of water.

6 *Answers may vary slightly.* The little girl asked her mother to buy her the truck. Her mother said she didn't have enough money with her. Then the little girl asked when she could have it. Her mother told her she would buy it the next day on the way to work.

7 *Answers may vary.* 1. garbage, waste 2. getting rid of garbage (plastic wrappings) 3. Because he or she feels we need a new law to control use of plastic products. OR Because he or she thinks we may soon be buried by plastic products. 4. a. Too much plastic wrap is used. b. There are other dangers from too much plastic wrap. c. Other cities have banned the use of plastic wraps.

8 *Answers will vary.*

UNIT 12

1 *Answers will vary but should contain this information:* 1. Yes, I am. 2. They caught me when I discovered their hideout. 3. No, no one was hurt. 4. I called the *Herald* with a secret message. 5. They wanted to steal some paintings. 6. Carol Fullerton worked for the Museum. 7. Yes, they are. They said I was very helpful to them.

2 1. drama 2. surrender 3. trio 4. motive 5. robbery

3 *Answers may vary slightly.* 2. I was going to go shopping, but it was too hot 3. . . .were going to go to a movie, but there was nothing we wanted to see 4. I was going to relax, but I just want to go back to work

4 1. . . .was going to play professional basketball, but he hurt his leg in a car accident. 2. He was going to go into business, but he discovered he made more money on weekends playing golf. 3. He was going to go into the Army when he was 17, but his mother would not sign the form.

5 1. let 2. choose 3. make 4. eat 5. let 6. let 7. decide 8. let 9. drink 10. make 11. have 12. let 13. pick

6 1. Angela made Linda take a few days off work. 2. She wants to let Linda relax a little before Linda comes back. 3. Angela treats her employees well and makes them feel comfortable at work.

7 *Answers will vary.*

8 *Answers will vary. Some possible answers:* 1. She ought to ask her supervisor or someone in the personnel office because she might not get the right answer from a co-worker. 2. He ought to check (find out) her U.S. size. OR He ought to find out the store's refund or exchange policy because the clothing might not fit his mother. 3. She ought to call the hospital and find out the room number and visiting hours. OR She ought to call her friend's family and find out what's wrong because her friend might be very sick or might not want visitors. 4. He ought to make a list before he goes shopping. OR He ought to check the cost per unit of the items he buys because sometimes the larger size is not really a bargain. OR He ought to use coupons because you can sometimes save money with them.

9 1. will 2. must 3. don't have to 4. should OR ought to 5. may 6. ought to OR should

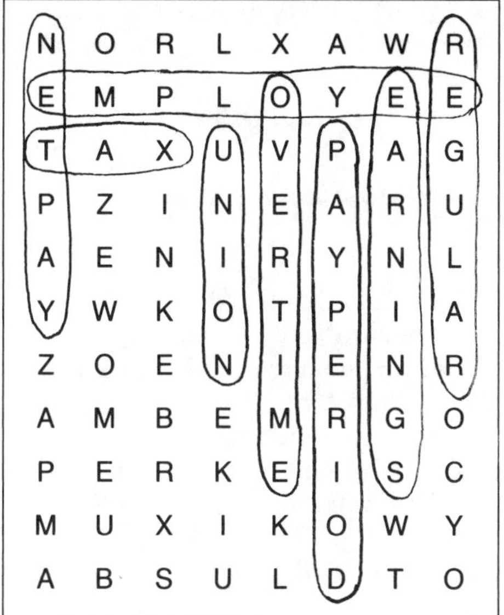

10 1. employee 2. pay period 3. earnings 4. regular 5. overtime 6. union 7. tax 8. net pay
A penny saved is a penny earned.

Answer Key for Midterm Test

I. 1. b. Then you should find a new one. 2. a. It's listed as good. 3. c. I've been working overtime. 4. c. I'm sure you'll be able to find one soon. 5. a. This is Jillian. Please call me tomorrow. 6. b. I know what you mean. 7. a. Sure. I'll be able to do it tonight.
II. 8. b. I was at the museum. 9. b. I'm taking pictures of the renovation. 10. a. To make room for the new paintings. 11. a. I don't believe it! 12. b. I think we will. 13. a. Yes, you did. 14. b. I will if I don't work too late. 15. c. That sounds like a good idea. 16. a. I'd like to return these shoes. 17. c. They're too small. 18. a. No, she didn't. 19. b. Here it is.
III. 20. since 21. to speak 22. gets back 23. 'll give 24. called 25. 've been trying 26. for
IV. 27. be able to 28. might 29. can 30. 'd better
V. 31. picks up 32. has dropped him off OR has been dropping him off 33. old enough 34. himself 35. themselves 36. too young
VI. 37. am writing 38. interesting 39. as cool as 40. While 41. saw 42. enjoying 43. But 44. will like 45. relaxing 46. play 47. b 48. a 49. b 50. c
VII. 51. c. It's great to be here, Tom. 52. a. That's right. I'm coaching. 53. b. The Children's Club. 54. c. For the past two summers. 55. a. To help out neighborhood kids. 56. c. Yes, I played on one for years. 57. b. If you practice, you will get better. 58. a. They'd better just enjoy playing the game. 59. a. No, I'm too young to retire. 60. b. Sure thing.

Answer Key for Final Test

I. 1. b. Taking long walks. 2. a. Every two weeks. 3. c. I know how you feel. 4. b. Why don't you ask at the hospital? 5. a. Take it easy. 6. b. I like the weather. 7. a. I'm sorry to hear that. 8. b. To get a driver's license. 9. c. I was waiting for the bus. 10. b. You should have practiced more.
II. 11. b. As soon as I finish writing this page. 12. a. For ten years. 13. c. After I graduated from college. 14. a. Writing about government, I think. 15. b. Important decisions are made there. 16. c. I was going to be President. 17. a. I was aggressive enough to be a good politician. 18. b. I wrote better than I talked. 19. a. Yes, I was. 20. b. They ought to be ready to work hard. 21. c. Don't mention it.
III. 22. is made 23. making 24. must 25. to fill 26. had to 27. was boiling 28. cooked 29. would 30. mustn't
IV. 31. 3 32. 2 33. 3 34. 4
V. 35. b 36. c 37. c
VI. 38. When it was done? 39. look that up 40. are caused OR were caused 41. those problems were 42. 'll call 43. finish
VII. 44. must 45. faster 46. more accurately 47. don't have to 48. ought to 49. make 50. should've
VIII. 51. b. Thanks, I'm sure I will. 52. As soon as I talk to Angela today. 53. c. I've been a reporter for about five years. 54. a. She said I'll cover politics. 55. a. I know. I was going to. 56. b. I think that's a good idea. 57. b. Yes, I was. 58. c. I've been using one for ages too. 59. a. OK. 60. b. Thanks for your help.

MIDTERM TEST

Name: ______________________________

Course: ______________________________

Date: ______________________________

Grade: ______________________________

I. Circle the correct answer in each conversation. Then write it on the line.

> **EXAMPLE:**
>
> A: This is my wife, Vilma.
>
> B: *Nice to meet you.*
> a. I think so too.
> (b) Nice to meet you.
> c. That's right.

1. A: I really hate my job.

   B: ______________________________
   a. You usually cover politics.
   b. Then you should find a new one.
   c. How long did you wait?

2. A: Can you please tell me the condition of Luis Goris? This is his wife.

   B: ______________________________
   a. It's listed as good.
   b. He's on the fifth floor, North Wing.
   c. Are you related to the patient?

3. A: What have you been doing lately?

   B: ______________________________
   a. The train broke down.
   b. I'll learn to drive.
   c. I've been working overtime.

4. A: I'm really discouraged about finding a job.

   B: ______________________________
   a. OK. Maybe you'll be able to help.
   b. I'm not. It's too tiring.
   c. I'm sure you'll be able to find one soon.

5. A: At the sound of the beep, please leave a short message.

   B: ______________________________
   a. This is Jillian. Please call me tomorrow.
   b. Sure. Please hold on while I get a pencil.
   c. I'm sorry. I dialed the wrong number.

6. A: I really miss my high school friends.

   B: ______________________________
   a. You'd better call the police.
   b. I know what you mean.
   c. Two heads are better than one.

7. A: Can you help me with this application form?

   B: ______________________________
   a. Sure. I'll be able to do it tonight.
   b. I can take care of myself.
   c. You should get a bit to eat with me.

8. LAN: I tried to reach you at the office this afternoon.

   MINH: ______________________________
   a. I'm not sure.
   b. I was at the museum.
   c. I haven't started yet.

II. Circle the correct answers to complete the conversation. Then write them.

> **EXAMPLE:**
>
> LAN: Sorry I'm late.
>
> MINH: That's OK. *I've been watching TV.*
> (a.) I've been watching TV.
> b. I've watched TV.
> c. I'll read a magazine.

9. LAN: What are you working on there?

MINH: ______________________

a. I started working there today.
b. I'm taking pictures of the renovation.
c. After they finish the new Children's Room.

10. LAN: The museum is already so big. Why do we need a new wing?

MINH: ______________________

a. To make room for the new paintings.
b. When they build a new restaurant.
c. If they want more people to visit the museum.

11. LAN: Speaking of sizes, the shoes we got May are too small.

MINH: ______________________ We checked them when she tried them on.

a. I don't believe it!
b. They'll fit next year.
c. That's a great idea.

12. LAN: It's true. I hope we'll be able to return them.

MINH: ______________________ We only bought them a few days ago.

a. I thought we couldn't.
b. I think we will.
c. I think we did.

13. LAN: Did I remind you to keep the receipt?

MINH: ______________________ It's right here in my wallet.

a. Yes, you did.
b. Yes, you are.
c. Yes, we have.

14. LAN: Good. Could you drop them off on your way home tomorrow?

MINH: ______________________

a. No, I'll be careful.
b. I will if I don't work too late.
c. I usually don't drop them off.

15. LAN: And ask for a refund. I think we can get a better pair at the mall.

MINH: ______________________

a. It'll be OK. Don't worry.
b. If you don't call them, I will.
c. That sounds like a good idea.

(Later at the mall)

16. CLERK: Can I help you?

MINH: ______________________

a. I'd like to return these shoes.
b. There seemed to be a problem.
c. I usually take a smaller size.

17. CLERK: What seems to be the problem?

MINH: ______________________

a. Yes, it is.
b. Yes. It seem to be.
c. They're too small.

18. CLERK: Did your daughter use them?

MINH: ______________________ We only bought them two days ago.

a. No, she didn't.
b. She doesn't like them.
c. She used to.

19. CLERK: If you have the receipt, we'll be glad to give you a refund.

MINH: Thanks. ______________________

a. We will.
b. Here it is.
c. Yes, you have.

III. Complete the conversations. Write the correct form of the verb and *for* or *since*.

EXAMPLE:

A: Have you seen (see) Officer Brady?

SERGEANT: Not ______ (20. for/since) 9:00 this morning. Why?

CLERK: The Chief is on the telephone. He asked ______ (21. speak) to him.

SERGEANT: If he ______ (22. get back), I ______ (23. give) him the message.

CLERK: Thanks.

(Five minutes later)

SERGEANT: Brady, the Chief just ________ (24. call) you, five minutes ago.

BRADY: That's strange. I ________ (25. try) to reach him ________ (26. for/since) an hour.

IV. Complete the conversation with the words in the box.

has to	can	might	be able to	had better

EXAMPLE:
Angela *has to* to choose the stories for tomorrow's paper.

ANGELA: I want to run the Evans Collier story tomorrow. Will you ________ (27) to finish it by tonight?

BRAD: I ________ (28) finish tonight if I ________ (29) reach Collier by telephone. I need to ask him a few more questions. But I'm not sure.

ANGELA: We ________ (30) get this story out right away. The *Tribune* is covering it too.

V. Complete the letter with a *-self/-selves* pronoun, the correct form of the two-word verb and *enough* or *too* + adjective.

EXAMPLE:
Dear Dr. Cousins:

I'm driving *myself* crazy with this problem. I keep *thinking it over* (think over/it), but I still don't know know what to do. It's just *too hard* (hard) for me to decide. I hope you can help.

Right now a baby sitter ________ (31. pick up) my son after school. Every evening since he was four years old, she ________ (32. drop off/him) at home at 6:00, when I get home from work. Now my son is ten years old, and he says he's ________ (33. old) to take care of ________ (34). But the baby sitter tells me children that age can't be responsible for ________ (35).

Is he ________ (36. young) to be alone for two hours? Please help me decide.

Confused Parent

VI. Complete the article with the correct form of the verb, the comparative form of the adjective or the correct word.

EXAMPLE:

I usually *write* (write) about outdoor sports in this column. *However* (Therefore/However), Houston has been *as hot as* (hot) a Texas barbecue for the past two weeks.

So this week, I ________ (37. write) about some indoor activities. There are plenty of ________ (38. interested/interesting), air conditioned sports in this city. You can get some exercise in one of Houston's bowling alleys and still feel ________ (39. cool) a cucumber. ________ (40. While/As soon as) I was visiting Bowl-A-Rama last week, I ________ (41. see) many families ________ (42. enjoy) themselves cheaply.

________ (43. But/So) sometimes even athletes don't like strenuous activity. If that's how you feel this week, you ________ (44. like) ________ (45. relax) with the new

Spanish film, ¡Jugamos!, about a soccer team as it tours Europe. I used to _______________ (46. play) this game, so I can tell you this film shows how professional really do it.

Now read the article again and circle the letter of each correct answer.

> **EXAMPLE:**
>
> In paragraph 2, *themselves* refers to:
> (a.) the families
> b. the bowling alleys
> c. the writer

47. For the last two weeks, Texas has been having a:
    a. barbecue.
    b. heat wave.
    c. lot of indoor sports.

48. In paragraph 3, *strenuous* probably means:
    a. tiring
    b. relaxing
    c. cool

49. In paragraph 3, *used to* means that the writer of the article:
    a. plays soccer a lot.
    b. doesn't play soccer anymore.
    c. uses soccer as an exercise.

50. The main idea of this column is:
    a. Bowling is a good sport for families to enjoy together.
    b. Houston has hot weather in the summer.
    c. Houston has interesting indoor activities.

VII. Midterm Listening Comprehension Test (Optional)

Tom is interviewing Derek Mahoney for a television program. You will hear Tom's part of the conversation. Circle the correct answers for Derek's part of the conversation. (The Midterm Listening Comprehension Test is recorded on the cassette after Unit 6 Pronunciation Exercises.)

51. DEREK: a. Yes, it is, Tom.
    b. Well, I think so, Tom.
    c. It's great to be here, Tom.
52. DEREK: a. That's right. I'm coaching.
    b. Yes, I usually coach.
    c. Sur, I've coached.
53. DEREK: a. To help out neighborhood kids.
    b. The Children's Club.
    c. During the summer.
54. DEREK: a. I did it in the summer.
    b. Yes, I have.
    c. For the past two summers.
55. DEREK: a. To help out neighborhood kids.
    b. I decided to play football.
    c. I decided last year.
56. DEREK: a. Yes, I was one for three years.
    b. Yes, I used one for ages.
    c. Yes, I played on one for years.
57. DEREK: a. Nothing, really. I'm just bored.
    b. If you practice, you will get better.
    c. It's very discouraging.
58. DEREK: a. They'd better just enjoy playing the game.
    b. Don't worry, you'll find one soon.
    c. It's too hot to play football today.
59. DEREK: a. No, I'm too young to retire.
    b. Yes, but I miss my local team.
    c. Yes, it reminds me of that too.
60. DEREK: a. Don't worry.
    b. Sure thing.
    c. Sorry to hear that.

FINAL TEST

Name: ______

Course: ______

Date: ______

Grade: ______

I. Circle the correct answer in each conversation. Then write it on the line.

EXAMPLE:

A: When are you going to start your new business?

B: As soon as I save enough money.

ⓐ As soon as I save enough money.
b. I was going to save enough money.
c. I ought to save enough money.

1. A: What's your favorite pastime?

   B: ______
   a. I took a long walk last Saturday.
   b. Taking long walks.
   c. I think I'll take a walk.

2. A: How often are we paid on this job?

   B: ______
   a. Every two weeks.
   b. $400 a week.
   c. Yes, we are.

3. A: It's hard being unemployed.

   B: ______
   a. I have a wife and two kids.
   b. Sounds OK to me.
   c. I know how you feel.

4. A: I don't know how to find a good dermatologist.

   B: ______
   a. He's right over there.
   b. Why don't you ask at the hospital?
   c. You must get a lot of rest.

5. A: I'm really upset that I didn't get that promotion.

   B: ______
   a. Take it easy.
   b. You're pulling my leg!
   c. They ought to give her a trophy.

6. A: What do you like about Miami?

   B: ______
   a. I like Toronto.
   b. I like it a lot, but I miss my hometown.
   c. I like the weather.

7. A: I just got some bad news. A friend of mine was demoted.

   B: ______
   a. I'm sorry to hear that.
   b. Was he badly hurt?
   c. I've never been there.

8. A: Why did you sign up for driving lessons?

   B: ______
   a. I got a driver's license.
   b. To get a driver's license.
   c. He didn't sign up yet.

9. A: What were you doing when it started to rain yesterday?

   B: ______
   a. I used to wait for the bus.
   b. I waited for the bus.
   c. I was waiting for the bus.

10. A: I just failed my driver's test.

    B: ______
    a. You might practice more.
    b. You should have practiced more.
    c. You'll practice more.

II. Circle the correct answers to complete the conversation. Then write them.

EXAMPLE:

MICHAEL: Can I interview you for my English class, Dad?

PETE: Sure you can.

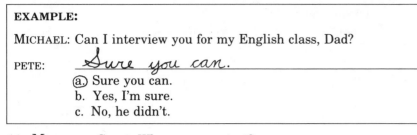

(a.) Sure you can.
b. Yes, I'm sure.
c. No, he didn't.

11. MICHAEL: Great. When can we start?

PETE: ______________________

a. About an hour ago.
b. As soon as I finish writing this page.
c. Yes, we can.

(A few minutes later)

12. MICHAEL: OK. Here's my first question. How long have you been a reporter?

PETE: ______________________

a. For ten years.
b. Ten years ago.
c. Yes, I've been a reporter.

13. MICHAEL: Wow. That's a long time. When did you decide to become a journalist?

PETE: ______________________

a. As soon as I graduate from college.
b. I was going to graduate from college.
c. After I graduated from college.

14. MICHAEL: What do you like best about your job?
PETE: Hmm. Let me think a minute.

____

a. Writing about government, I think.
b. I wrote about government.
c. Yes, I like it very much.

15. MICHAEL: Why is that so great?

PETE: ______________________

a. Because it's really great.
b. Important decisions are made there.
c. I made important decisions.

16. MICHAEL: Did you ever want to do something different?
PETE: Sure—when I was twelve years old.

____

a. I was President.
b. I was different.
c. I was going to be President.

17. MICHAEL: Did you think you'd be good at that?
PETE: Yes, I did.

____

a. I was aggressive enough to be a good politician.
b. I was too aggressive to be a good politician.
c. I was too young to be President of a big country.

18. MICHAEL: Why did you change your mind?
PETE: Well, when I had to make speeches in school I found out something.

____

a. So I went there.
b. I wrote better than I talked.
c. Then it happened.

19. MICHAEL: You must have been a very good writer.

PETE: ______________________

a. Yes, I was.
b. Yes, I had.
c. Yes, I had to.

20. MICHAEL: What advice can you give new reporters?

PETE: ______________________

a. They can work hard at their jobs.
b. They ought to be ready to work hard.
c. They should have worked harder.

21. MICHAEL: Thanks, Dad.

PETE: ______________________

a. Take it easy.
b. Yes, go on.
c. Don't mention it.

III. Complete Rosa's speech with the correct form of the verb or the correct modal.

> **EXAMPLE:**
>
> Last summer I visited Italy, and I got interested in
> *cooking* (cook).

My grandmother showed me how spaghetti ______ (22. make) there. Actually, ______ (23. make) good spaghetti isn't hard, but you ______ (24. can/must) follow some simple steps. She said ______ (25. fill) a big pot with water. But first, of course, she ______ (26. had to/should've) make sure she had the right amount—two gallons of water for one pound of spaghetti. While the water ______ (27. boil) hard, she dropped the spaghetti into the pot. However, before she did that, she added some oil to the water. Grandma told me that after it ______ (28. cook) for about twelve minutes, it ______ (29. will/would) be done. You ______ (30. ought to/mustn't) cook spaghetti too long.

IV. Number Rosa's notes for her speech in the correct order to make clear instructions.

31. ____ drop spaghetti into the boiling water
32. ____ add oil
33. __1__ put two gallons of water into the pot
34. ____ cook the spaghetti for twelve minutes

V. Read the editorial and then answer the questions.

The state legislature will soon vote on a bill that would force companies to pay for annual physical examinations for employees who use computers. Companies would also have to pay for glasses for these employees. The bill's supporters say that studies have proved long hours at the computer can cause neck and back problems. They point out that we cannot know the long-term effects of this technology, so we ought to protect the worker now. Opponents argue that if this bill is passed, workers will feel unnecessary fear about working on computers.

Circle the letter of each correct answer.

35. One fact presented in this editorial is:
    a. We ought to protect the employees who work at computers now.
    b. Studies have shown that neck and back problems are caused by working at a computer.
    c. Companies ought to pay for physical examinations of employees who work at computers.
36. One opinion in this editorial is:
    a. The legislature is considering a bill about employees who use computers.
    b. The bill would force companies to pay for glasses for employees who use computers.
    c. With a law like this, workers will be afraid to work with computers.
37. *Long-term* probably means:
    a. in the past.
    b. at the present time.
    c. over a long period of time.

VI. Complete the conversation with the correct form of the verbs and the correct word order.

> **EXAMPLE:**
>
> ANGELA: I need some more information about that study before I finish this editorial. First, do you know *who did the study* (who/do/the study)?

BRAD: Let me look at my notes. I think it was the National Academy of Orthopedics.

ANGELA: Can you find out

_______________ ?
38. when/do/it

BRAD: I'll have to

_______________ .
39. look up/that

ANGELA: The study said that some neck and back problems

_______________ by
40. cause

computer use. Also, please try to find out

_______________ .
41. what/be/those problems

BRAD: OK. I _______________
42. call

the Academy as soon as we

_______________ .
43. finish

VII. Complete the paragraph with the correct words and the correct forms of the adverbs.

EXAMPLE:

We support this bill because we feel that employers

should (might/should) act more *responsibly* (responsible).

VIII. Final Listening Comprehension Test (Optional)

Brad is talking to a new reporter, Crystal Chase. You will hear Brad's part of the conversation. Circle the correct answers for Crystal's part of the conversation. (The Final Listening Comprehension Test is recorded on the cassette after Unit 12 Pronunciation Exercises.)

51. CRYSTAL: a. Thanks, I like my work.
b. Thanks, I'm sure I will.
c. Thanks, I liked that job.

52. CRYSTAL: a. As soon as I talk to Angela today.
b. After I read the ad in the paper.
c. For the last two weeks.

53. CRYSTAL: a. When?
b. No. I'd prefer not to.
c. I've been one for about five years.

54. CRYSTAL: a. She said I'll cover politics.
b. Yes, I wonder if she'll tell me.
c. Yes, she'll tell me tomorrow.

55. CRYSTAL: a. I know. I was going to.
b. I know. I owe her some money.
c. What did she say?

56. CRYSTAL: a. Where did she go?
b. I think that's a good idea.
c. I make my own clothes.

57. CRYSTAL: a. Yes, I did.
b. Yes, I was.
c. Yes, you were.

58. CRYSTAL: a. She used to use one too.
b. He prefers to use the typewriter.
c. I've been using one for ages too.

59. CRYSTAL: a. OK.
b. Yes, I do.
c. Yes, I must.

60. CRYSTAL: a. What's happening?
b. Thanks for your help.
c. Yes, I ought to.